Writer: **Daniel Corey**

Artist: **Anthony Diecidue**

Letters and Design: **Dave Lanphear**

Colors (issues 3 and 4): **Perry Freeze**

Based on characters created by
Sir Arthur Conan Doyle

www.professorjamesmoriarty.com
www.twitter.com/dangerkatt
info@dangerkatt.com

DANGERKATT
CREATIVE STUDIO

MORIARTY VOLUME 1: THE DARK CHAMBER
ISBN: 978-1-60706-450-3
First printing

Published by Image Comics, Inc. Office of publication: 2134 Allston Way, 2nd Floor, Berkeley, CA 94704.
Copyright © 2011 DangerKatt Creative Studio. Originally published in single magazine form as MORIARTY
#1-4. All rights reserved. MORIARTY™ (including all prominent characters featured herein), its logo and all
character likenesses are trademarks of DangerKatt Creative Studio, unless otherwise noted. Image Comics®
and its logos are registered trademarks and copyrights of Image Comics, Inc. All rights reserved. No part of this
publication may be reproduced or transmitted in any form or by any means (except for short excerpts for review
purposes) without the express written permission of Image Comics, Inc. All names, characters, events and locales
in this publication are entirely fictional. Any resemblance to actual persons (living and/or dead), events or places,
without satiric intent, is coincidental. Printed in Korea.

International Rights Representative: Christine Meyer (christine@gfloystudio.com)

IMAGE COMICS, INC.

Robert Kirkman - chief operating officer
Erik Larsen - chief financial officer
Todd McFarlane - president
Marc Silvestri - chief executive officer
Jim Valentino - vice-president

Eric Stephenson - publisher
Todd Martinez - sales & licensing coordinator
Sarah deLaine - pr & marketing coordinator
Branwyn Bigglestone - accounts manager
Emily Miller - administrative assistant
Jamie Parreno - marketing assistant
Kevin Yuen - digital rights coordinator
Tyler Shainline - production manager
Drew Gill - art director
Jonathan Chan - senior production artist
Monica Garcia - production artist
Vincent Kukua - production artist
Jana Cook - production artist

www.imagecomics.com

THE STRAND MAGAZINE.

Vol. 1   July, 1914   No. 1

Regarding the Bad Guy.
A literary reflection on the life and character of
PROFESSOR JAMES MORIARTY.

By Daniel Corey.

THIS may be a statement of the obvious, but I am a lifetime fan of Sherlock Holmes and a longtime respecter of Sir Arthur Conan Doyle. To deduce this, one needs but to close this book and look at the cover.

Reading the Holmes adventures as a kid, I thought of them as great literature. And they certainly are such, as scholars the world over will tell you. But when you really break them down and take a close look, they are the stuff of great pulp. They involve visits from mysterious strangers, danger, intrigue, secret codes, artifacts and folklore from far away lands — the sorts of things everyone wants in a yarn. These elements have endeared Sherlock to us all these years.

But what about the other guy, this mysterious Professor

Moriarty? Very little is known about him, really. Your average Joe on the street knows Moriarty as Holmes' arch nemesis, but the truth is that he is barely present in Doyle's stories. Holmes mentions Moriarty and his criminal network here and there, but it is really popular culture that has exhorted him to the level of ever-present villain. Doyle actually created Moriarty as an excuse to kill off Holmes when he himself had tired of the stories.

Moriarty was introduced to the world in a story called *The Final Problem*, in which the two foes meet on a mountain pass overlooking Reichenbach Falls and fight each other to their supposed deaths. *The Final Problem* is told from the viewpoint of the good Dr. Watson (as is the case with most of the Holmes stories), so Moriarty himself never really appears "on stage." Holmes tells Watson about Moriarty, recounts a meeting with him, but Watson never really sees the man. At one point, as he and Holmes are departing Victoria Station via the Continental Express, Watson reports to the reader of seeing "a tall man pushing his way furiously through the crowd, and waving his hand as if he desired to have the train stopped." This is the only sighting of Moriarty that exists in the official canon of Holmes, apart from Holmes' own third-person accounts.

Moriarty would only have involvement in one other story, *The Valley of Fear*. In this novel-length adventure, Moriarty is a peripheral player in the attempted assassination of a nobleman. It's a great story, but as it makes small deviations in continuity with the other stories, it is often overlooked.

So, why not bring the bad guy to the foreground? In creating *The Dark Chamber*, I set out to exalt this barely-mentioned-yet-world-famous criminal to the role of protagonist. Sure, he's been portrayed numerous times on film and television, but I wanted to create a long, feature-length examination and figure out what makes him tick. And what better way to probe the man's psyche than to put him on the skids, challenge him to rebuild his former criminal empire? The idea was just too much fun to pass by.

In other extracanonical renderings of Holmes, Moriarty has been played on both the large and small screens by some fantastic actors, including the great Sir Laurence Olivier, who portrayed the Professor in *The Seven-Per-Cent Solution*, based on the novel by Nicholas Meyer. Portrayals that resonated with me personally include the wonderful Daniel Davis in the *Star Trek: The Next Generation* episode titled *Elementary, Dear Data* (yes, I'm a geek – just deal with it), as well as the venerable Paul Freeman (Belloq from *Raiders of the Lost Ark!*) in the comical *Without a Clue*.

The idea has been posited by critics, theorists and other important mucky-mucks that Moriarty never existed, that he was a construct of Holmes' mind: the result of Holmes' craving for a real challenge. I don't know if Doyle intended this, but it is an interesting point to ponder.

As for me, I think he's real. I mean *really* real. I think all this notion of him being a work of fiction is merely a trick that he's devised to throw us off his trail, and that he is still out there, lurking in shadow…perhaps watching you now, as you read this…

✧ ✧ ✧

Daniel Corey
July 11, 1914

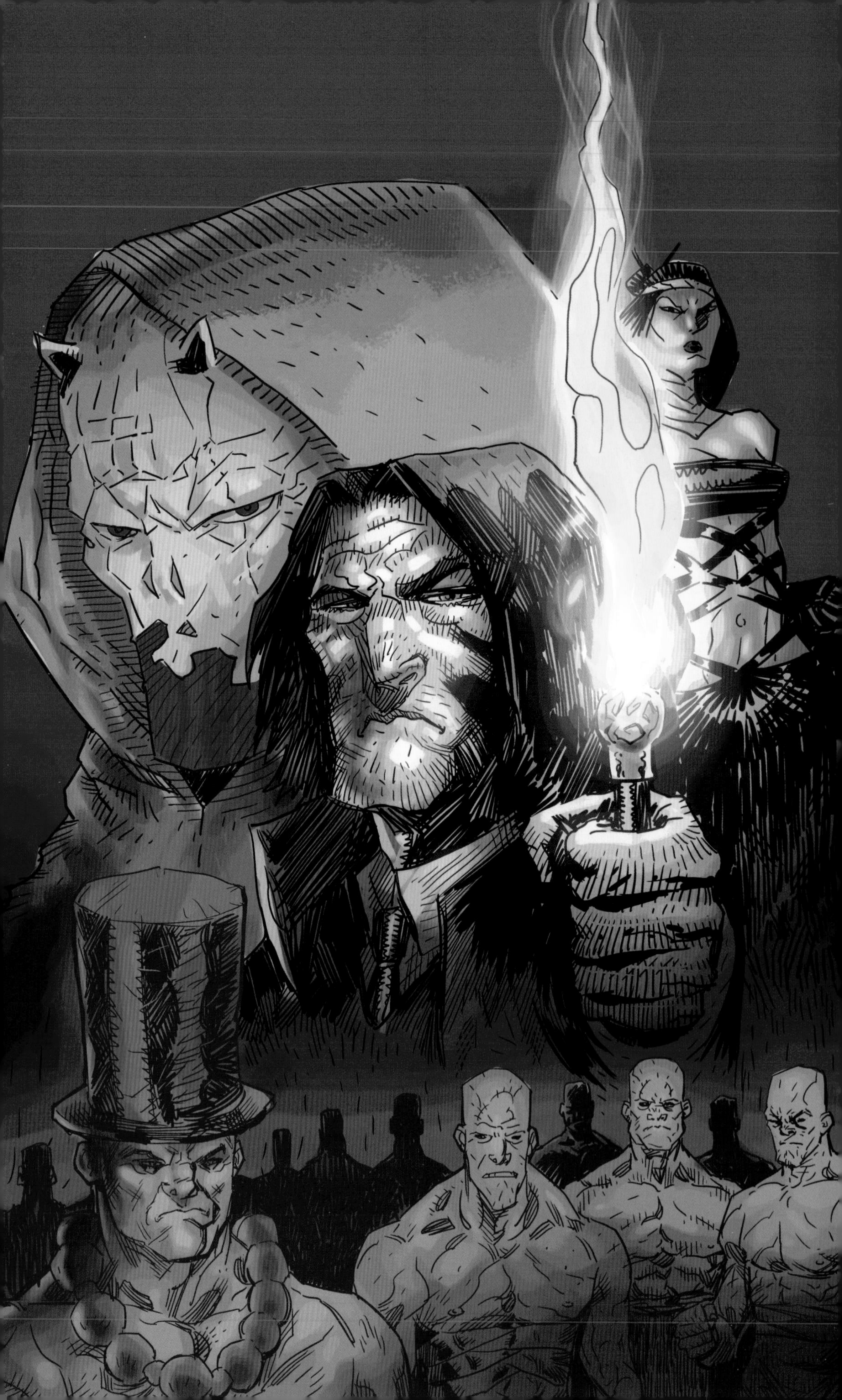

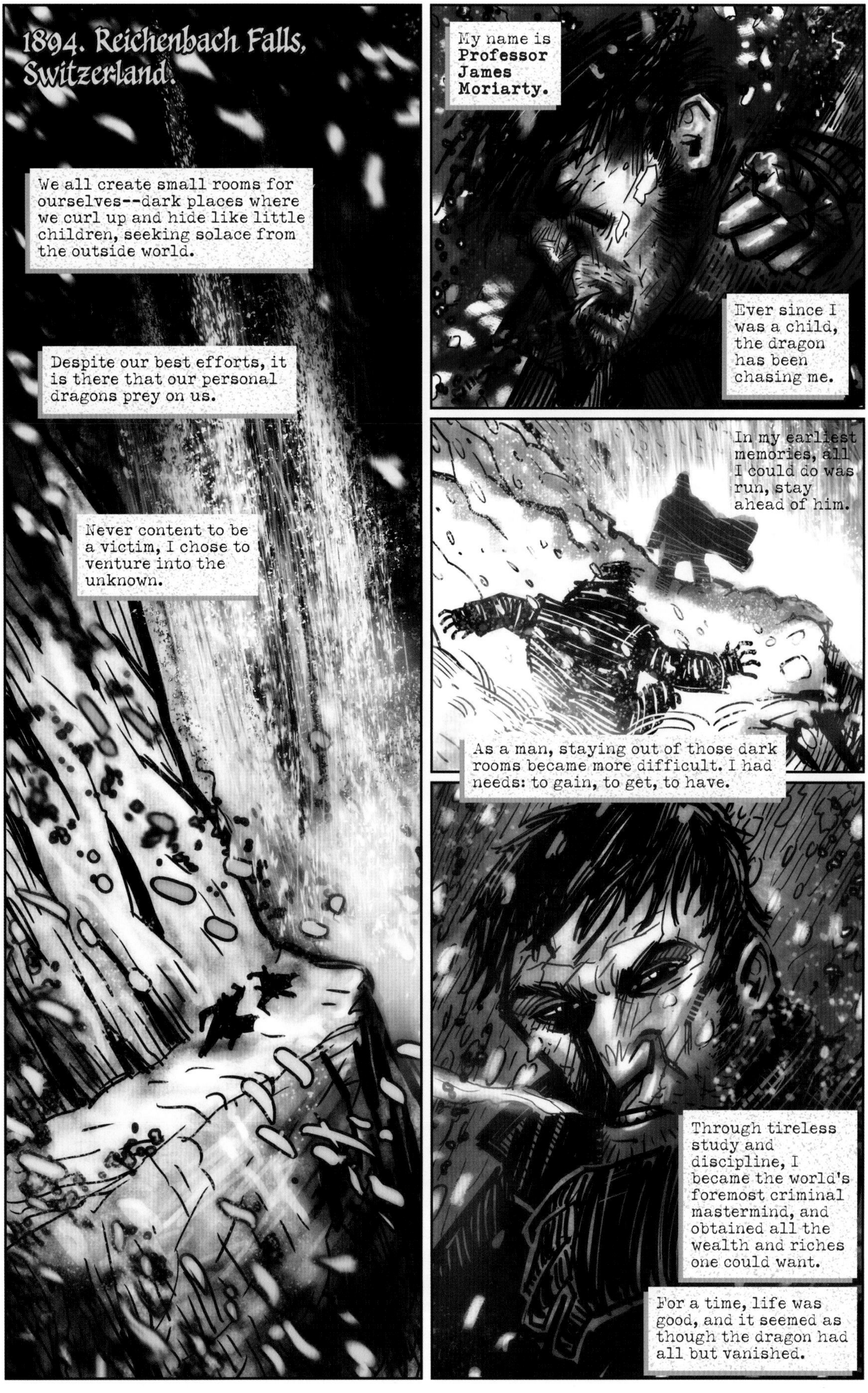
1894. Reichenbach Falls, Switzerland.
We all create small rooms for ourselves--dark places where we curl up and hide like little children, seeking solace from the outside world.
Despite our best efforts, it is there that our personal dragons prey on us.
Never content to be a victim, I chose to venture into the unknown.
My name is Professor James Moriarty.
Ever since I was a child, the dragon has been chasing me.
In my earliest memories, all I could do was run, stay ahead of him.
As a man, staying out of those dark rooms became more difficult. I had needs: to gain, to get, to have.
Through tireless study and discipline, I became the world's foremost criminal mastermind, and obtained all the wealth and riches one could want.
For a time, life was good, and it seemed as though the dragon had all but vanished.

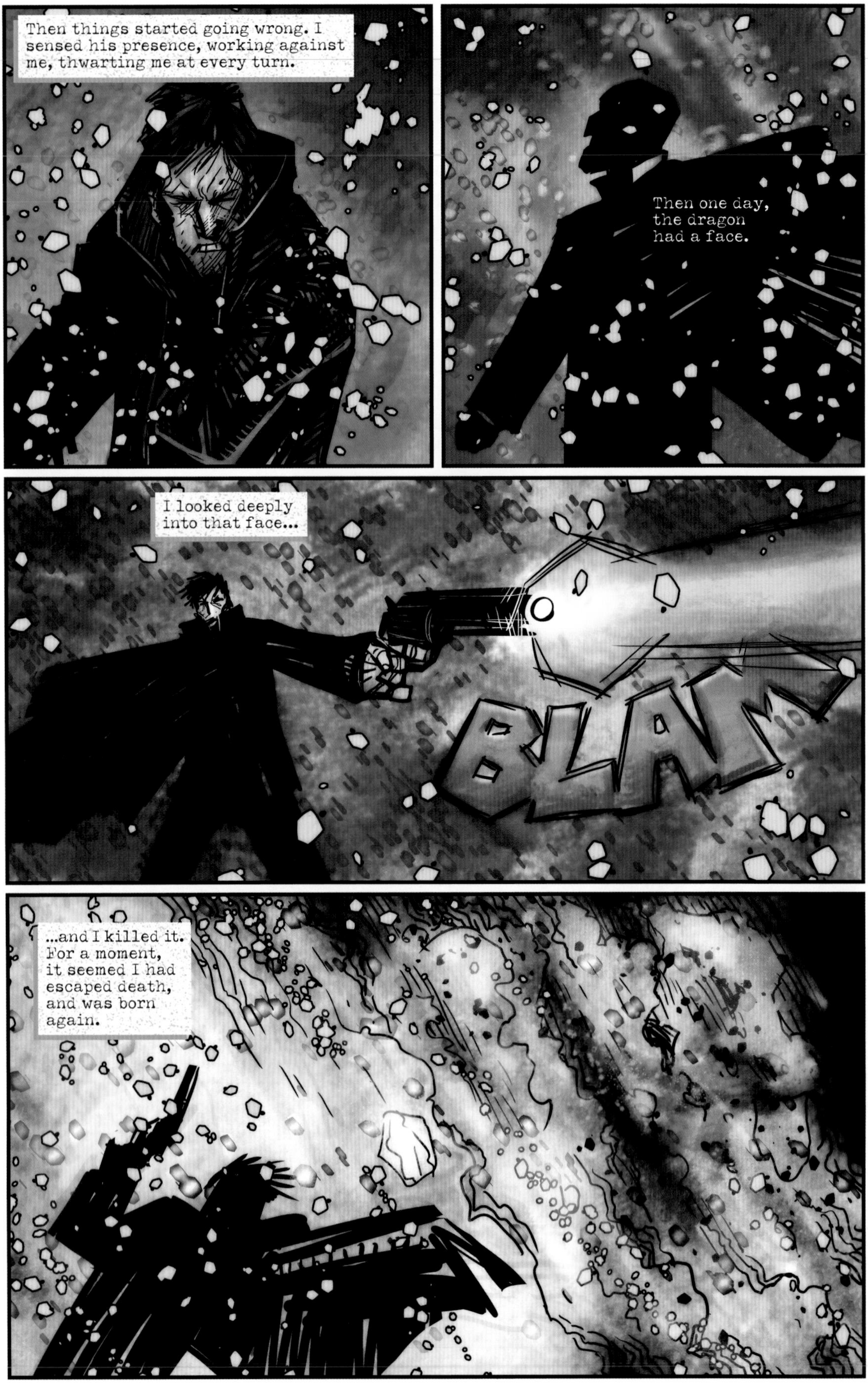

Then things started going wrong. I sensed his presence, working against me, thwarting me at every turn.
Then one day, the dragon had a face.
I looked deeply into that face...
BLAM
...and I killed it. For a moment, it seemed I had escaped death, and was born again.

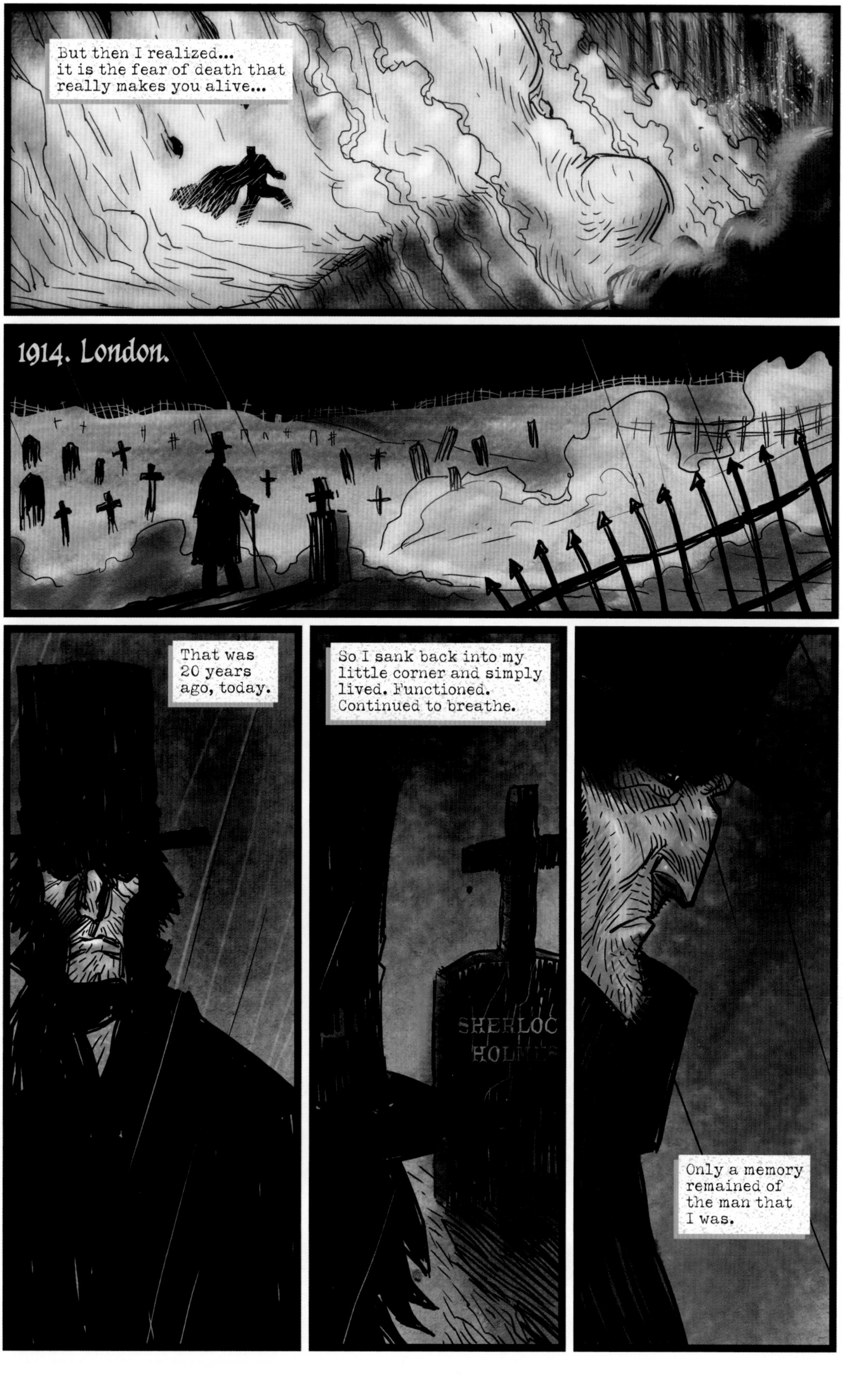
But then I realized...
it is the fear of death that
really makes you alive...
1914. London.
That was
20 years
ago, today.
So I sank back into my
little corner and simply
lived. Functioned.
Continued to breathe.
SHERLOC
HOLM
Only a memory
remained of
the man that
I was.

I never desired the label of 'criminal.' I simply wanted to control my own destiny, live in such grand significance that I could outpace the dragon.

I once ran a vast network that controlled all aspects of the European underworld.

I SAW IT PLAIN AS THE DAY. I LOOKED INSIDE, AN' IT PLAYED OUT 'AFORE ME EYES.

WHAT DID?

END OF THE WORLD, GUV. HE MADE ME LOOK. I SAW IT. WE ALL DID.

WHO MADE YOU?

TARTARUS. THE DEVIL 'IMSELF.

MUCH OBLIGED, GUV. BUT THIS AIN'T GONNA STOP IT.

THAT IS CERTAIN. GOOD DAY TO YOU.

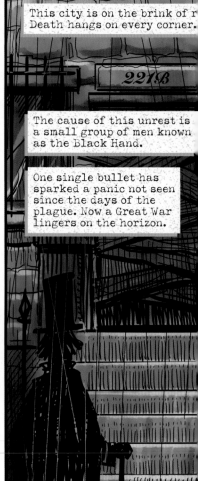

This city is on the brink of r Death hangs on every corner.

The cause of this unrest is a small group of men known as the Black Hand.

One single bullet has sparked a panic not seen since the days of the plague. Now a Great War lingers on the horizon.

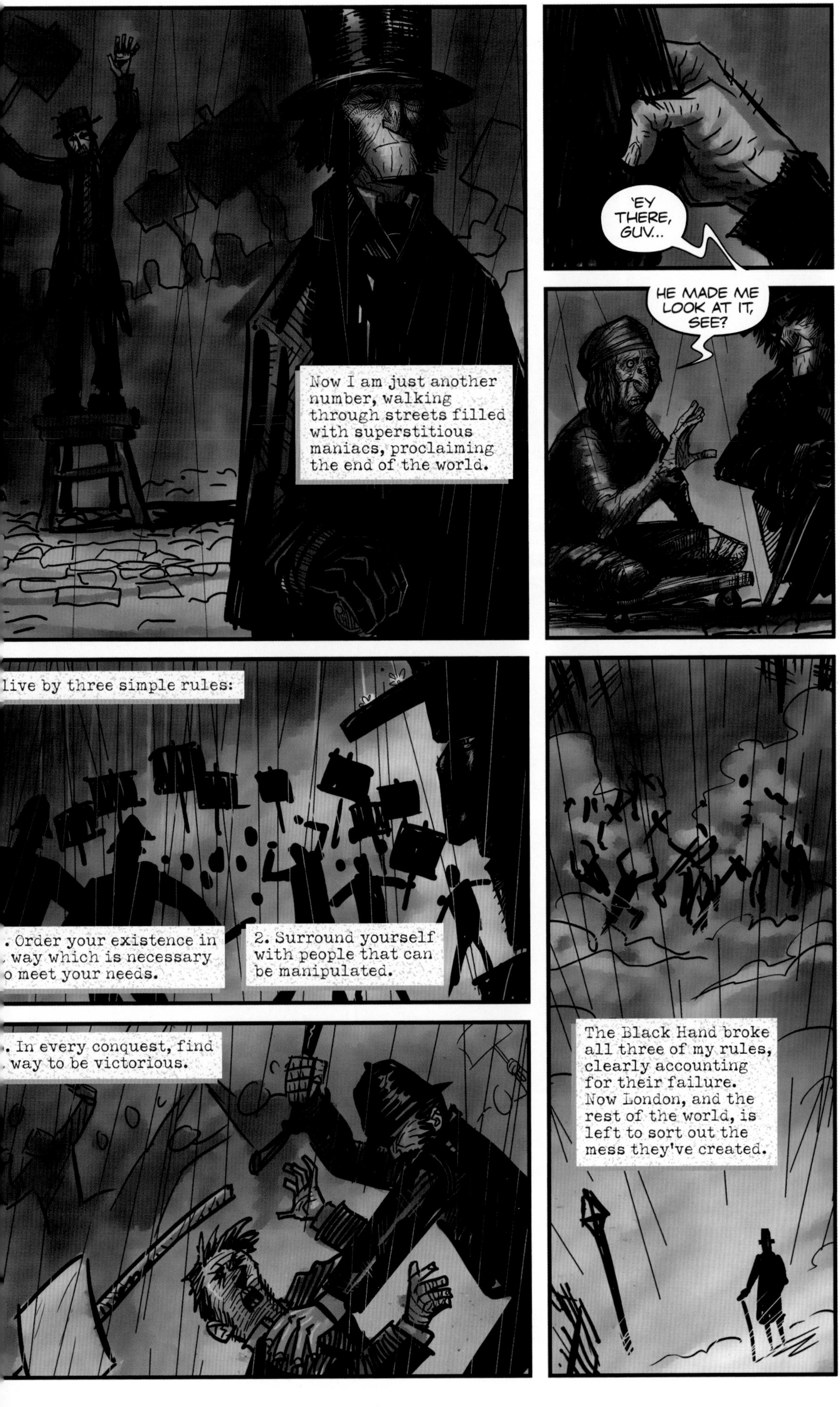
Now I am just another number, walking through streets filled with superstitious maniacs, proclaiming the end of the world.
'EY THERE, GUV...
HE MADE ME LOOK AT IT, SEE?
live by three simple rules:
. Order your existence in
way which is necessary
o meet your needs.
2. Surround yourself with people that can be manipulated.
. In every conquest, find
way to be victorious.
The Black Hand broke all three of my rules, clearly accounting for their failure. Now London, and the rest of the world, is left to sort out the mess they've created.

G'DAY, MISTER TRUMBOLD.

MR. BIRCH. PLEASE TELL ME THERE IS NEWS OTHER THAN THE KILLING OF THIS ARCHDUKE FERDINAND.

NOT MUCH, SIR. RIGHTLY SO. SECRET SOCIETIES CAUSING WARS...

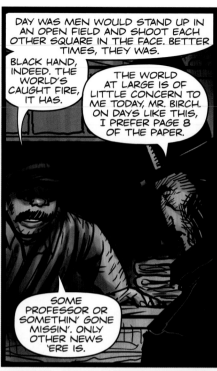

DAY WAS MEN WOULD STAND UP IN AN OPEN FIELD AND SHOOT EACH OTHER SQUARE IN THE FACE. BETTER TIMES, THEY WAS.

BLACK HAND, INDEED. THE WORLD'S CAUGHT FIRE, IT HAS.

THE WORLD AT LARGE IS OF LITTLE CONCERN TO ME TODAY, MR. BIRCH. ON DAYS LIKE THIS, I PREFER PAGE 8 OF THE PAPER.

SOME PROFESSOR OR SOMETHIN' GONE MISSIN'. ONLY OTHER NEWS 'ERE IS.

YES, RUPERT THOMASON OF DURHAM UNIVERSITY, PROFESSOR OF PHYSICS. HE WAS AN ASSOCIATE OF MINE IN A DIFFERENT LIFE.

REALLY, SIR? WELL, MAYBE YOU COULD USE SOME OF 'AT FANCY DETECTING WORK AND FIND 'IM.

IF THERE'S A PAYCHECK IN IT, CERTAINLY. GOOD DAY, MR. BIRCH.

After Holmes died, so did Professor Moriarty. Now Moriarty is simply known as 'Trumbold.'

I have become a sort of investigator for the criminal element, taking small jobs, helping petty men escape blackmail, finding keys that open doors to paltry treasure-- favors, really, and for a fraction of the life and salary that I was once accustomed to.

My main business is import/export. I run this as a front, keeping an eye on the waterfront for what- ever pittance of business may come my way.

This is an attempt to accomplish Rule Number One: ordering your existence.

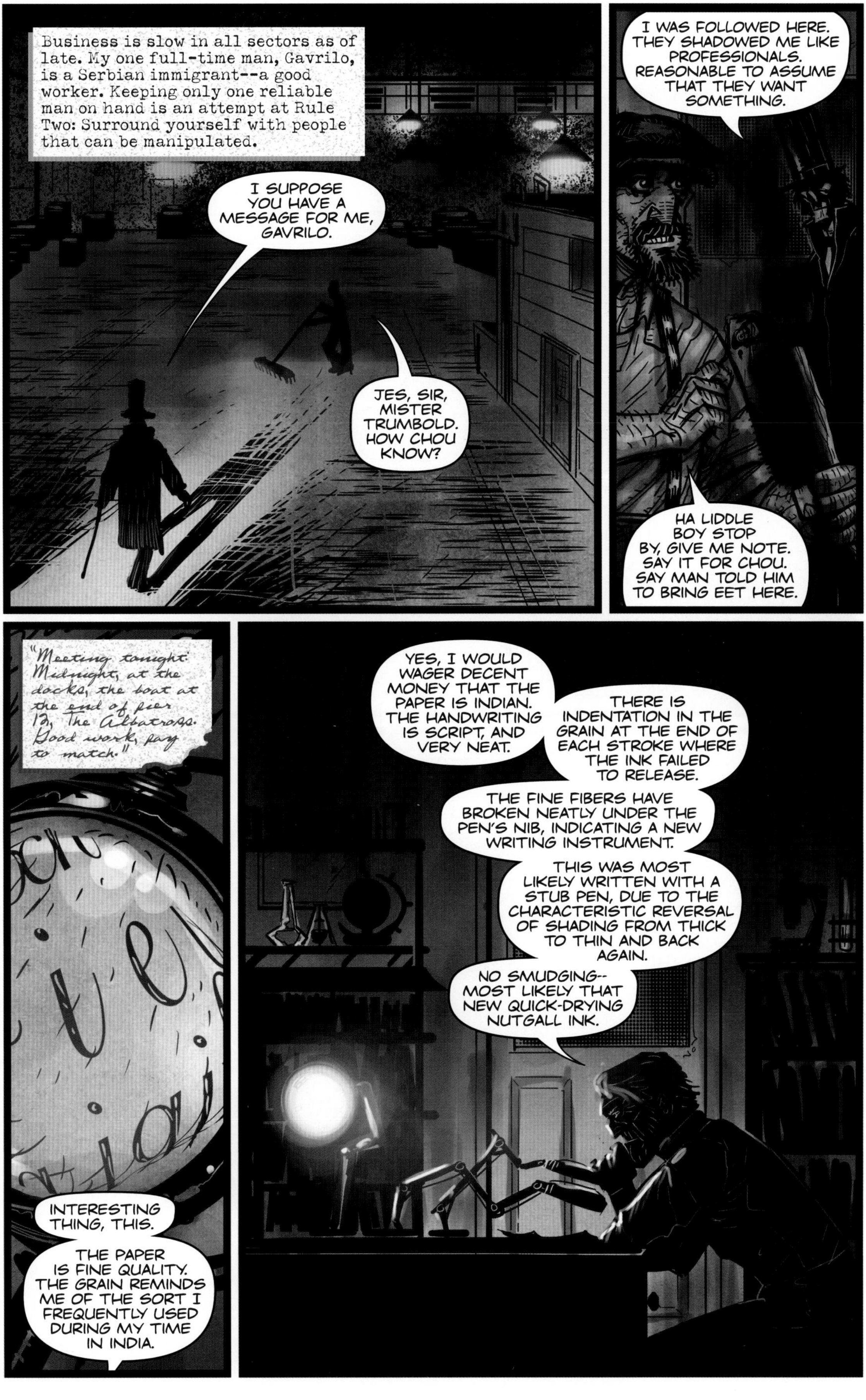
Business is slow in all sectors as of late. My one full-time man, Gavrilo, is a Serbian immigrant--a good worker. Keeping only one reliable man on hand is an attempt at Rule Two: Surround yourself with people that can be manipulated.
I SUPPOSE YOU HAVE A MESSAGE FOR ME, GAVRILO.
JES, SIR, MISTER TRUMBOLD. HOW CHOU KNOW?
I WAS FOLLOWED HERE. THEY SHADOWED ME LIKE PROFESSIONALS. REASONABLE TO ASSUME THAT THEY WANT SOMETHING.
HA LIDDLE BOY STOP BY, GIVE ME NOTE. SAY IT FOR CHOU. SAY MAN TOLD HIM TO BRING EET HERE.
"Meeting tonight: Midnight, at the docks, the boat at the end of pier 13, The Albatross. Good work, pay to match."
INTERESTING THING, THIS.
THE PAPER IS FINE QUALITY. THE GRAIN REMINDS ME OF THE SORT I FREQUENTLY USED DURING MY TIME IN INDIA.
YES, I WOULD WAGER DECENT MONEY THAT THE PAPER IS INDIAN. THE HANDWRITING IS SCRIPT, AND VERY NEAT.
THERE IS INDENTATION IN THE GRAIN AT THE END OF EACH STROKE WHERE THE INK FAILED TO RELEASE.
THE FINE FIBERS HAVE BROKEN NEATLY UNDER THE PEN'S NIB, INDICATING A NEW WRITING INSTRUMENT.
THIS WAS MOST LIKELY WRITTEN WITH A STUB PEN, DUE TO THE CHARACTERISTIC REVERSAL OF SHADING FROM THICK TO THIN AND BACK AGAIN.
NO SMUDGING-- MOST LIKELY THAT NEW QUICK-DRYING NUTGALL INK.

AN EDUCATED MAN, A MAN OF MEANS COMPOSED THIS MESSAGE.

CLEARLY AN ENGLISHMAN, AND LIKELY A GOVERNMENT MAN WITH MILITARY EXPERIENCE.

HE IS, HOWEVER, LEFT-HANDED, WHICH WE MAY TAKE AS A WARNING, GAVRILO. THE HEBREWS BELIEVED THAT THE HAND SYMBOLIZED POWER, AND THE LEFT HAND MEANT THE POWER TO SHAME SOCIETY, REPRESENTING NATURAL EVIL.

MOST LIKELY, THE WRITER COMES FROM HUMBLE, WORKING-CLASS ROOTS AND WORKED HIS WAY UP. A MAN OF HIGHER BREEDING WOULD HAVE LEARNED TO WRITE WITH HIS RIGHT HAND.

ALTHOUGH THE AMBITION OF SUCH A CLOAK AND DAGGER OPERATION INDICATES THE TENACITY OF A YOUNGER MAN, THE NEATNESS OF THE PRESENTATION AND APPARENT WORK ETHIC OF THE WRITER INDICATES A STEADY HAND, ONE OF EXPERIENCE-- PERHAPS A MAN 37, 38 YEARS OF AGE.

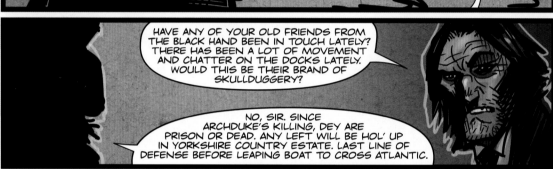

HAVE ANY OF YOUR OLD FRIENDS FROM THE BLACK HAND BEEN IN TOUCH LATELY? THERE HAS BEEN A LOT OF MOVEMENT AND CHATTER ON THE DOCKS LATELY. WOULD THIS BE THEIR BRAND OF SKULLDUGGERY?

NO, SIR. SINCE ARCHDUKE'S KILLING, DEY ARE PRISON OR DEAD. ANY LEFT WILL BE HOL' UP IN YORKSHIRE COUNTRY ESTATE. LAST LINE OF DEFENSE BEFORE LEAPING BOAT TO CROSS ATLANTIC.

I HAVE AN ERRAND FOR YOU. I NEED YOU TO CONTACT A MAN AT THE SCOTLAND YARD INTELLIGENCE DESK. HIS NAME IS *INSPECTOR LeSTRADE.*

HE MUST TELL YOU IF A NEW GOVERNMENT BUREAU CALLED *DIRECTORATE OF MILITARY INTELLIGENCE SECTION 5* HAS ANY SHIPS ON REGISTER AT PIER 12 IN THE HARBOR.

JUST TELL HIM THE "OLD PROFESSOR" HAS COME TO CALL ON THE LAST FAVOR HE OWES.

I'LL BE AT THE BOAR'S HEAD TAVERN ON HIGH STREET. SEND A TELEGRAM AT 8 PM TO INFORM ME OF HIS RESPONSE.

TAKE THIS.

I'M AFRAID WE'LL HAVE TO SHUT UP SHOP FOR A TIME, UNTIL THIS CLEARS UP. I'VE ALREADY PUT A CHECK IN THE POST TO HOLD YOU OVER.

I WOULD LAY LOW FOR A WHILE, IF I WERE YOU.

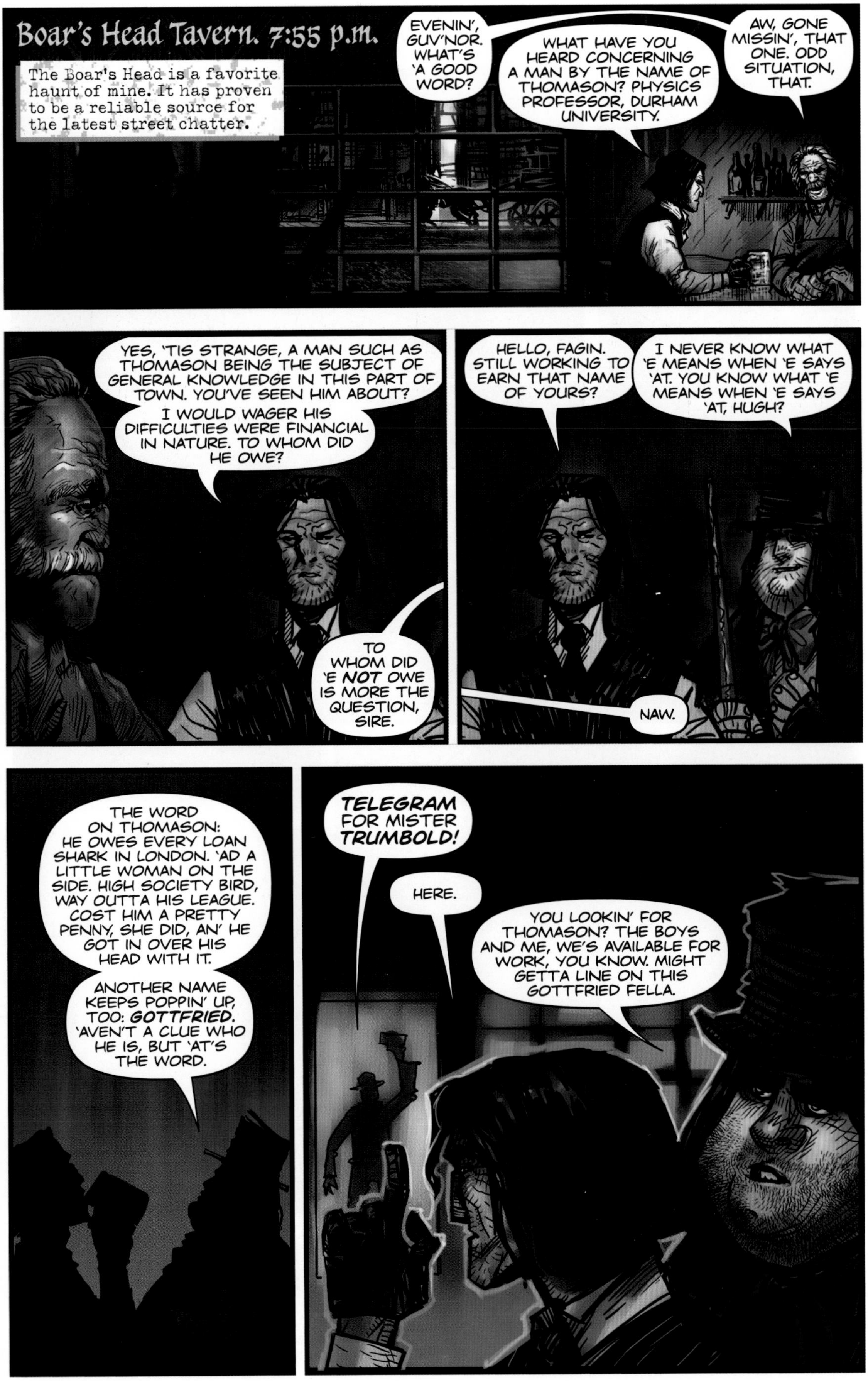

Boar's Head Tavern. 7:55 p.m.
The Boar's Head is a favorite haunt of mine. It has proven to be a reliable source for the latest street chatter.
EVENIN', GUV'NOR. WHAT'S 'A GOOD WORD?
WHAT HAVE YOU HEARD CONCERNING A MAN BY THE NAME OF THOMASON? PHYSICS PROFESSOR, DURHAM UNIVERSITY.
AW, GONE MISSIN', THAT ONE. ODD SITUATION, THAT.
YES, 'TIS STRANGE, A MAN SUCH AS THOMASON BEING THE SUBJECT OF GENERAL KNOWLEDGE IN THIS PART OF TOWN. YOU'VE SEEN HIM ABOUT?
I WOULD WAGER HIS DIFFICULTIES WERE FINANCIAL IN NATURE. TO WHOM DID HE OWE?
TO WHOM DID 'E NOT OWE IS MORE THE QUESTION, SIRE.
HELLO, FAGIN. STILL WORKING TO EARN THAT NAME OF YOURS?
I NEVER KNOW WHAT 'E MEANS WHEN 'E SAYS 'AT. YOU KNOW WHAT 'E MEANS WHEN 'E SAYS 'AT, HUGH?
NAW.
THE WORD ON THOMASON: HE OWES EVERY LOAN SHARK IN LONDON. 'AD A LITTLE WOMAN ON THE SIDE. HIGH SOCIETY BIRD, WAY OUTTA HIS LEAGUE. COST HIM A PRETTY PENNY, SHE DID, AN' HE GOT IN OVER HIS HEAD WITH IT.
ANOTHER NAME KEEPS POPPIN' UP, TOO: GOTTFRIED. 'AVEN'T A CLUE WHO HE IS, BUT 'AT'S THE WORD.
TELEGRAM FOR MISTER TRUMBOLD!
HERE.
YOU LOOKIN' FOR THOMASON? THE BOYS AND ME, WE'S AVAILABLE FOR WORK, YOU KNOW. MIGHT GETTA LINE ON THIS GOTTFRIED FELLA.

NO, FAGIN. JUST CURIOUS. WOULD THOMASON'S BIRD HAVE A NAME, PERCHANCE?

NO, SIRE. NOT 'AT I KNOW OF.

I COULD USE YOUR SERVICES IN ANOTHER MATTER. TWO MEN HAVE BEEN FOLLOWING ME. THEY SHOULD BE NEAR THE ALLEY AT PIER 12 ON THE WATERFRONT AROUND MIDNIGHT.

I WANT YOU AND YOUR BOYS TO TAKE CARE OF THEM. I WILL BE LEAVING HERE IN TWO MINUTES, AND YOU CAN GET AN EYE ON THEM.

TAKE CARE OF, TAKE CARE OF?

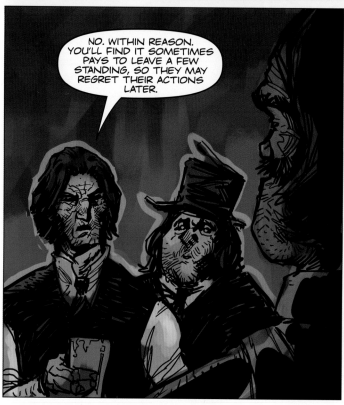

NO. WITHIN REASON. YOU'LL FIND IT SOMETIMES PAYS TO LEAVE A FEW STANDING, SO THEY MAY REGRET THEIR ACTIONS LATER.

WHATEVEH YOU SAY, SIRE.

Albatross is Section 5 boat. STOP.   -G

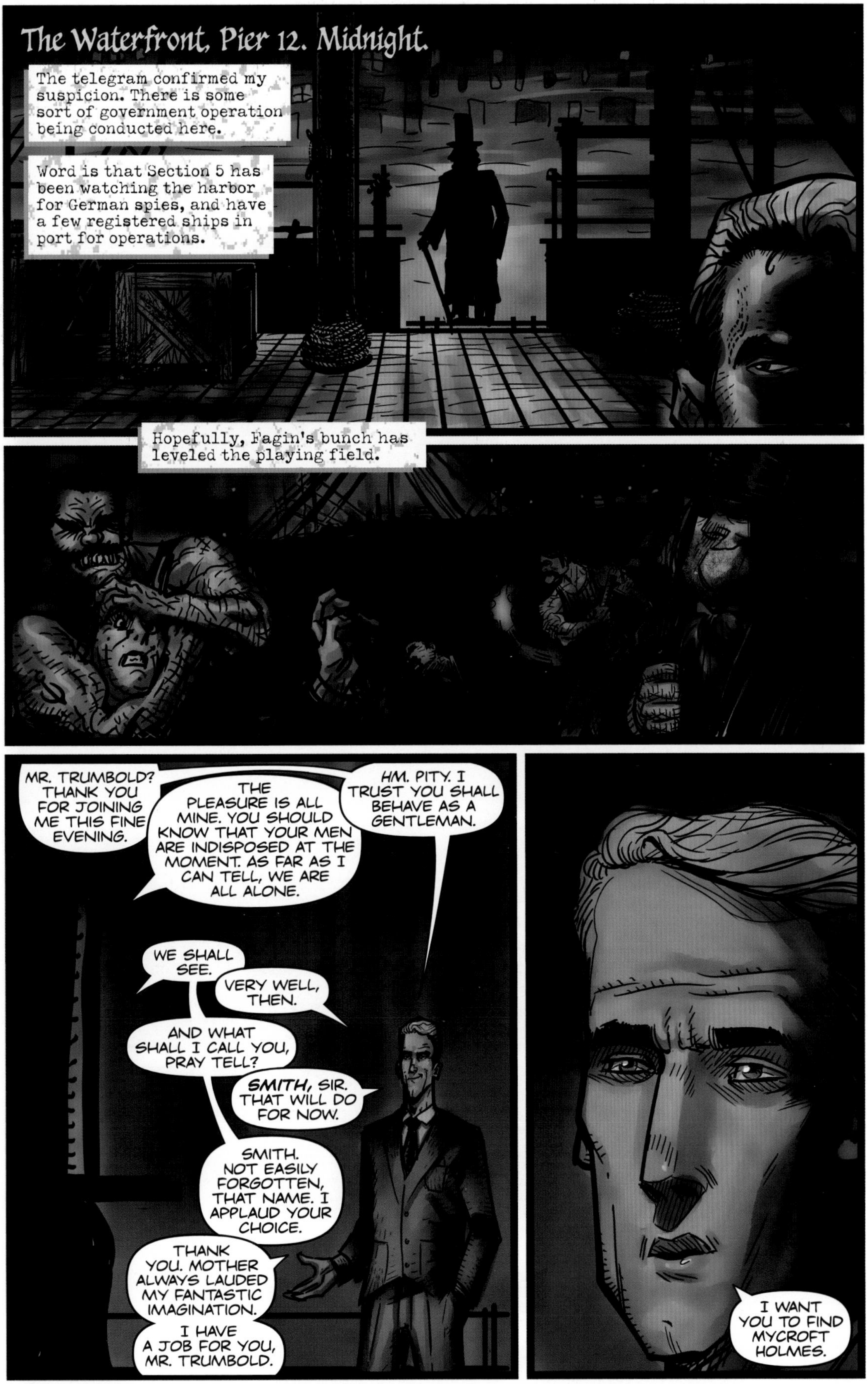
The Waterfront, Pier 12. Midnight.
The telegram confirmed my suspicion. There is some sort of government operation being conducted here.
Word is that Section 5 has been watching the harbor for German spies, and have a few registered ships in port for operations.
Hopefully, Fagin's bunch has leveled the playing field.
MR. TRUMBOLD? THANK YOU FOR JOINING ME THIS FINE EVENING.
THE PLEASURE IS ALL MINE. YOU SHOULD KNOW THAT YOUR MEN ARE INDISPOSED AT THE MOMENT. AS FAR AS I CAN TELL, WE ARE ALL ALONE.
HM. PITY. I TRUST YOU SHALL BEHAVE AS A GENTLEMAN.
WE SHALL SEE.
VERY WELL, THEN.
AND WHAT SHALL I CALL YOU, PRAY TELL?
SMITH, SIR. THAT WILL DO FOR NOW.
SMITH. NOT EASILY FORGOTTEN, THAT NAME. I APPLAUD YOUR CHOICE.
THANK YOU. MOTHER ALWAYS LAUDED MY FANTASTIC IMAGINATION.
I HAVE A JOB FOR YOU, MR. TRUMBOLD.
I WANT YOU TO FIND MYCROFT HOLMES.

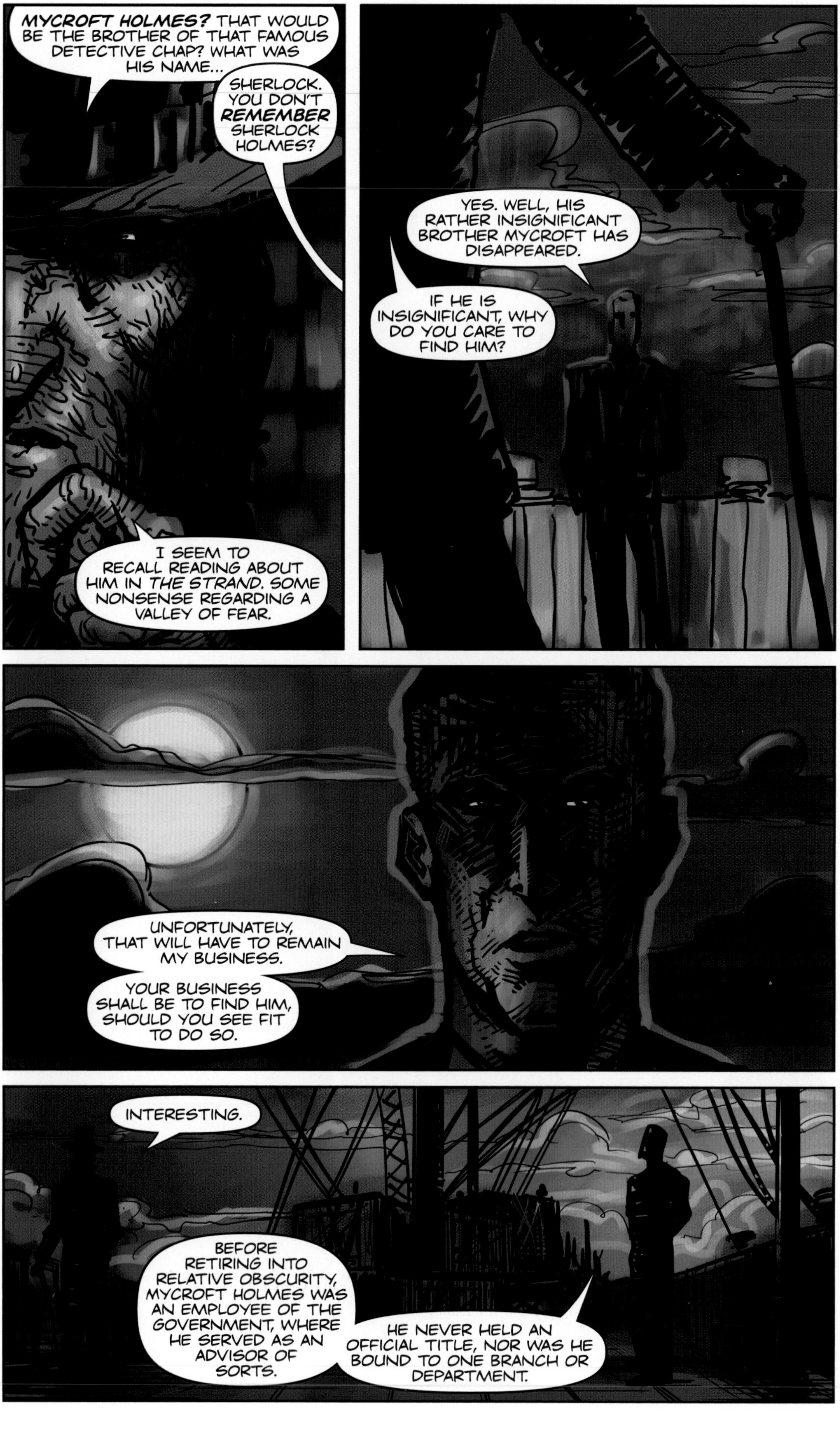
MYCROFT HOLMES? THAT WOULD BE THE BROTHER OF THAT FAMOUS DETECTIVE CHAP? WHAT WAS HIS NAME...
SHERLOCK. YOU DON'T REMEMBER SHERLOCK HOLMES?
I SEEM TO RECALL READING ABOUT HIM IN THE STRAND. SOME NONSENSE REGARDING A VALLEY OF FEAR.
YES. WELL, HIS RATHER INSIGNIFICANT BROTHER MYCROFT HAS DISAPPEARED.
IF HE IS INSIGNIFICANT, WHY DO YOU CARE TO FIND HIM?
UNFORTUNATELY, THAT WILL HAVE TO REMAIN MY BUSINESS.
YOUR BUSINESS SHALL BE TO FIND HIM, SHOULD YOU SEE FIT TO DO SO.
INTERESTING.
BEFORE RETIRING INTO RELATIVE OBSCURITY, MYCROFT HOLMES WAS AN EMPLOYEE OF THE GOVERNMENT, WHERE HE SERVED AS AN ADVISOR OF SORTS.
HE NEVER HELD AN OFFICIAL TITLE, NOR WAS HE BOUND TO ONE BRANCH OR DEPARTMENT.

"THE MAN WAS A WALKING DATA BANK, A CENTRAL EXCHANGE OF INFORMATION THAT MADE OUT THE BALANCE IN ALL BRANCHES OF GOVERNMENT."

"AFTER HIS RETIREMENT, SECURITY SERVICES KEPT AN EYE ON HIM, BUT I'M AFRAID TO SAY THAT WE LOST INTEREST AFTER A TIME."

"IT WAS QUICKLY APPARENT HE POSED NO THREAT TO STATE SECURITY, AS HIS PERSONAL INTERESTS ORBITED A SEEMINGLY INSIGNIFICANT MICROCOSM."

"HE COFOUNDED THE DIOGENES CLUB FOR SOCIALLY INEPT POLITICAL TYPES SUCH AS HIMSELF, BUT IN RECENT MONTHS, HIS VISITS HAVE BEEN ERRATIC AT BEST."

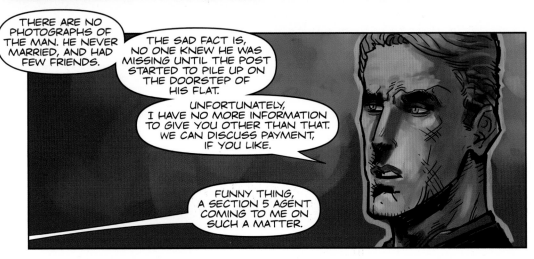

THERE ARE NO PHOTOGRAPHS OF THE MAN. HE NEVER MARRIED, AND HAD FEW FRIENDS.

THE SAD FACT IS, NO ONE KNEW HE WAS MISSING UNTIL THE POST STARTED TO PILE UP ON THE DOORSTEP OF HIS FLAT.

UNFORTUNATELY, I HAVE NO MORE INFORMATION TO GIVE YOU OTHER THAN THAT. WE CAN DISCUSS PAYMENT, IF YOU LIKE.

FUNNY THING, A SECTION 5 AGENT COMING TO ME ON SUCH A MATTER.

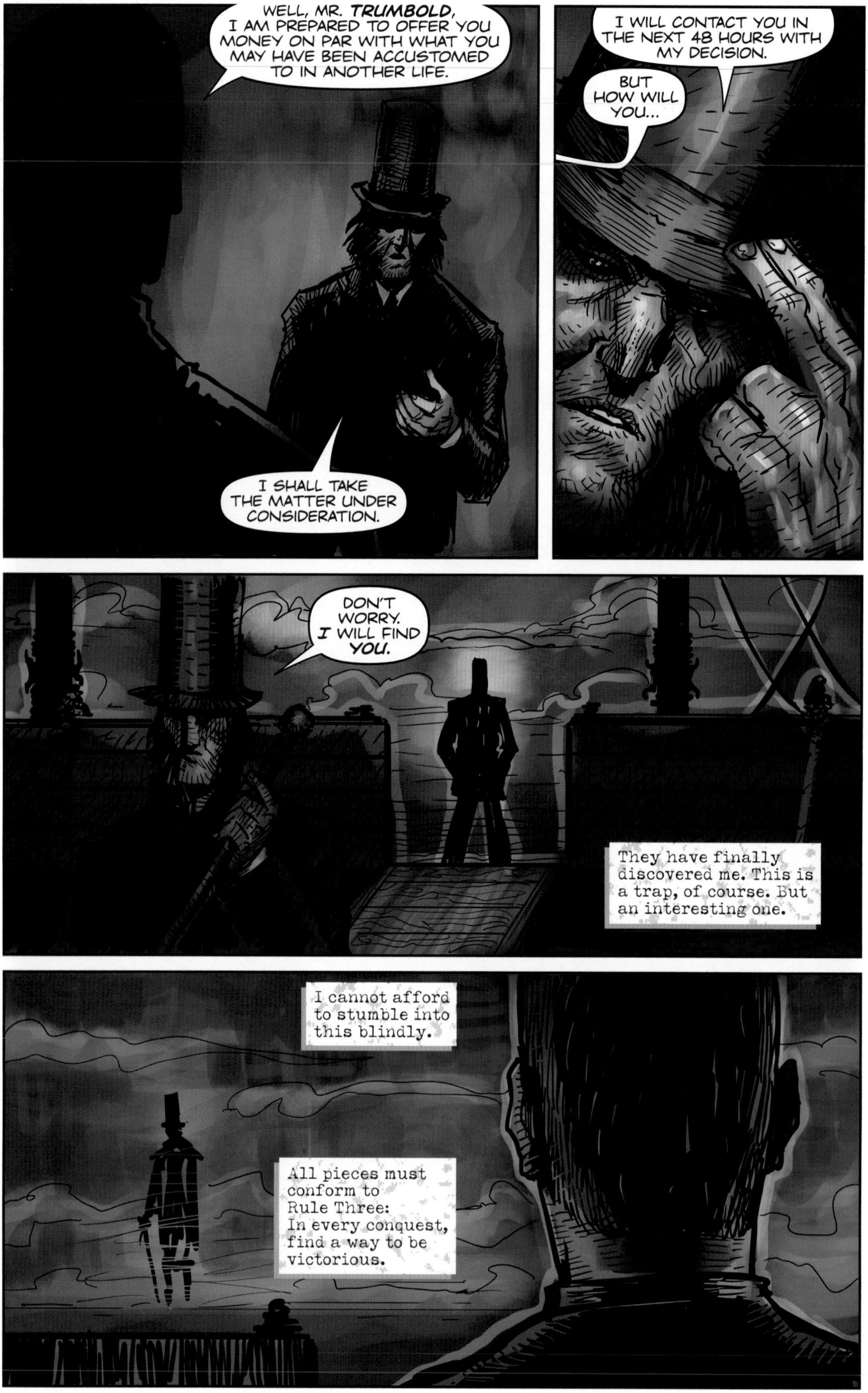
WELL, MR. TRUMBOLD, I AM PREPARED TO OFFER YOU MONEY ON PAR WITH WHAT YOU MAY HAVE BEEN ACCUSTOMED TO IN ANOTHER LIFE.
I SHALL TAKE THE MATTER UNDER CONSIDERATION.
I WILL CONTACT YOU IN THE NEXT 48 HOURS WITH MY DECISION.
BUT HOW WILL YOU...
DON'T WORRY. I WILL FIND YOU.
They have finally discovered me. This is a trap, of course. But an interesting one.
I cannot afford to stumble into this blindly.
All pieces must conform to Rule Three: In every conquest, find a way to be victorious.

More inquiries need to be made among the street element regarding Rupert Thomason.

Thanks to the absurd recollections of Dr. Watson, people seem to remember Holmes as something of a master of disguise. No one knows how bad at it he actually was.

Laughable, really.

I cannot see a direct connection between the disappearance of Thomason and Mycroft Holmes, but it all seems very odd in the timing.

Two such learned men disappearing at the same time is curious, to say the very least. I have decided to treat both cases as one for the time being.

Fagin's story on Thomason seems to be credible to some extent. He does owe every loan shark in town. There are no accounts of his involvement with a woman, though speculations abound.

This Gottfried is something of a familiar name about town--a radical of some sort. He lends money on the street to fund his feeble political efforts.

I don't yet know if he is mixed up with this lot. There are many strange ones lurking about these days, so it is difficult to say at this point.

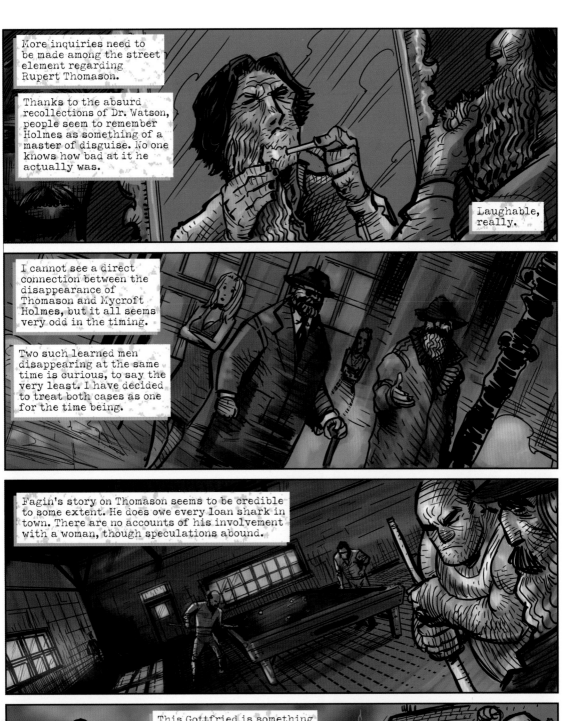
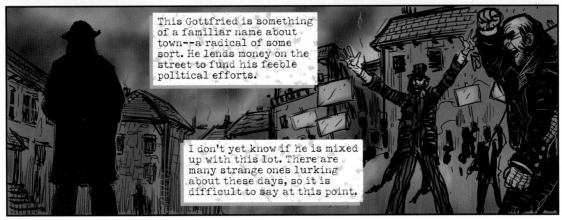

Durham University.

The next logical place of inquiry would be Thomason's employer: my old stomping grounds of Durham University.

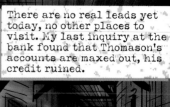

There are no real leads yet today, no other places to visit. My last inquiry at the bank found that Thomason's accounts are maxed out, his credit ruined.

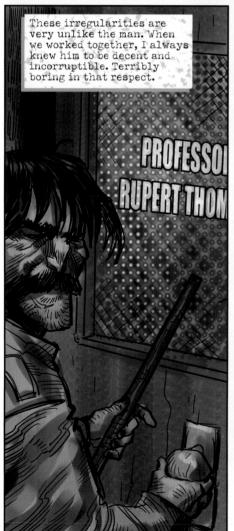

These irregularities are very unlike the man. When we worked together, I always knew him to be decent and incorruptible. Terribly boring in that respect.

PROFESSOR
RUPERT THOM

At last, an item of interest: a letter from Tomokichi Fukurai, professor of psychology at Tokyo University.

The letter is dated as received a week ago, just before Thomason's disappearance. It states, very simply:

"I am pleased to hear your experiments with Nensha are successful thus far. I look forward to meeting you in the fall."

Nensha?

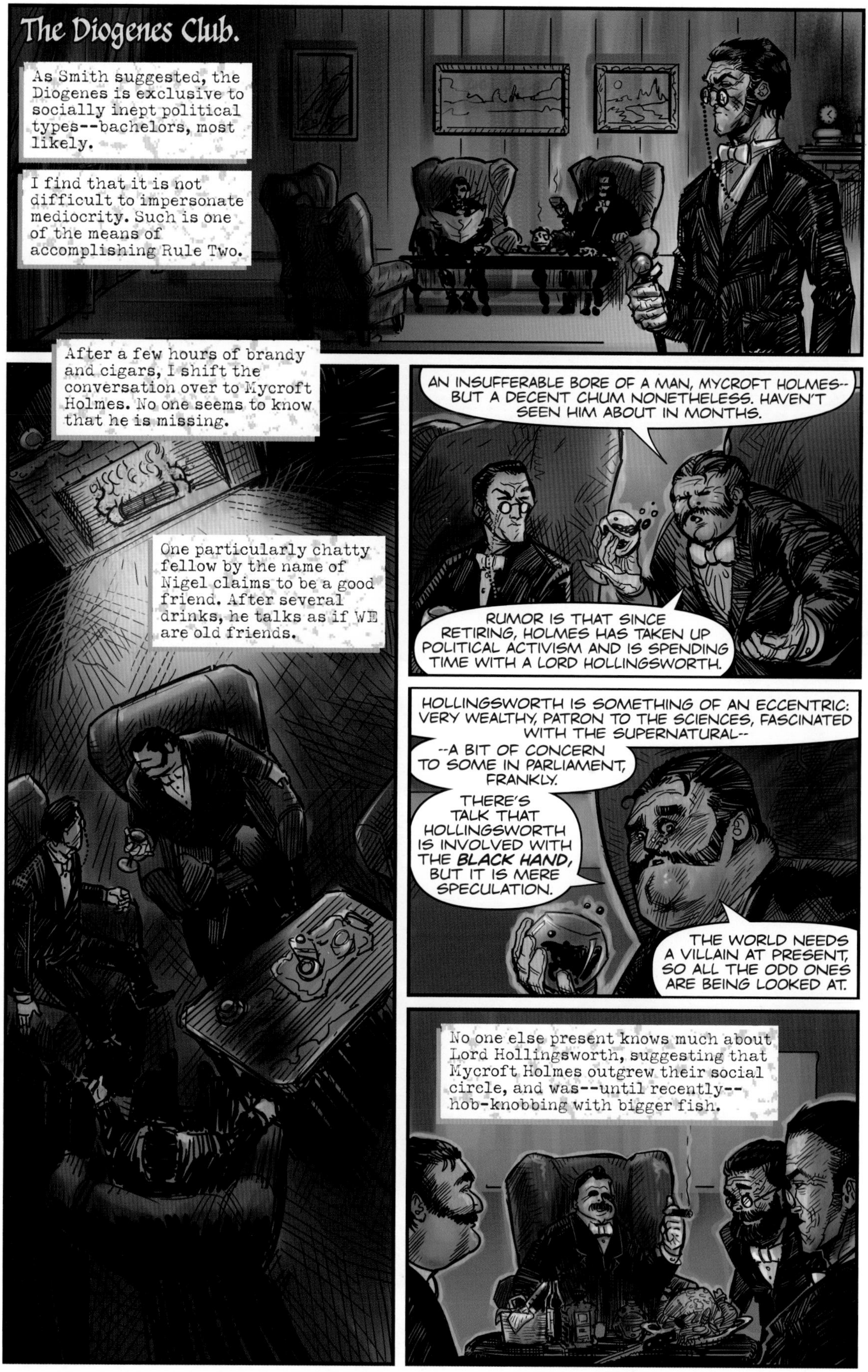
The Diogenes Club.
As Smith suggested, the Diogenes is exclusive to socially inept political types--bachelors, most likely.
I find that it is not difficult to impersonate mediocrity. Such is one of the means of accomplishing Rule Two.
After a few hours of brandy and cigars, I shift the conversation over to Mycroft Holmes. No one seems to know that he is missing.
One particularly chatty fellow by the name of Nigel claims to be a good friend. After several drinks, he talks as if WE are old friends.
AN INSUFFERABLE BORE OF A MAN, MYCROFT HOLMES-- BUT A DECENT CHUM NONETHELESS. HAVEN'T SEEN HIM ABOUT IN MONTHS.
RUMOR IS THAT SINCE RETIRING, HOLMES HAS TAKEN UP POLITICAL ACTIVISM AND IS SPENDING TIME WITH A LORD HOLLINGSWORTH.
HOLLINGSWORTH IS SOMETHING OF AN ECCENTRIC: VERY WEALTHY, PATRON TO THE SCIENCES, FASCINATED WITH THE SUPERNATURAL--
--A BIT OF CONCERN TO SOME IN PARLIAMENT, FRANKLY.
THERE'S TALK THAT HOLLINGSWORTH IS INVOLVED WITH THE BLACK HAND, BUT IT IS MERE SPECULATION.
THE WORLD NEEDS A VILLAIN AT PRESENT, SO ALL THE ODD ONES ARE BEING LOOKED AT.
No one else present knows much about Lord Hollingsworth, suggesting that Mycroft Holmes outgrew their social circle, and was--until recently--hob-knobbing with bigger fish.

Mycrofts Flat. Later.

Time for a visit to Mycroft's flat.

I have several pieces with no common links. Two men missing, both acting out of character. Rupert Thomason: philanderer and spendthrift? Mycroft Holmes: political radical and high society man?

Nothing looks terribly out of place, other than this rather exquisite silver cigarette case of the finest craftsmanship. A bit extravagant for Holmes.

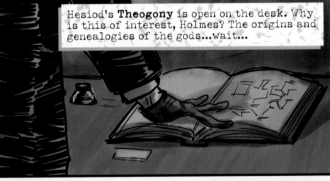

Hesiod's **Theogony** is open on the desk. Why is this of interest, Holmes? The origins and genealogies of the gods...wait...

Tartarus. The beggar on the street blamed his woes on Tartarus. Curious.

Chapter VII
Tartarus

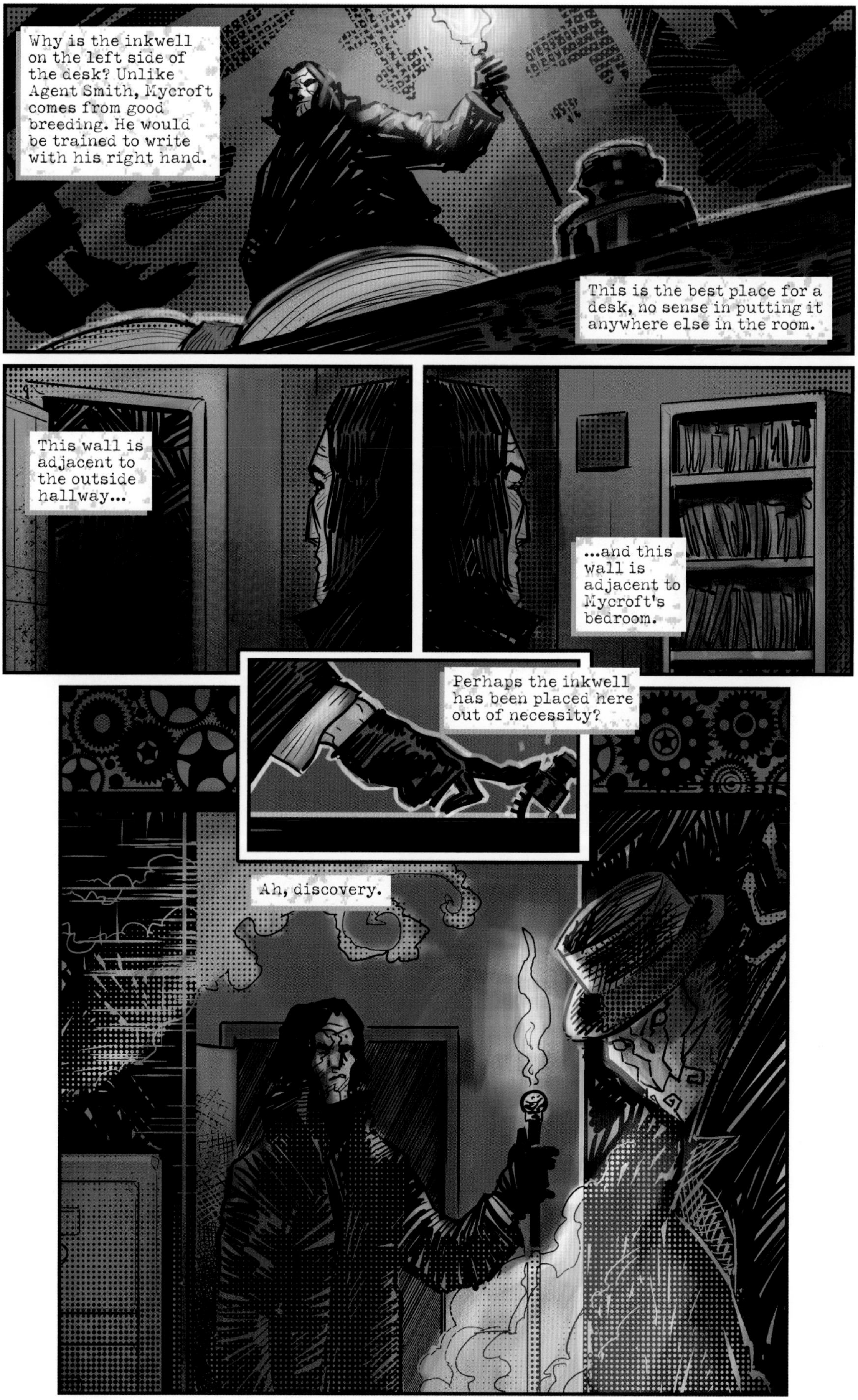
Why is the inkwell on the left side of the desk? Unlike Agent Smith, Mycroft comes from good breeding. He would be trained to write with his right hand.
This is the best place for a desk, no sense in putting it anywhere else in the room.
This wall is adjacent to the outside hallway...
...and this wall is adjacent to Mycroft's bedroom.
Perhaps the inkwell has been placed here out of necessity?
Ah, discovery.

Mycroft Holmes, man of mystery. Seems I under-estimate you, good sir.

A costume, no doubt worn to your more exclusive, sordid-type affairs. The smell of cigars and alcohol are apparent. There's an envelope in the pocket of the cloak...

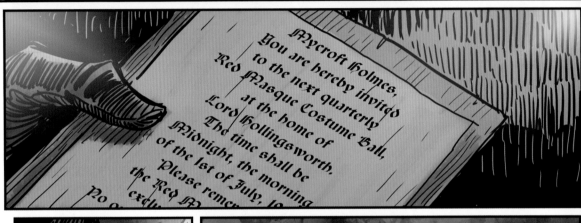

Mycroft Holmes,
You are hereby invited to the next quarterly Red Masque Costume Ball, at the home of Lord Hollingsworth,
The time shall be Midnight, the morning of the 1st of July, 18_
Please remember the Red M_ exclu_
No o_

I must attend a party tonight, it seems.

Only a few hours left to prowl before the event. Mostly financial records here, nothing of interest.

Wait...

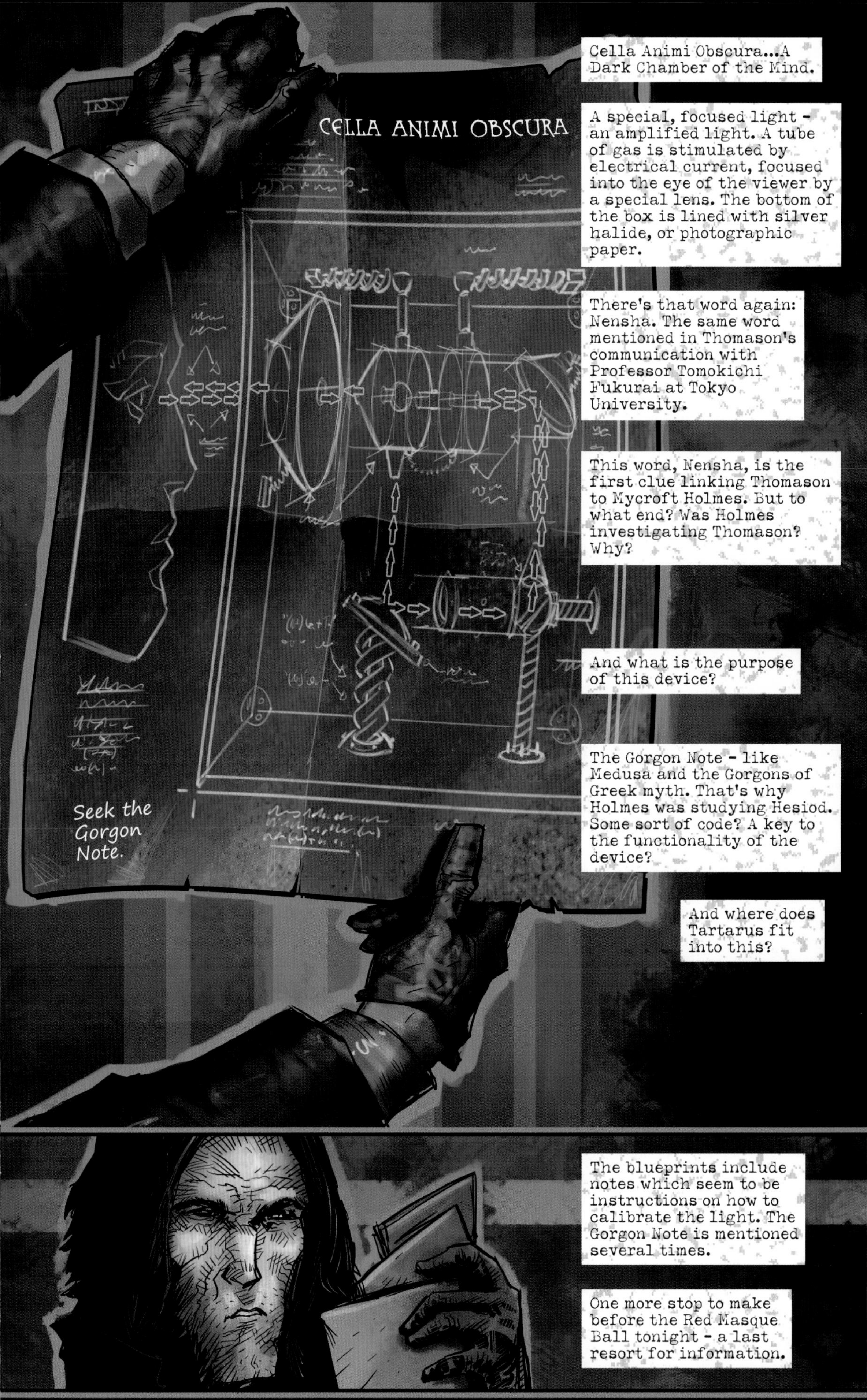
Cella Animi Obscura...A Dark Chamber of the Mind.
CELLA ANIMI OBSCURA
A special, focused light - an amplified light. A tube of gas is stimulated by electrical current, focused into the eye of the viewer by a special lens. The bottom of the box is lined with silver halide, or photographic paper.
There's that word again: Nensha. The same word mentioned in Thomason's communication with Professor Tomokichi Fukurai at Tokyo University.
This word, Nensha, is the first clue linking Thomason to Mycroft Holmes. But to what end? Was Holmes investigating Thomason? Why?
And what is the purpose of this device?
Seek the Gorgon Note.
The Gorgon Note - like Medusa and the Gorgons of Greek myth. That's why Holmes was studying Hesiod. Some sort of code? A key to the functionality of the device?
And where does Tartarus fit into this?
The blueprints include notes which seem to be instructions on how to calibrate the light. The Gorgon Note is mentioned several times.
One more stop to make before the Red Masque Ball tonight - a last resort for information.

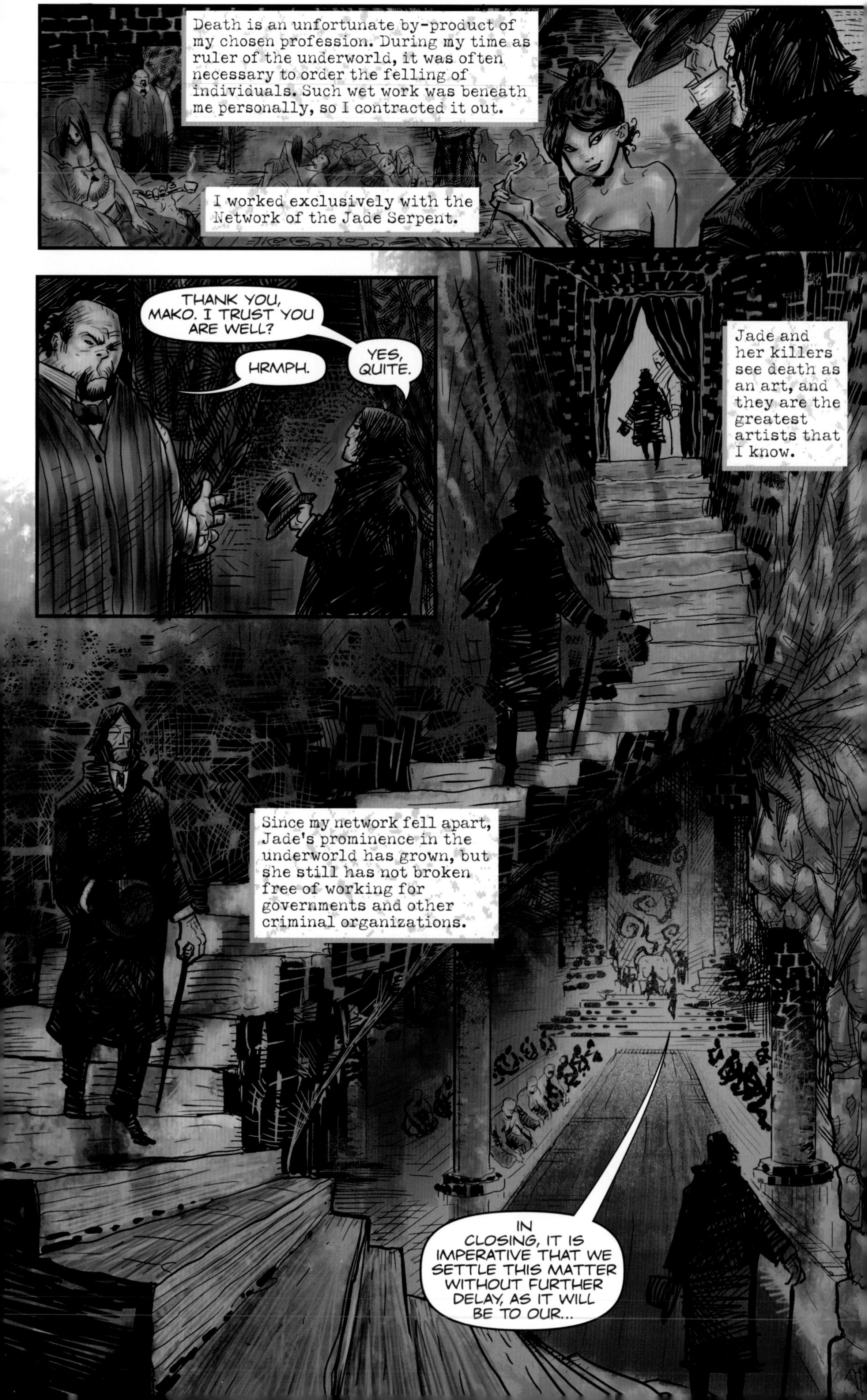

Death is an unfortunate by-product of my chosen profession. During my time as ruler of the underworld, it was often necessary to order the felling of individuals. Such wet work was beneath me personally, so I contracted it out.
I worked exclusively with the Network of the Jade Serpent.
THANK YOU, MAKO. I TRUST YOU ARE WELL?
HRMPH.
YES, QUITE.
Jade and her killers see death as an art, and they are the greatest artists that I know.
Since my network fell apart, Jade's prominence in the underworld has grown, but she still has not broken free of working for governments and other criminal organizations.
IN CLOSING, IT IS IMPERATIVE THAT WE SETTLE THIS MATTER WITHOUT FURTHER DELAY, AS IT WILL BE TO OUR...

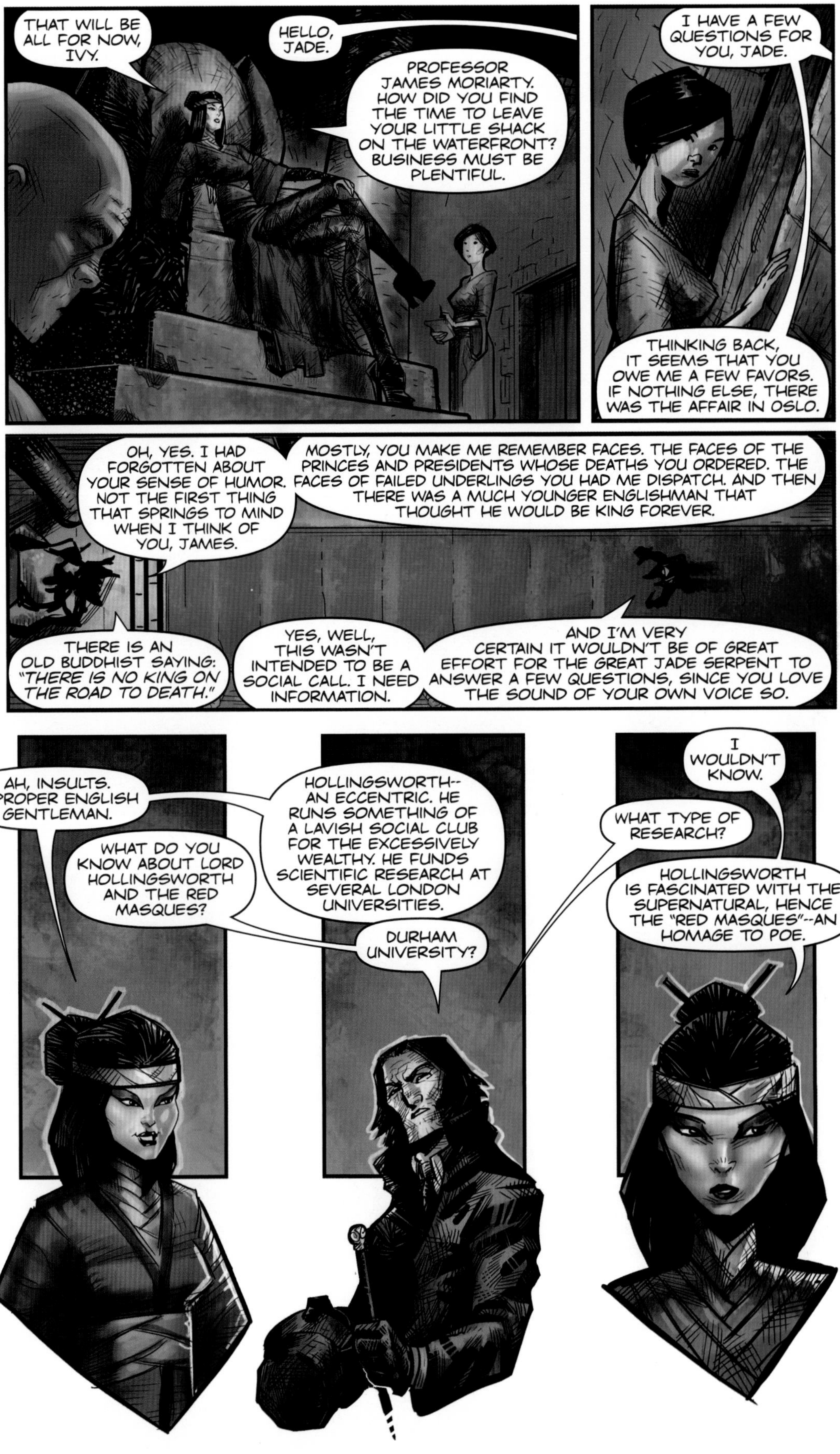
THAT WILL BE ALL FOR NOW, IVY.
HELLO, JADE.
PROFESSOR JAMES MORIARTY. HOW DID YOU FIND THE TIME TO LEAVE YOUR LITTLE SHACK ON THE WATERFRONT? BUSINESS MUST BE PLENTIFUL.
I HAVE A FEW QUESTIONS FOR YOU, JADE.
THINKING BACK, IT SEEMS THAT YOU OWE ME A FEW FAVORS. IF NOTHING ELSE, THERE WAS THE AFFAIR IN OSLO.
OH, YES. I HAD FORGOTTEN ABOUT YOUR SENSE OF HUMOR. NOT THE FIRST THING THAT SPRINGS TO MIND WHEN I THINK OF YOU, JAMES.
MOSTLY, YOU MAKE ME REMEMBER FACES. THE FACES OF THE PRINCES AND PRESIDENTS WHOSE DEATHS YOU ORDERED. THE FACES OF FAILED UNDERLINGS YOU HAD ME DISPATCH. AND THEN THERE WAS A MUCH YOUNGER ENGLISHMAN THAT THOUGHT HE WOULD BE KING FOREVER.
THERE IS AN OLD BUDDHIST SAYING: "THERE IS NO KING ON THE ROAD TO DEATH."
YES, WELL, THIS WASN'T INTENDED TO BE A SOCIAL CALL. I NEED INFORMATION.
AND I'M VERY CERTAIN IT WOULDN'T BE OF GREAT EFFORT FOR THE GREAT JADE SERPENT TO ANSWER A FEW QUESTIONS, SINCE YOU LOVE THE SOUND OF YOUR OWN VOICE SO.
AH, INSULTS. A PROPER ENGLISH GENTLEMAN.
WHAT DO YOU KNOW ABOUT LORD HOLLINGSWORTH AND THE RED MASQUES?
HOLLINGSWORTH-- AN ECCENTRIC. HE RUNS SOMETHING OF A LAVISH SOCIAL CLUB FOR THE EXCESSIVELY WEALTHY. HE FUNDS SCIENTIFIC RESEARCH AT SEVERAL LONDON UNIVERSITIES.
DURHAM UNIVERSITY?
I WOULDN'T KNOW.
WHAT TYPE OF RESEARCH?
HOLLINGSWORTH IS FASCINATED WITH THE SUPERNATURAL, HENCE THE "RED MASQUES"--AN HOMAGE TO POE.

TELL ME ABOUT GOTTFRIED.

HE RUNS SOMETHING OF A STREET GANG CALLED THE SONS OF CHAOS. A LIMP IDEALIST WHO WORKS THE STREETS FOR PETTY CASH. NOT UNLIKE YOU, JAMES.

LOVELY.

WHAT DOES NENSHA MEAN? A JAPANESE WORD, YES?

TO ENGLISH SPEAKERS, IT IS BETTER CALLED PROJECTED THERMOGRAPHY, OR SPIRIT PHOTOGRAPHY.

A FEW YEARS AGO, A PROFESSOR AT TOKYO UNIVERSITY CALLED TOMOKICHI FUKURAI EXPERIMENTED WITH CLAIRVOYANTS, CLAIMING THAT SOME PEOPLE NOT ONLY HAVE THE ABILITY TO SEE INTO THE SPIRIT WORLD, BUT CAN BURN IMAGES ONTO SURFACES.

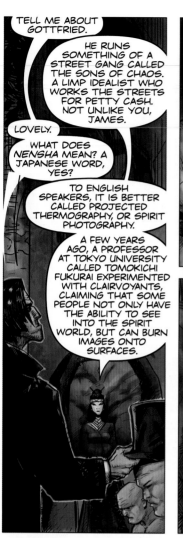

HAVE YOU BEEN IN COMMUNICATION WITH THE BLACK HAND RECENTLY?

OH, JAMES. THAT LOT IS ENTIRELY BENEATH YOU, EVEN.

NO, MY SUPERIORS IN JAPAN WANT TO STAY LOYAL TO THE ENTENTE CORDIALE, GIVEN THE RECENT REAFFIRMATION OF THE ANGLO-JAPANESE ALLIANCE.

I MAY HAVE NEED TO CALL ON THEM.

YOU WILL NEED TO SET THAT UP BY OTHER MEANS, I'M AFRAID.

YES, WELL, YOU WOULDN'T WANT TO UPSET YOUR SUPERIORS. HOW DOES IT FEEL, TAKING ORDERS? NEVER BEING THE QUEEN OF YOUR OWN DOMAIN?

I USE THEM, THEY USE ME. AN HONEST LIVING IS HARD TO MAKE IN OUR LINE OF WORK THESE DAYS, YOU KNOW.

AT LEAST I HAVE MANAGED TO MAINTAIN A CERTAIN LEVEL OF DIGNITY. YOU ARE SCRAPING THE BOTTOM OF THE BARREL.

WELL, I GUESS YOU'VE BEEN TO THE BOTTOM BEFORE. THERE WAS THAT TIME THAT YOU MANAGED TO DO YOUR OWN DIRTY WORK--

--HIGH ON THAT MOUNTAIN IN SWITZERLAND...

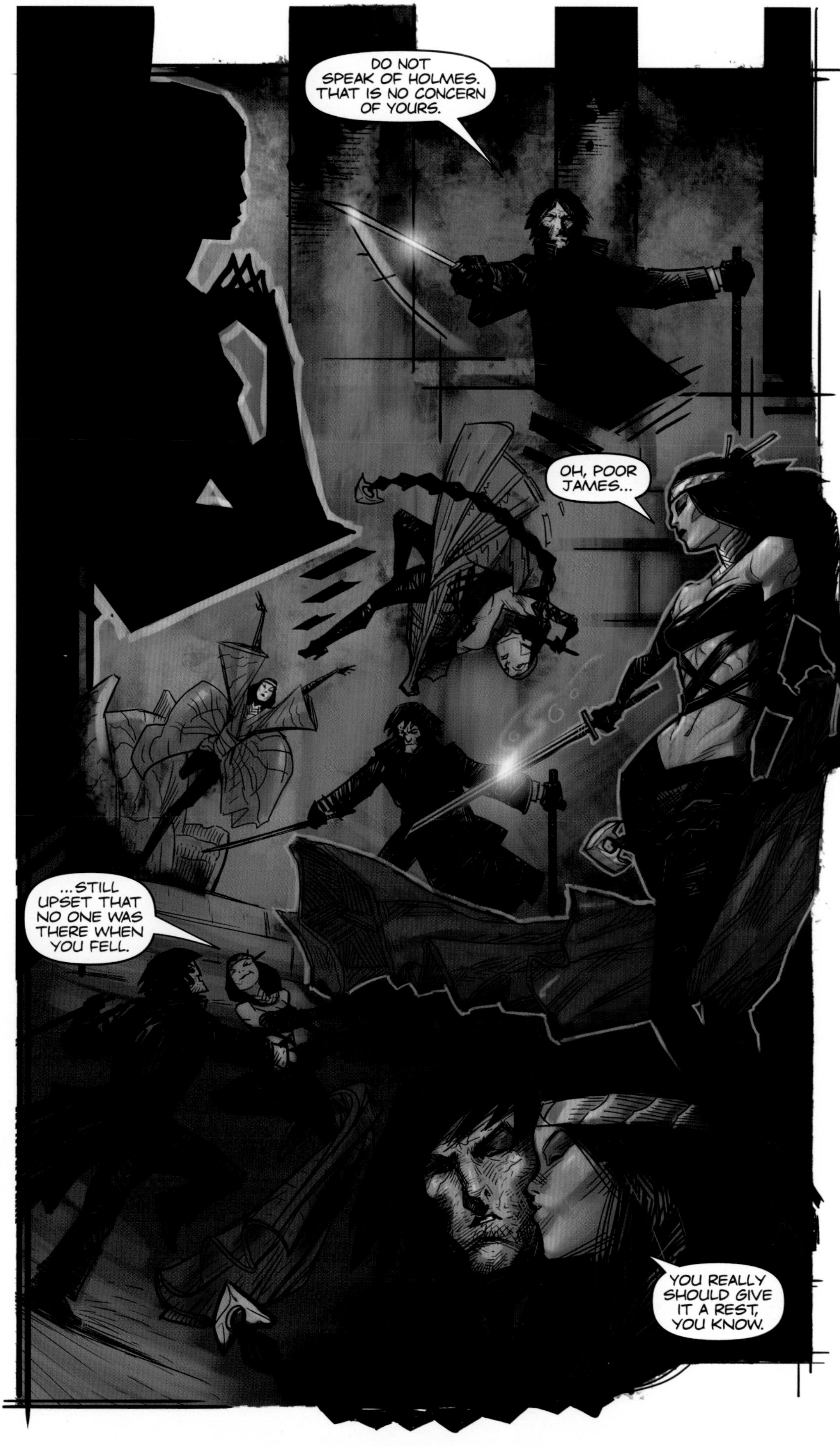
DO NOT SPEAK OF HOLMES. THAT IS NO CONCERN OF YOURS.
OH, POOR JAMES...
...STILL UPSET THAT NO ONE WAS THERE WHEN YOU FELL.
YOU REALLY SHOULD GIVE IT A REST, YOU KNOW.

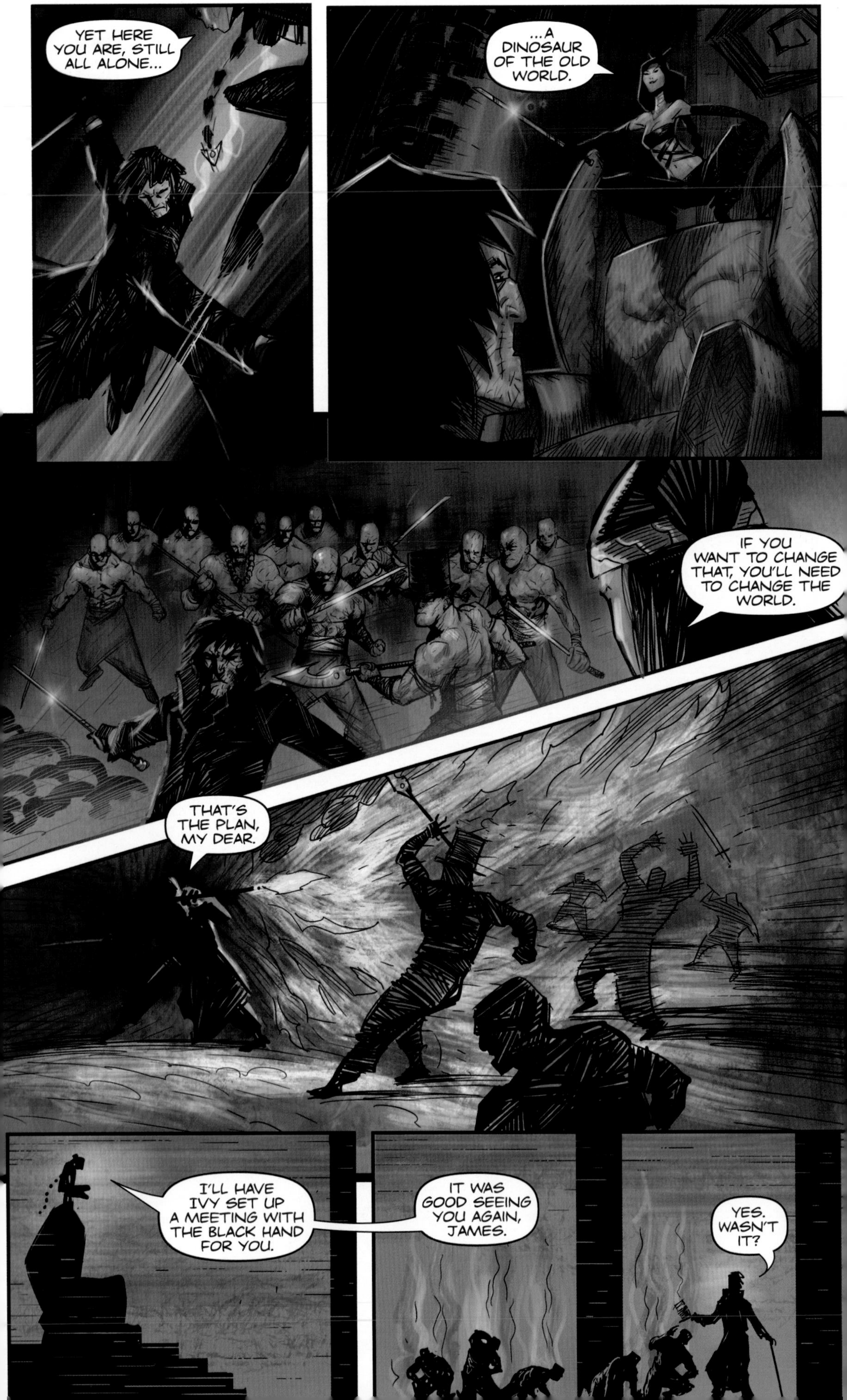
YET HERE YOU ARE, STILL ALL ALONE...
...A DINOSAUR OF THE OLD WORLD.
IF YOU WANT TO CHANGE THAT, YOU'LL NEED TO CHANGE THE WORLD.
THAT'S THE PLAN, MY DEAR.
I'LL HAVE IVY SET UP A MEETING WITH THE BLACK HAND FOR YOU.
IT WAS GOOD SEEING YOU AGAIN, JAMES.
YES. WASN'T IT?

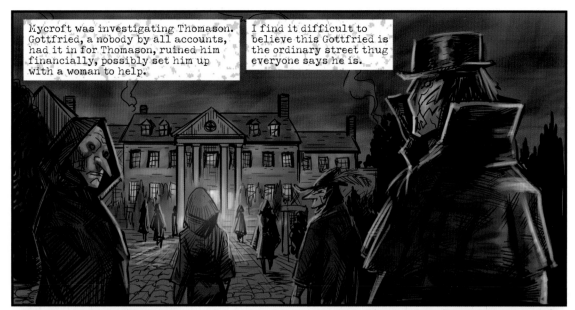

Mycroft was investigating Thomason. Gottfried, a nobody by all accounts, had it in for Thomason, ruined him financially, possibly set him up with a woman to help.

I find it difficult to believe this Gottfried is the ordinary street thug everyone says he is.

GOOD EVENING, MY FRIENDS! WELCOME TO THE RED MASQUE COSTUME BALL!

WE ARE CLOSER THAN EVER, GENTLEMEN. I AM PLEASED TO TELL YOU THAT BY THE NEXT TIME WE MEET, OUR LABOR SHALL BE MET WITH SUCCESS.

MANY HAVE OPPOSED US, BUT THE RED MASQUES KNOW THAT THERE IS A DARKNESS TO THE SOUL OF MAN THAT CONTAINS THE POWER TO LIGHT A THOUSAND ROOMS. WE INTEND TO TAP THAT POWER.

THE ENEMY HAS STOLEN FROM OUR FLOCK, BUT PROFESSOR THOMASON'S WORK CONTINUES.

There it is. Thomason worked for Hollingsworth, and Holmes was investigating both men.

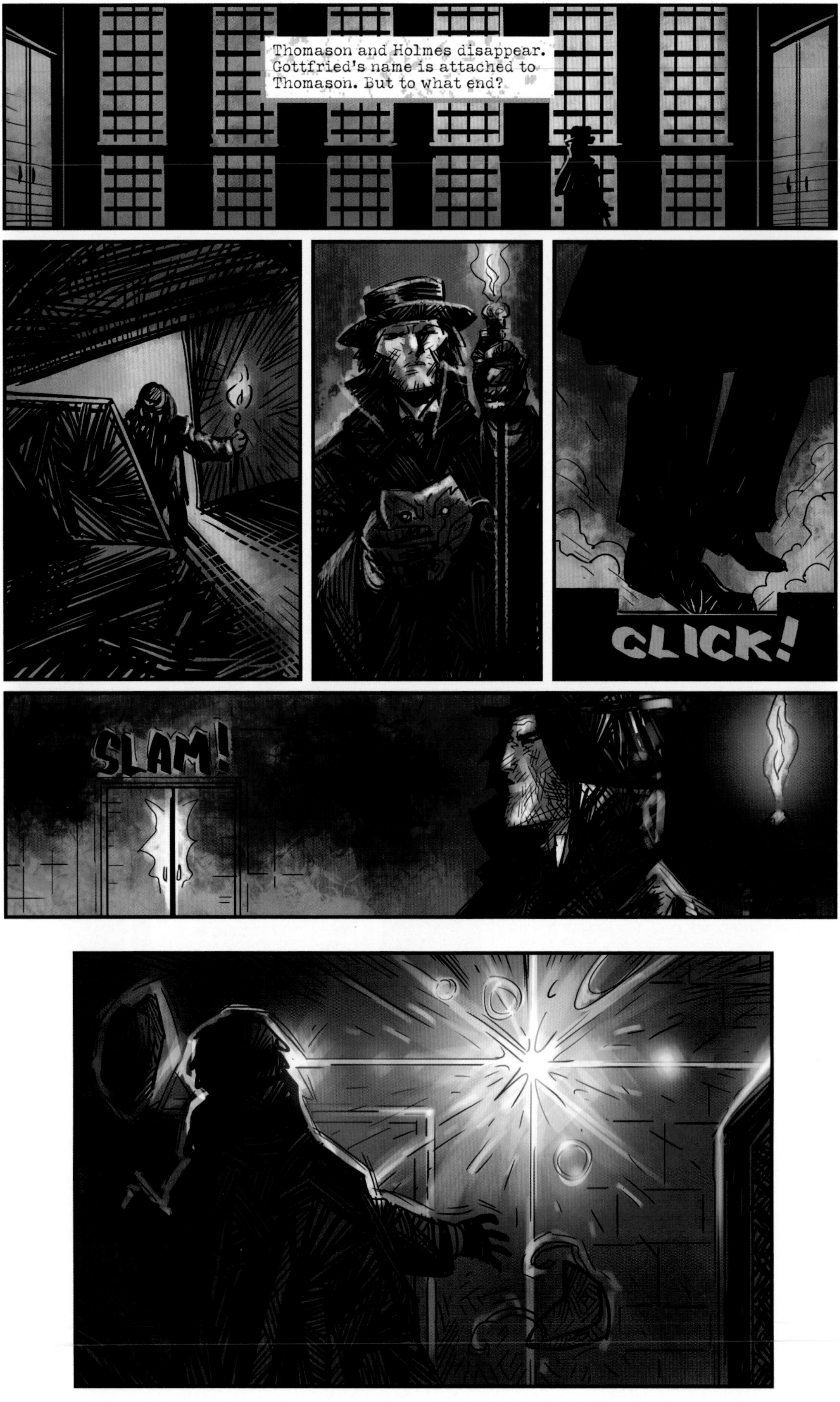
Thomason and Holmes disappear. Gottfried's name is attached to Thomason. But to what end?
CLICK!
SLAM!

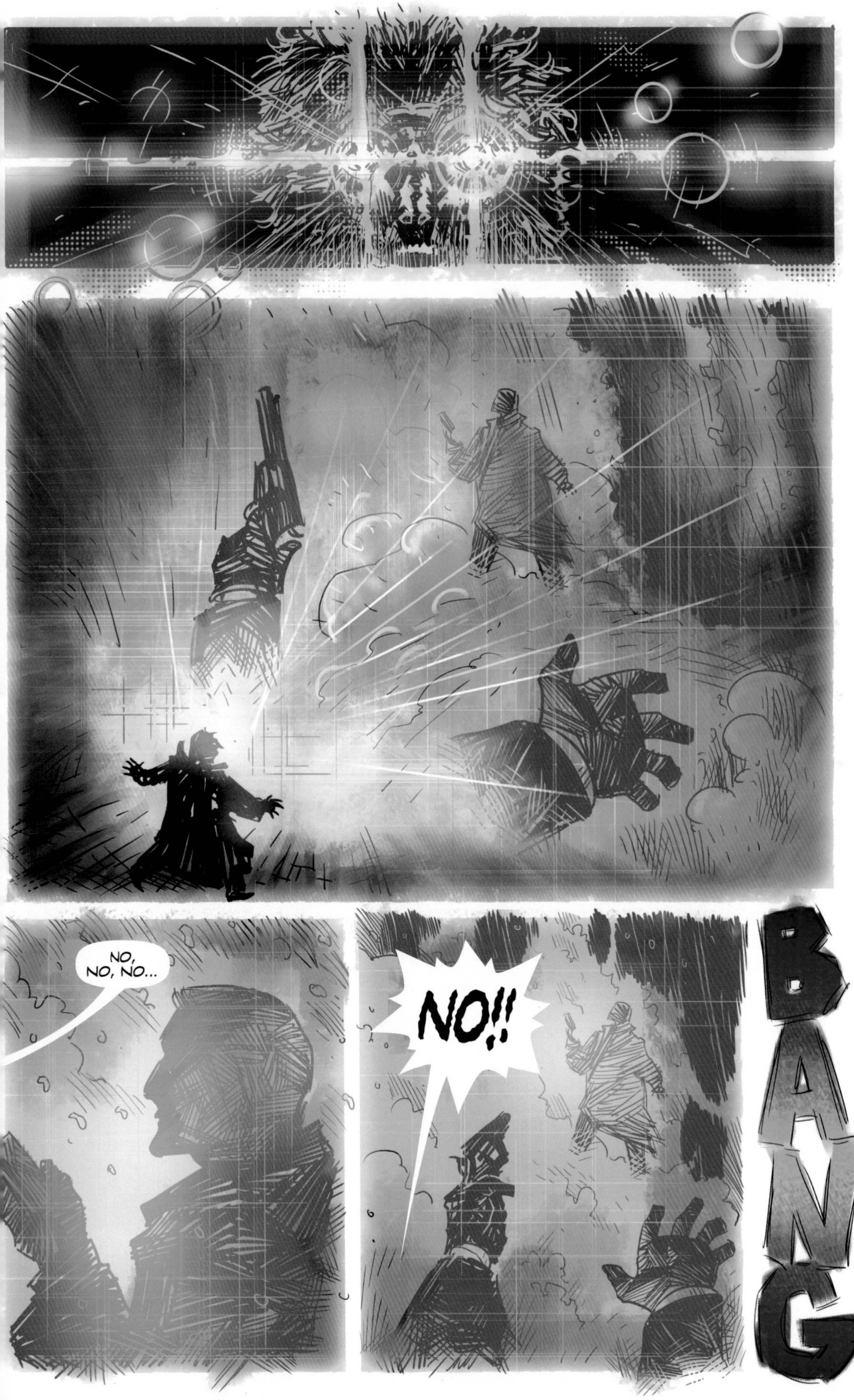
NO, NO, NO...
NO!!
BANG

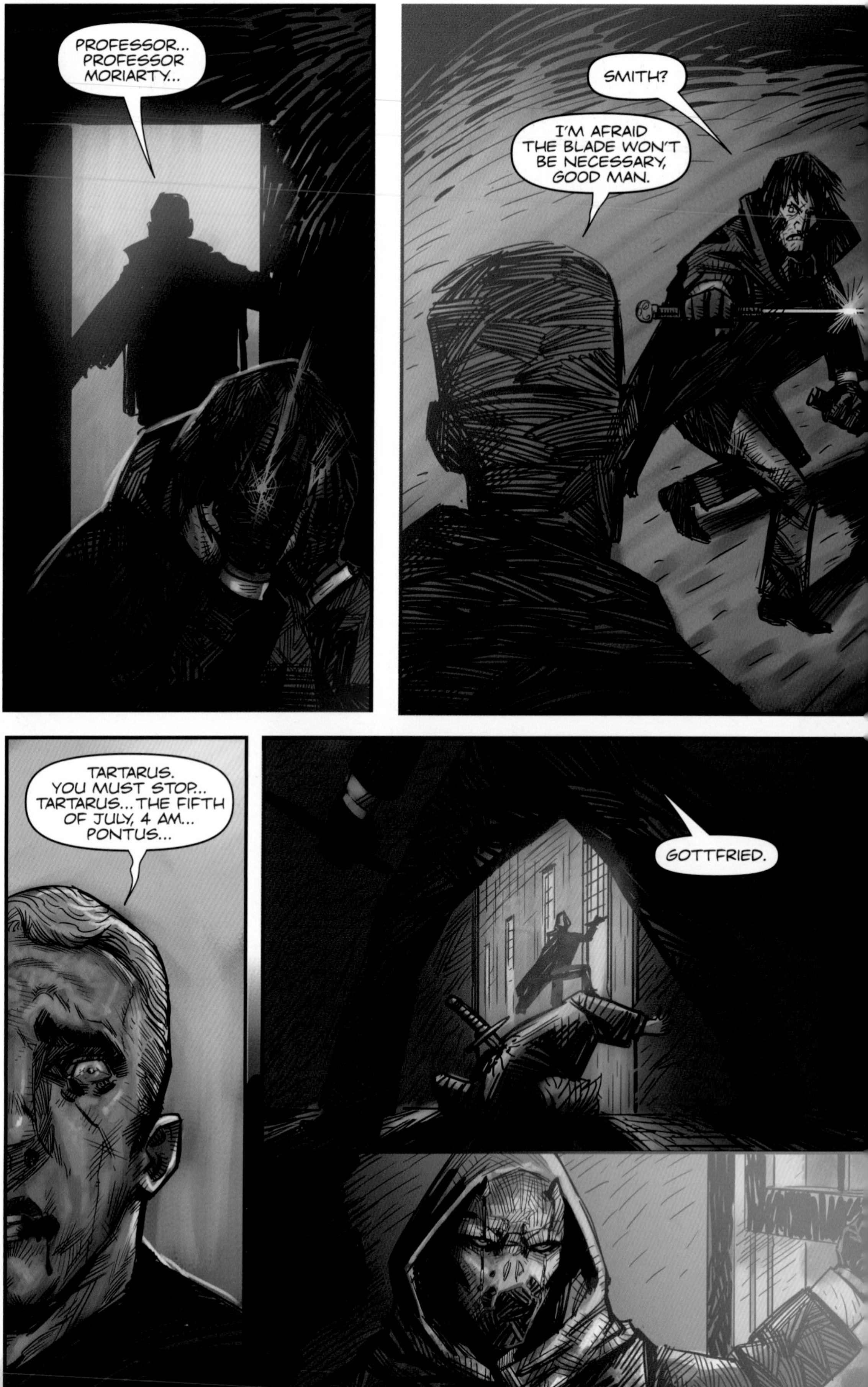
PROFESSOR... PROFESSOR MORIARTY...
SMITH?
I'M AFRAID THE BLADE WON'T BE NECESSARY, GOOD MAN.
TARTARUS. YOU MUST STOP... TARTARUS... THE FIFTH OF JULY, 4 AM... PONTUS...
GOTTFRIED.

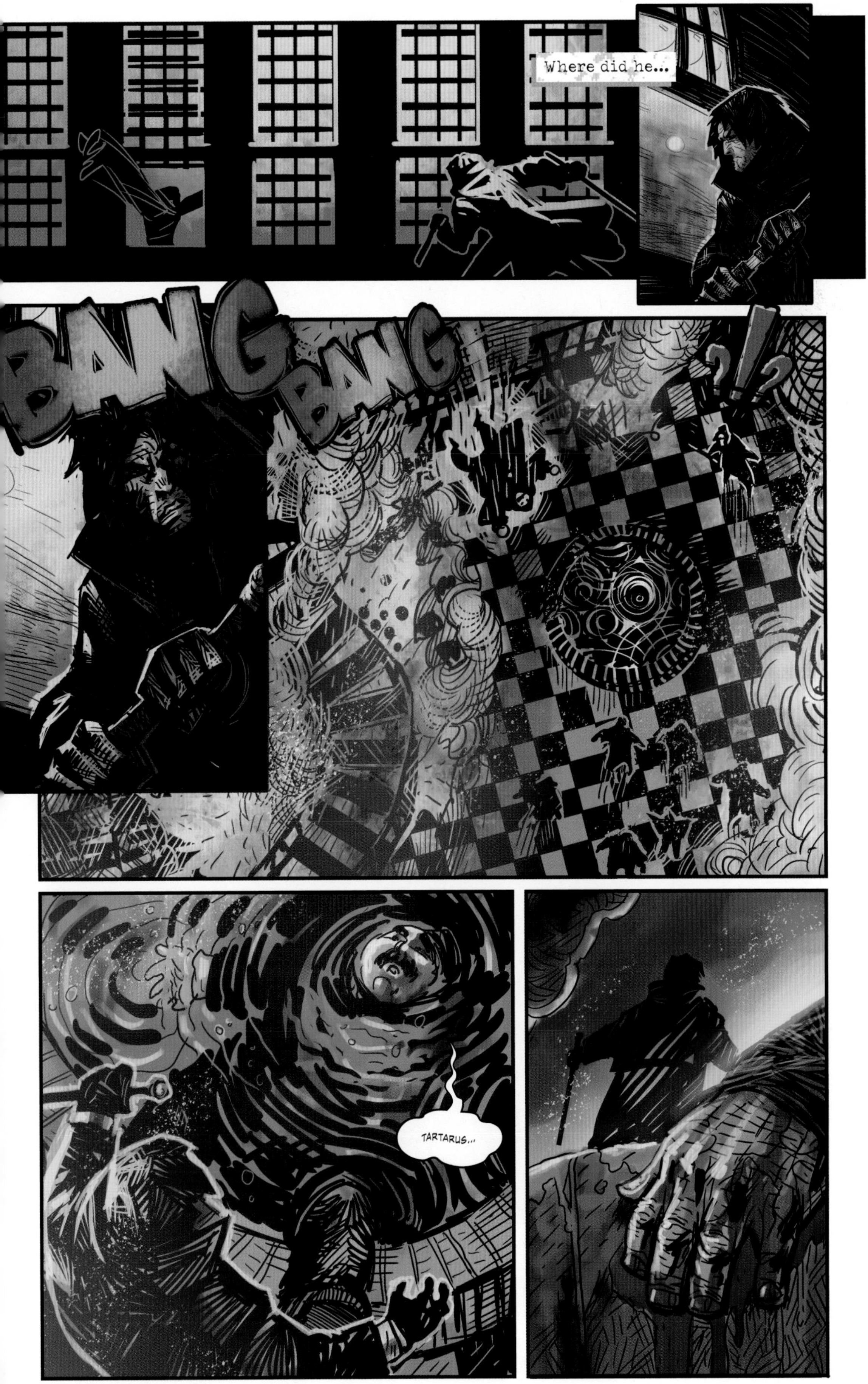
Where did he...
BANG
BANG
?!?
TARTARUS...

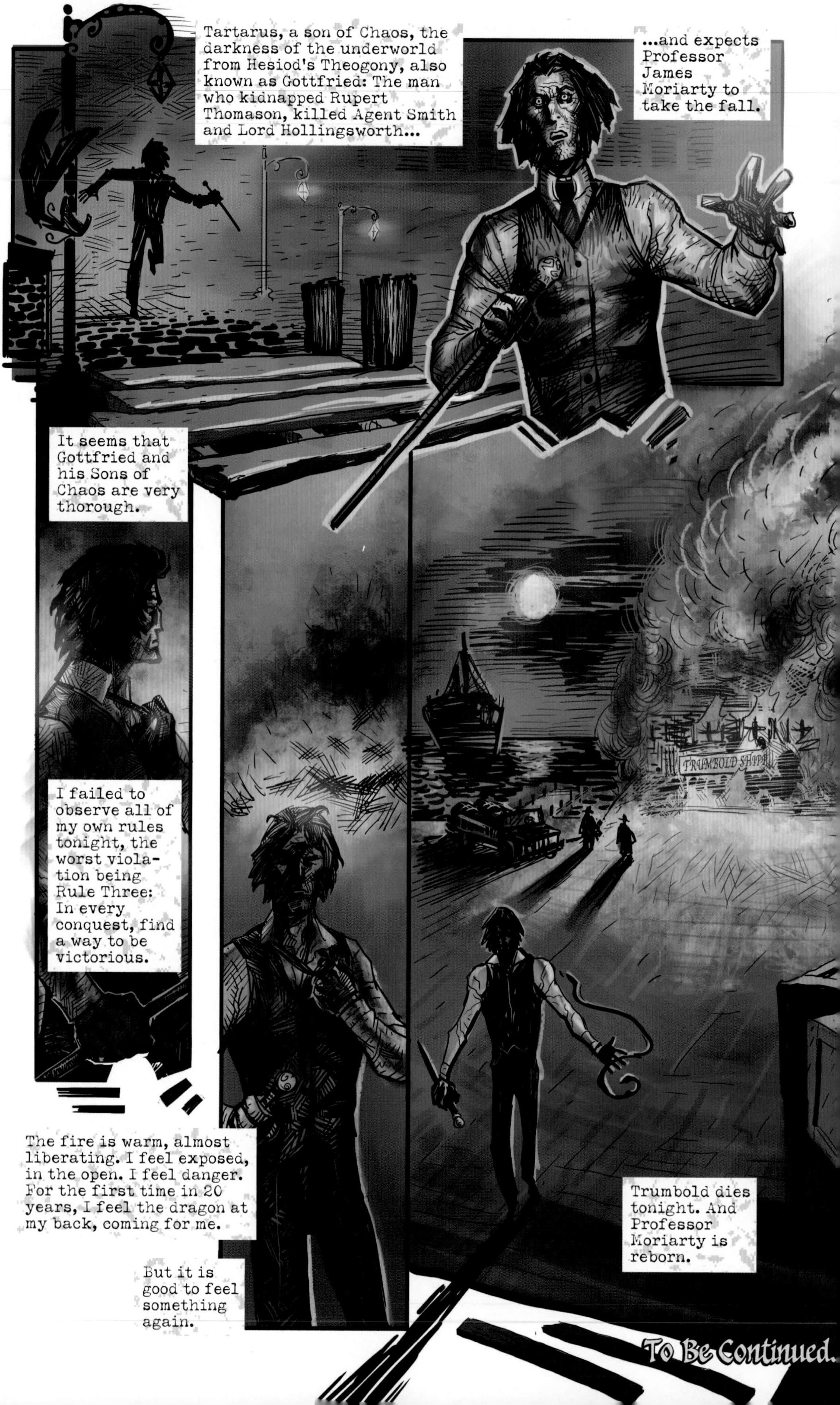
Tartarus, a son of Chaos, the darkness of the underworld from Hesiod's Theogony, also known as Gottfried: The man who kidnapped Rupert Thomason, killed Agent Smith and Lord Hollingsworth...
...and expects Professor James Moriarty to take the fall.
It seems that Gottfried and his Sons of Chaos are very thorough.
I failed to observe all of my own rules tonight, the worst violation being Rule Three: In every conquest, find a way to be victorious.
TRUMBOLD SHIPS
The fire is warm, almost liberating. I feel exposed, in the open. I feel danger. For the first time in 20 years, I feel the dragon at my back, coming for me.
But it is good to feel something again.
Trumbold dies tonight. And Professor Moriarty is reborn.
To Be Continued.

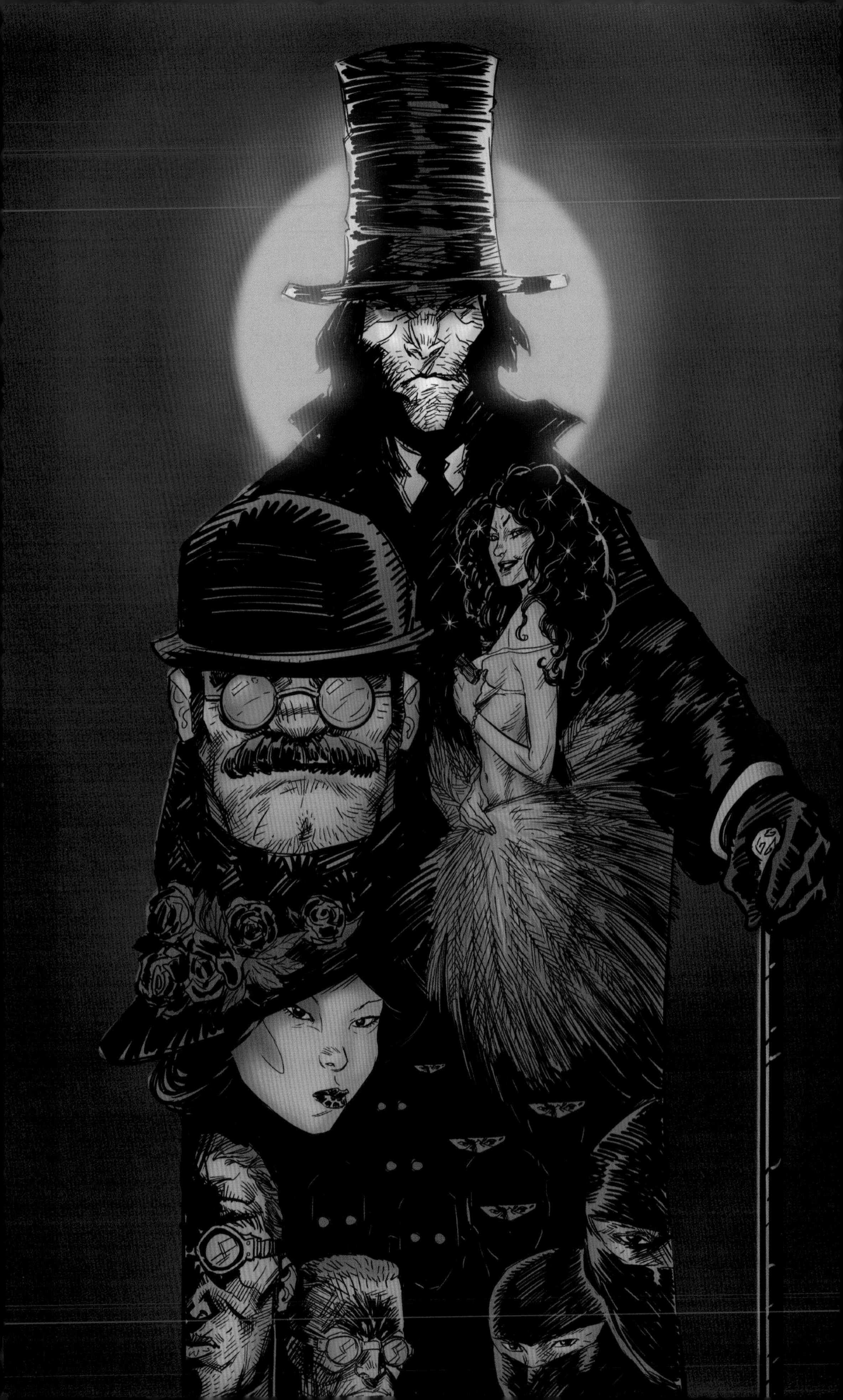

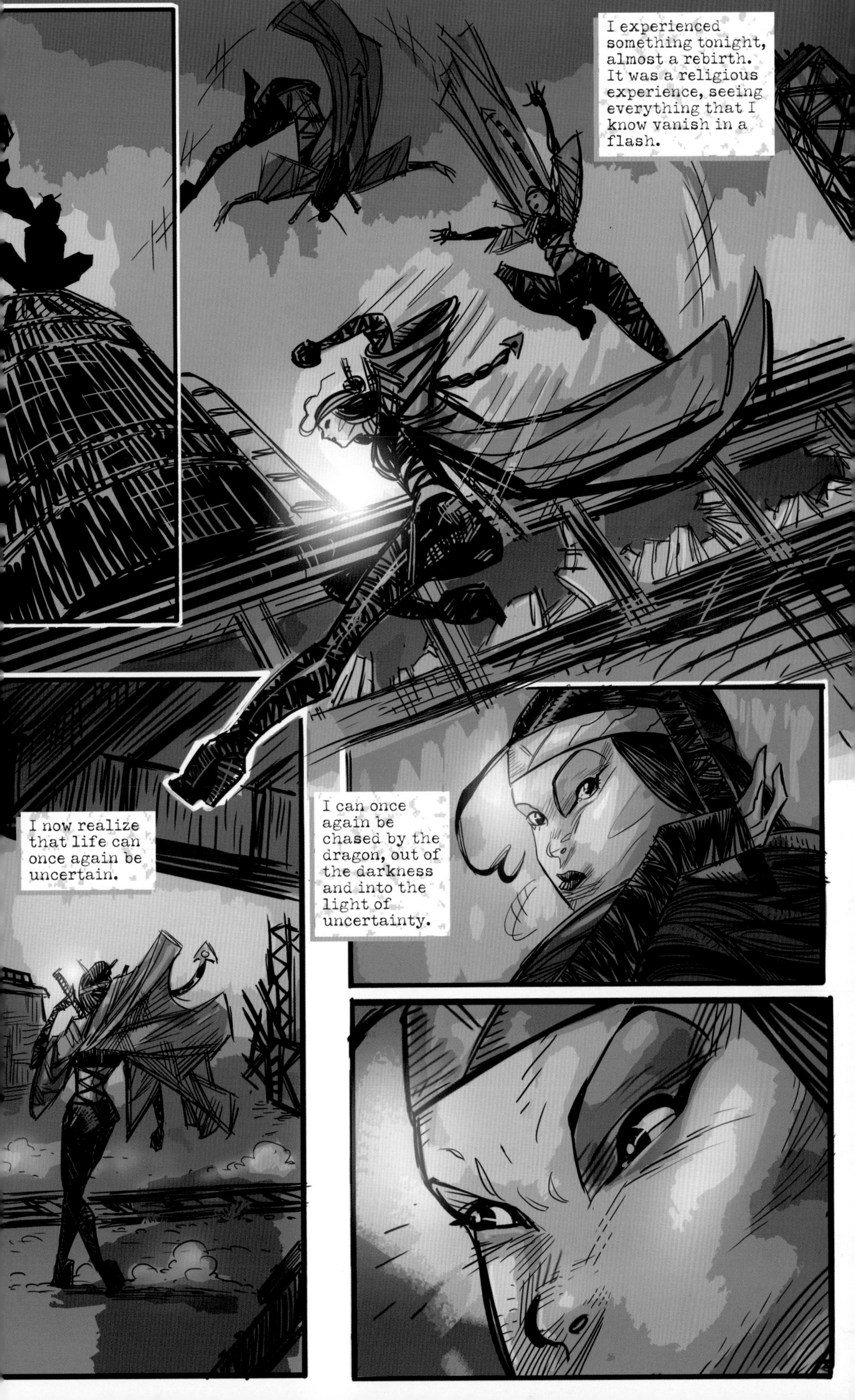
I experienced something tonight, almost a rebirth. It was a religious experience, seeing everything that I know vanish in a flash.
I now realize that life can once again be uncertain.
I can once again be chased by the dragon, out of the darkness and into the light of uncertainty.

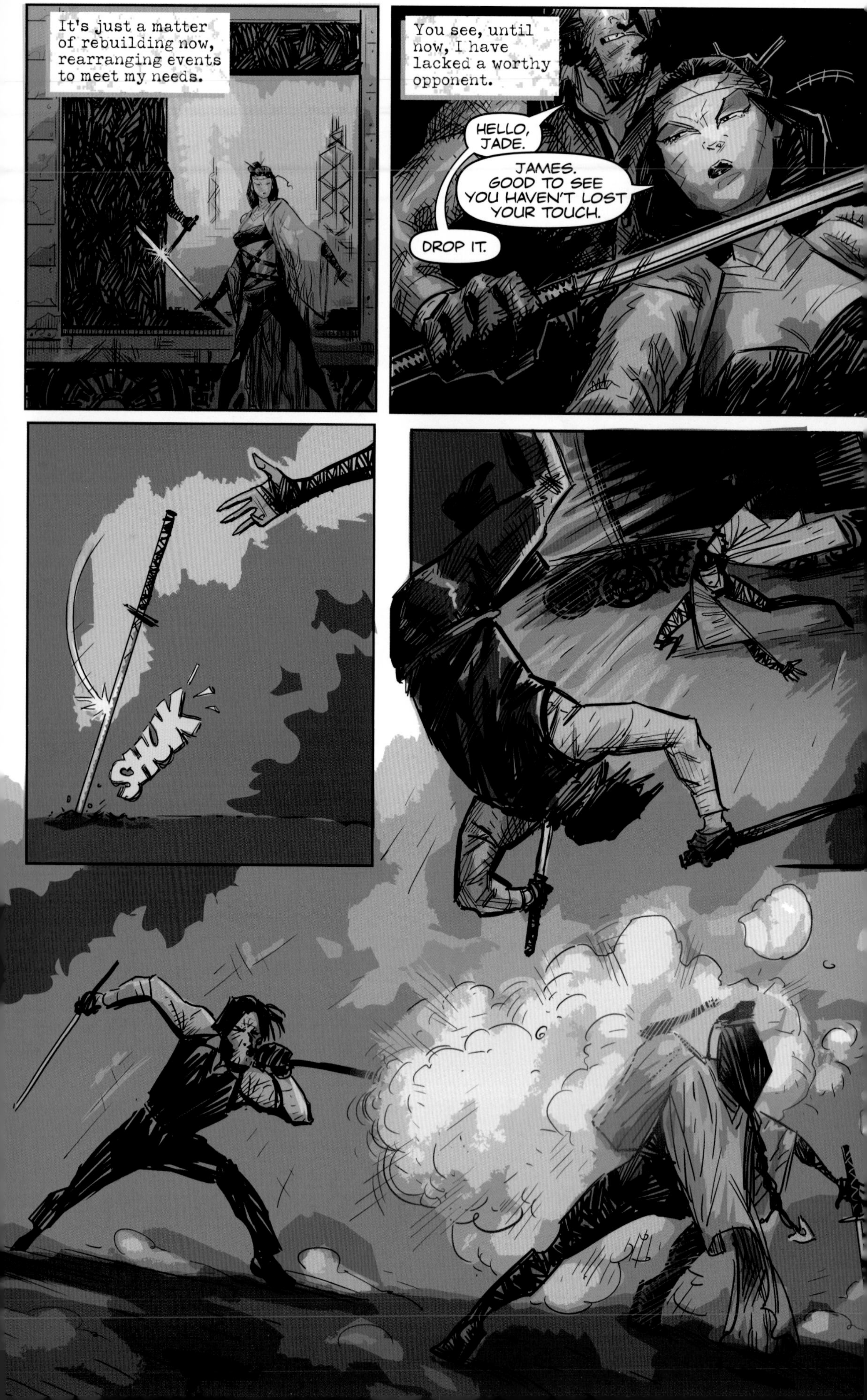
It's just a matter of rebuilding now, rearranging events to meet my needs.
You see, until now, I have lacked a worthy opponent.
HELLO, JADE.
JAMES. GOOD TO SEE YOU HAVEN'T LOST YOUR TOUCH.
DROP IT.
SHUK

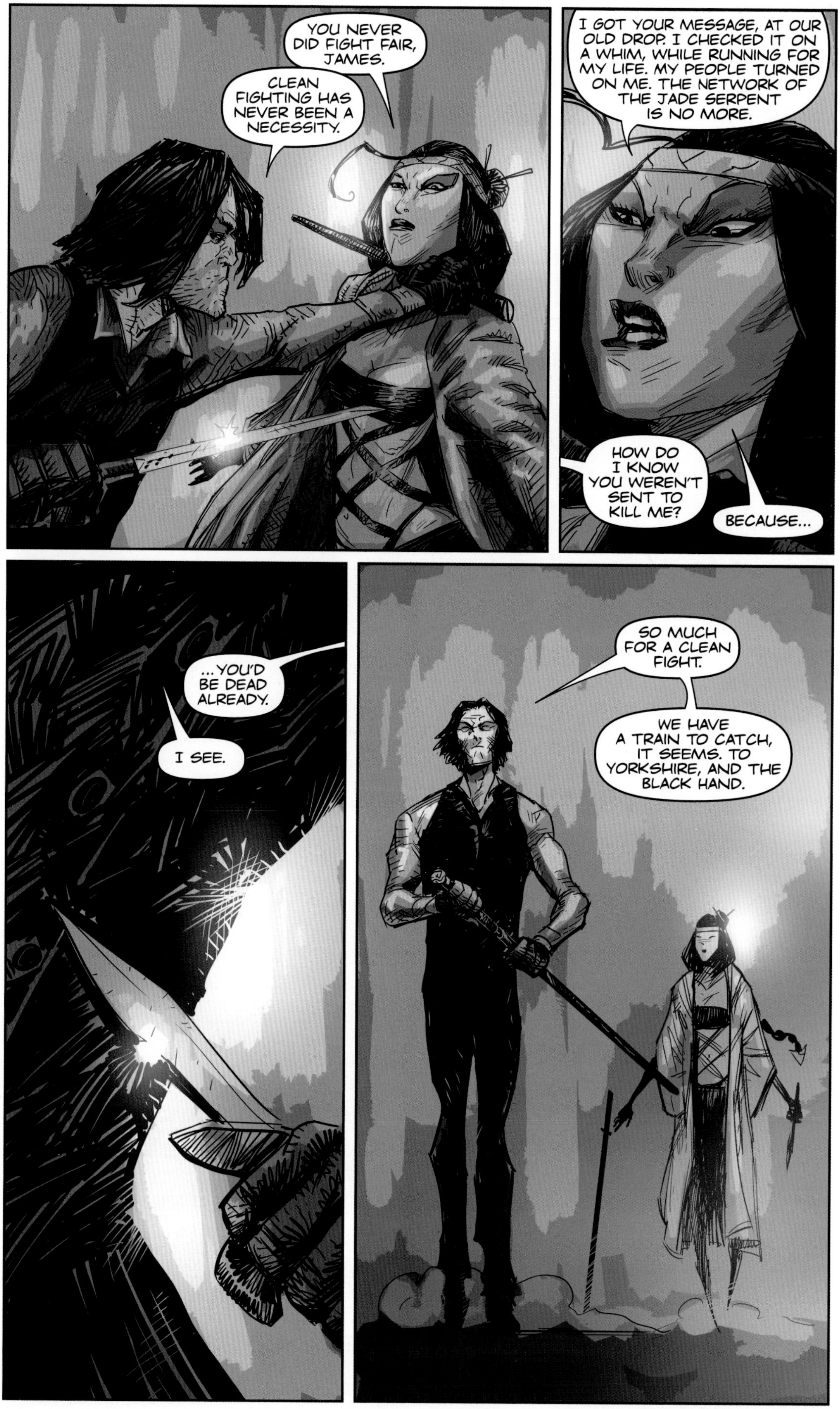
YOU NEVER DID FIGHT FAIR, JAMES.
CLEAN FIGHTING HAS NEVER BEEN A NECESSITY.
I GOT YOUR MESSAGE, AT OUR OLD DROP. I CHECKED IT ON A WHIM, WHILE RUNNING FOR MY LIFE. MY PEOPLE TURNED ON ME. THE NETWORK OF THE JADE SERPENT IS NO MORE.
HOW DO I KNOW YOU WEREN'T SENT TO KILL ME?
BECAUSE...
...YOU'D BE DEAD ALREADY.
I SEE.
SO MUCH FOR A CLEAN FIGHT.
WE HAVE A TRAIN TO CATCH, IT SEEMS. TO YORKSHIRE, AND THE BLACK HAND.

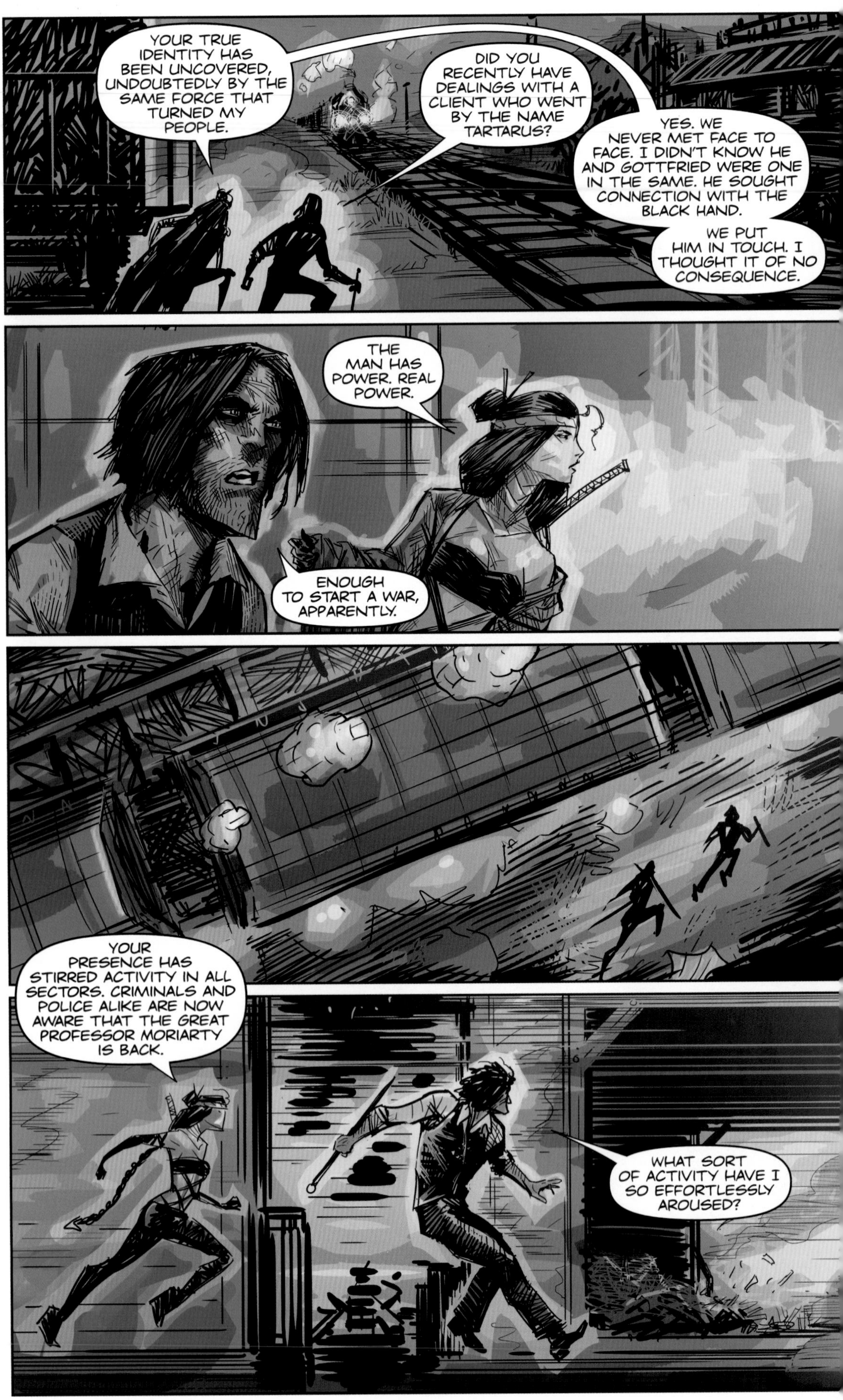
YOUR TRUE IDENTITY HAS BEEN UNCOVERED, UNDOUBTEDLY BY THE SAME FORCE THAT TURNED MY PEOPLE.
DID YOU RECENTLY HAVE DEALINGS WITH A CLIENT WHO WENT BY THE NAME TARTARUS?
YES. WE NEVER MET FACE TO FACE. I DIDN'T KNOW HE AND GOTTFRIED WERE ONE IN THE SAME. HE SOUGHT CONNECTION WITH THE BLACK HAND.
WE PUT HIM IN TOUCH. I THOUGHT IT OF NO CONSEQUENCE.
THE MAN HAS POWER. REAL POWER.
ENOUGH TO START A WAR, APPARENTLY.
YOUR PRESENCE HAS STIRRED ACTIVITY IN ALL SECTORS. CRIMINALS AND POLICE ALIKE ARE NOW AWARE THAT THE GREAT PROFESSOR MORIARTY IS BACK.
WHAT SORT OF ACTIVITY HAVE I SO EFFORTLESSLY AROUSED?

THE BOX, JAMES.

EVERYONE WANTS THE BOX.

THE BOX. THE RED MASQUES HAD ONE, MORE LIKE A LARGE CHAMBER.

YES, BUT THEIRS ONLY SHOWED YOU THE PAST.

IT COULD NOT PREDICT THE FUTURE.

PREDICT THE FUTURE, YOU SAY?

MOST DEFINITELY.

THOMASON CREATED THE CHAMBER YOU FOUND AT HOLLINGSWORTH'S, BUT THAT WAS JUST THE TRIAL RUN. BEFORE HIS DISAPPEARANCE, HE HAD TRUE SUCCESS.

AT LEAST THAT IS THE RUMOR. MOST ARE SPECULATING THAT GOTTFRIED RUINED THOMASON, AND NOW OWNS BOTH HIM AND HIS BOX.

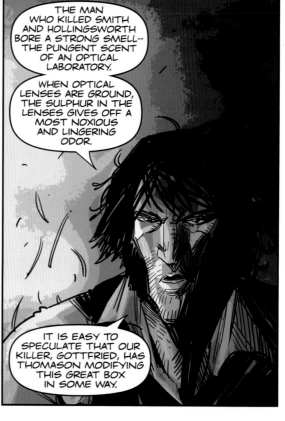

THE MAN WHO KILLED SMITH AND HOLLINGSWORTH BORE A STRONG SMELL-- THE PUNGENT SCENT OF AN OPTICAL LABORATORY.

WHEN OPTICAL LENSES ARE GROUND, THE SULPHUR IN THE LENSES GIVES OFF A MOST NOXIOUS AND LINGERING ODOR.

IT IS EASY TO SPECULATE THAT OUR KILLER, GOTTFRIED, HAS THOMASON MODIFYING THIS GREAT BOX IN SOME WAY.

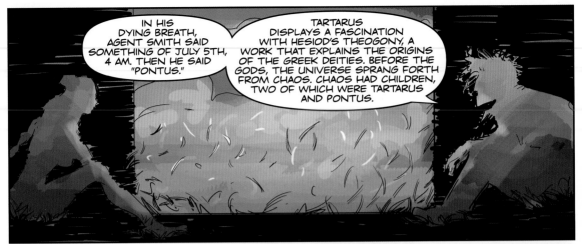

IN HIS DYING BREATH, AGENT SMITH SAID SOMETHING OF JULY 5TH, 4 AM. THEN HE SAID "PONTUS."

TARTARUS DISPLAYS A FASCINATION WITH HESIOD'S THEOGONY, A WORK THAT EXPLAINS THE ORIGINS OF THE GREEK DEITIES. BEFORE THE GODS, THE UNIVERSE SPRANG FORTH FROM CHAOS. CHAOS HAD CHILDREN, TWO OF WHICH WERE TARTARUS AND PONTUS.

WE KNOW THAT GOTTFRIED IS TARTARUS, ALTHOUGH HIS LOCALE IS UNKNOWN. BUT WE HAVE NO CLUE AS TO WHO THIS PONTUS IS.

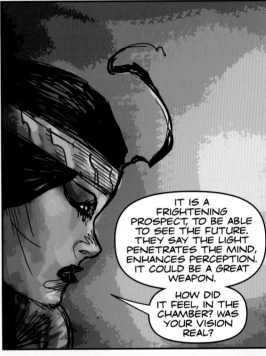

IT IS A FRIGHTENING PROSPECT, TO BE ABLE TO SEE THE FUTURE. THEY SAY THE LIGHT PENETRATES THE MIND, ENHANCES PERCEPTION. IT COULD BE A GREAT WEAPON.

HOW DID IT FEEL, IN THE CHAMBER? WAS YOUR VISION REAL?

WE RARELY GLIMPSE LITERAL REALITY. THE HUMAN MIND CAN ONLY WITHSTAND SO MUCH FEAR.

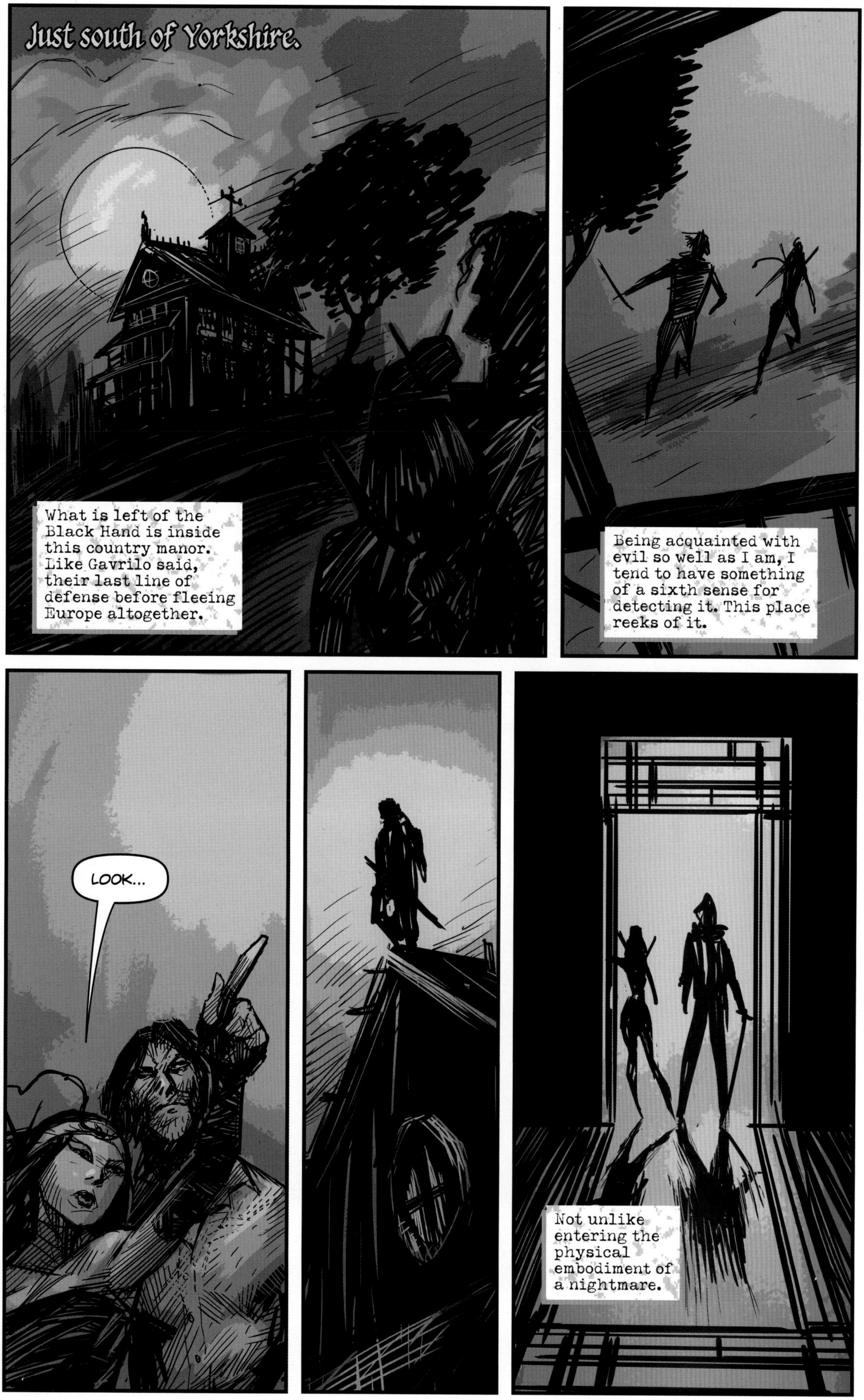
Just south of Yorkshire.
What is left of the Black Hand is inside this country manor. Like Gavrilo said, their last line of defense before fleeing Europe altogether.
Being acquainted with evil so well as I am, I tend to have something of a sixth sense for detecting it. This place reeks of it.
LOOK...
Not unlike entering the physical embodiment of a nightmare.

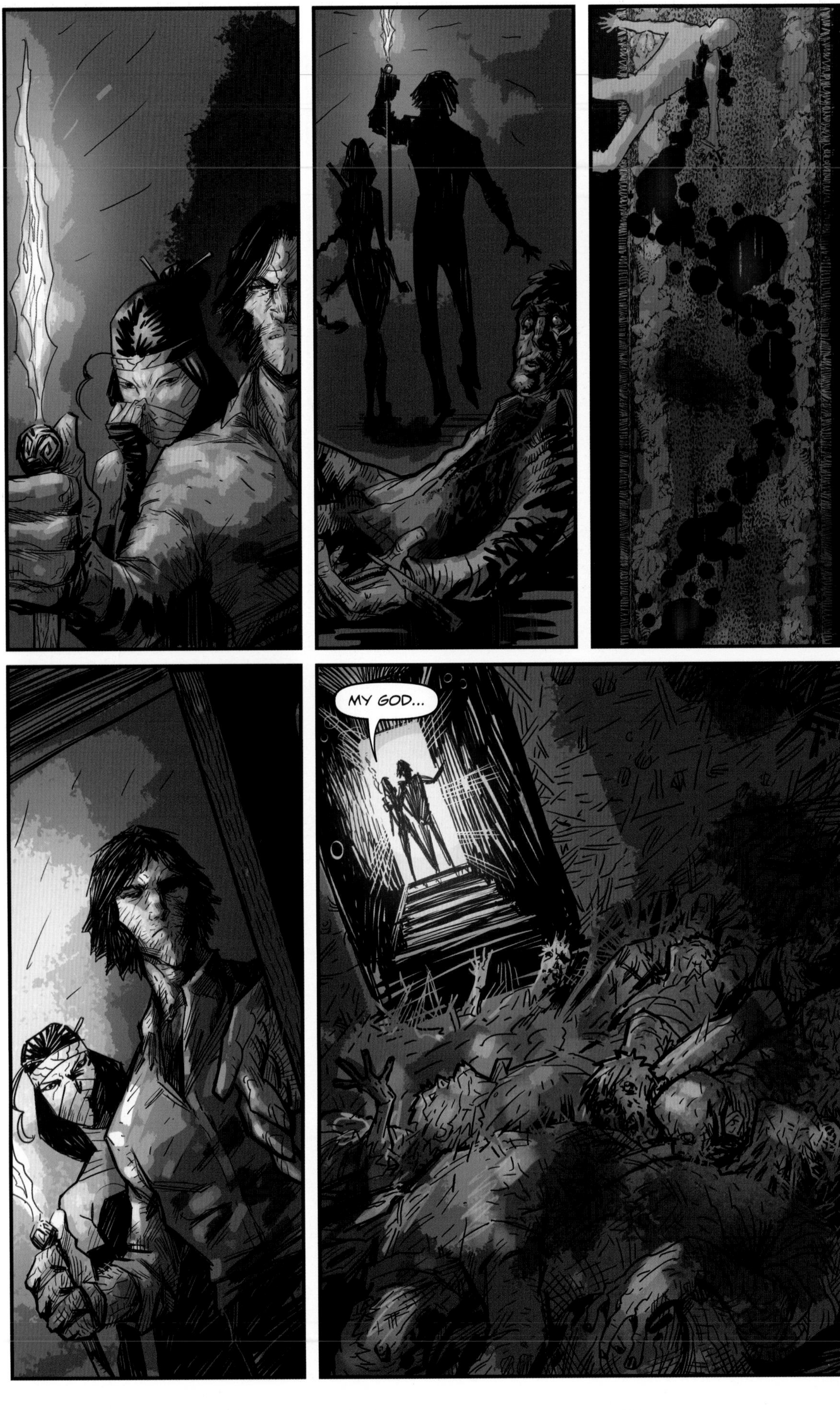
MY GOD...

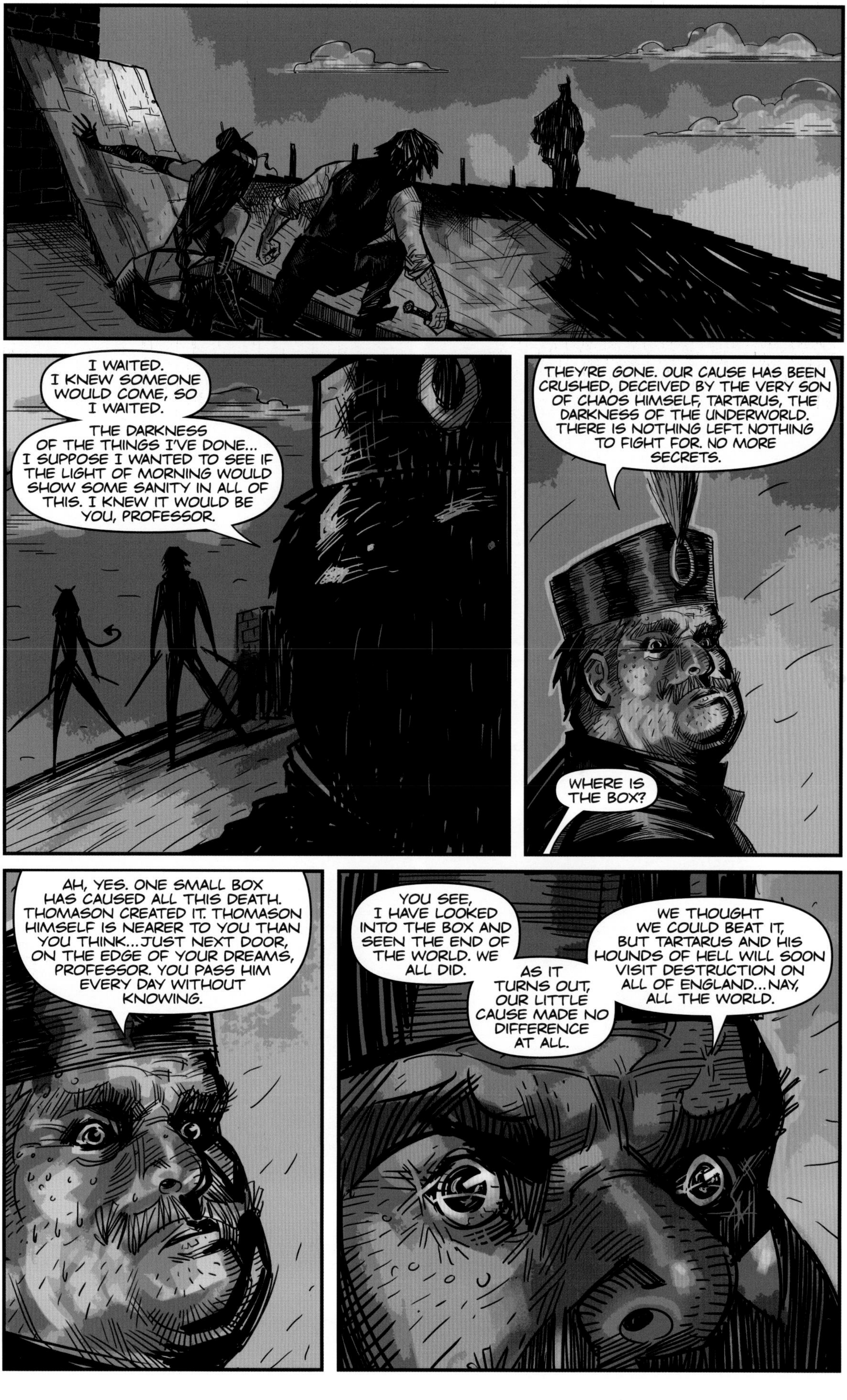
I WAITED. I KNEW SOMEONE WOULD COME, SO I WAITED.
THE DARKNESS OF THE THINGS I'VE DONE... I SUPPOSE I WANTED TO SEE IF THE LIGHT OF MORNING WOULD SHOW SOME SANITY IN ALL OF THIS. I KNEW IT WOULD BE YOU, PROFESSOR.
THEY'RE GONE. OUR CAUSE HAS BEEN CRUSHED, DECEIVED BY THE VERY SON OF CHAOS HIMSELF, TARTARUS, THE DARKNESS OF THE UNDERWORLD. THERE IS NOTHING LEFT. NOTHING TO FIGHT FOR. NO MORE SECRETS.
WHERE IS THE BOX?
AH, YES. ONE SMALL BOX HAS CAUSED ALL THIS DEATH. THOMASON CREATED IT. THOMASON HIMSELF IS NEARER TO YOU THAN YOU THINK...JUST NEXT DOOR, ON THE EDGE OF YOUR DREAMS, PROFESSOR. YOU PASS HIM EVERY DAY WITHOUT KNOWING.
YOU SEE, I HAVE LOOKED INTO THE BOX AND SEEN THE END OF THE WORLD. WE ALL DID.
AS IT TURNS OUT, OUR LITTLE CAUSE MADE NO DIFFERENCE AT ALL.
WE THOUGHT WE COULD BEAT IT, BUT TARTARUS AND HIS HOUNDS OF HELL WILL SOON VISIT DESTRUCTION ON ALL OF ENGLAND...NAY, ALL THE WORLD.

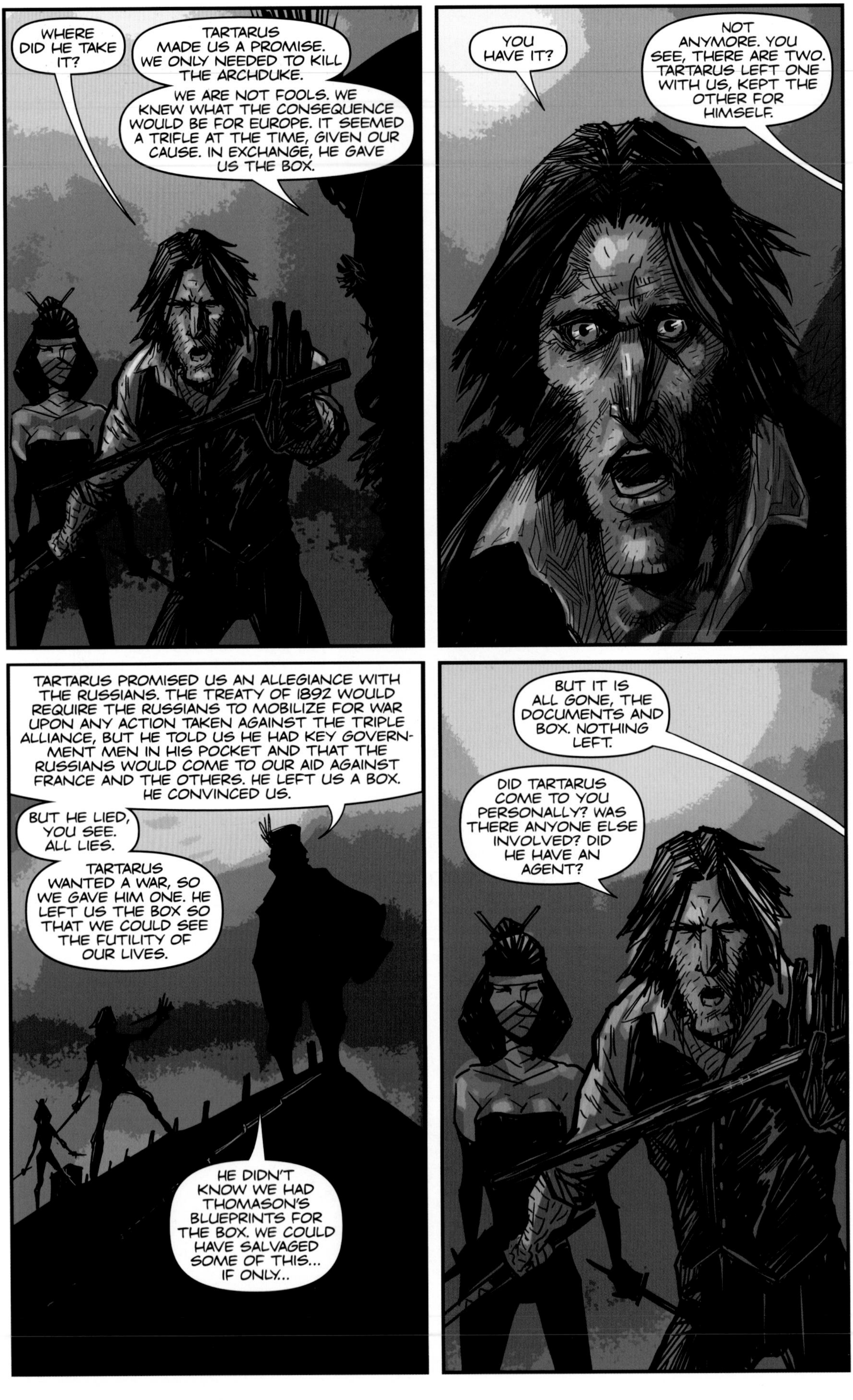
WHERE DID HE TAKE IT?
TARTARUS MADE US A PROMISE. WE ONLY NEEDED TO KILL THE ARCHDUKE.
WE ARE NOT FOOLS. WE KNEW WHAT THE CONSEQUENCE WOULD BE FOR EUROPE. IT SEEMED A TRIFLE AT THE TIME, GIVEN OUR CAUSE. IN EXCHANGE, HE GAVE US THE BOX.
YOU HAVE IT?
NOT ANYMORE. YOU SEE, THERE ARE TWO. TARTARUS LEFT ONE WITH US, KEPT THE OTHER FOR HIMSELF.
TARTARUS PROMISED US AN ALLEGIANCE WITH THE RUSSIANS. THE TREATY OF 1892 WOULD REQUIRE THE RUSSIANS TO MOBILIZE FOR WAR UPON ANY ACTION TAKEN AGAINST THE TRIPLE ALLIANCE, BUT HE TOLD US HE HAD KEY GOVERNMENT MEN IN HIS POCKET AND THAT THE RUSSIANS WOULD COME TO OUR AID AGAINST FRANCE AND THE OTHERS. HE LEFT US A BOX. HE CONVINCED US.
BUT HE LIED, YOU SEE. ALL LIES.
TARTARUS WANTED A WAR, SO WE GAVE HIM ONE. HE LEFT US THE BOX SO THAT WE COULD SEE THE FUTILITY OF OUR LIVES.
HE DIDN'T KNOW WE HAD THOMASON'S BLUEPRINTS FOR THE BOX. WE COULD HAVE SALVAGED SOME OF THIS... IF ONLY...
BUT IT IS ALL GONE, THE DOCUMENTS AND BOX. NOTHING LEFT.
DID TARTARUS COME TO YOU PERSONALLY? WAS THERE ANYONE ELSE INVOLVED? DID HE HAVE AN AGENT?

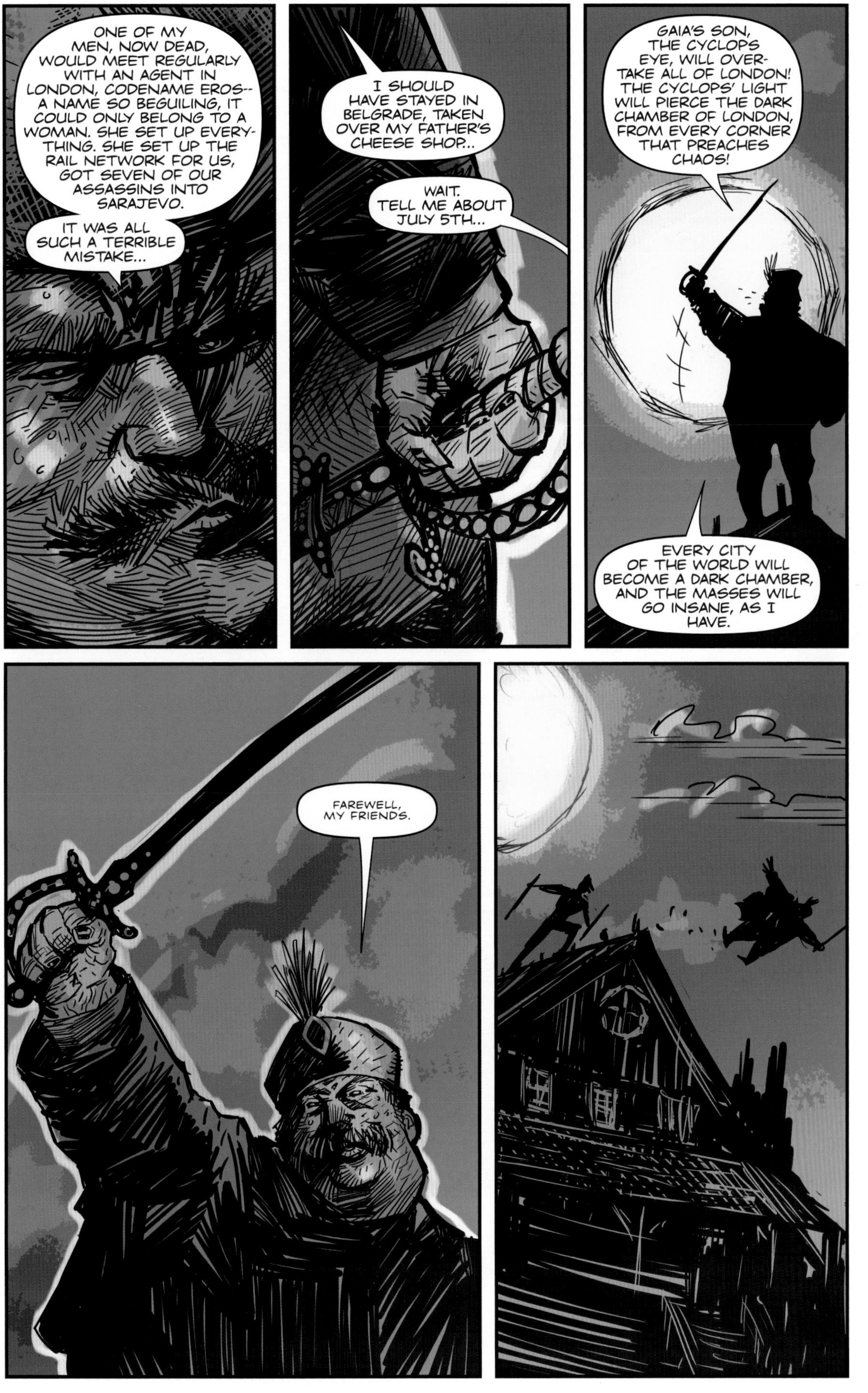
ONE OF MY MEN, NOW DEAD, WOULD MEET REGULARLY WITH AN AGENT IN LONDON, CODENAME EROS-- A NAME SO BEGUILING, IT COULD ONLY BELONG TO A WOMAN. SHE SET UP EVERYTHING. SHE SET UP THE RAIL NETWORK FOR US, GOT SEVEN OF OUR ASSASSINS INTO SARAJEVO.
IT WAS ALL SUCH A TERRIBLE MISTAKE...
I SHOULD HAVE STAYED IN BELGRADE, TAKEN OVER MY FATHER'S CHEESE SHOP...
WAIT. TELL ME ABOUT JULY 5TH...
GAIA'S SON, THE CYCLOPS EYE, WILL OVERTAKE ALL OF LONDON! THE CYCLOPS' LIGHT WILL PIERCE THE DARK CHAMBER OF LONDON, FROM EVERY CORNER THAT PREACHES CHAOS!
EVERY CITY OF THE WORLD WILL BECOME A DARK CHAMBER, AND THE MASSES WILL GO INSANE, AS I HAVE.
FAREWELL, MY FRIENDS.

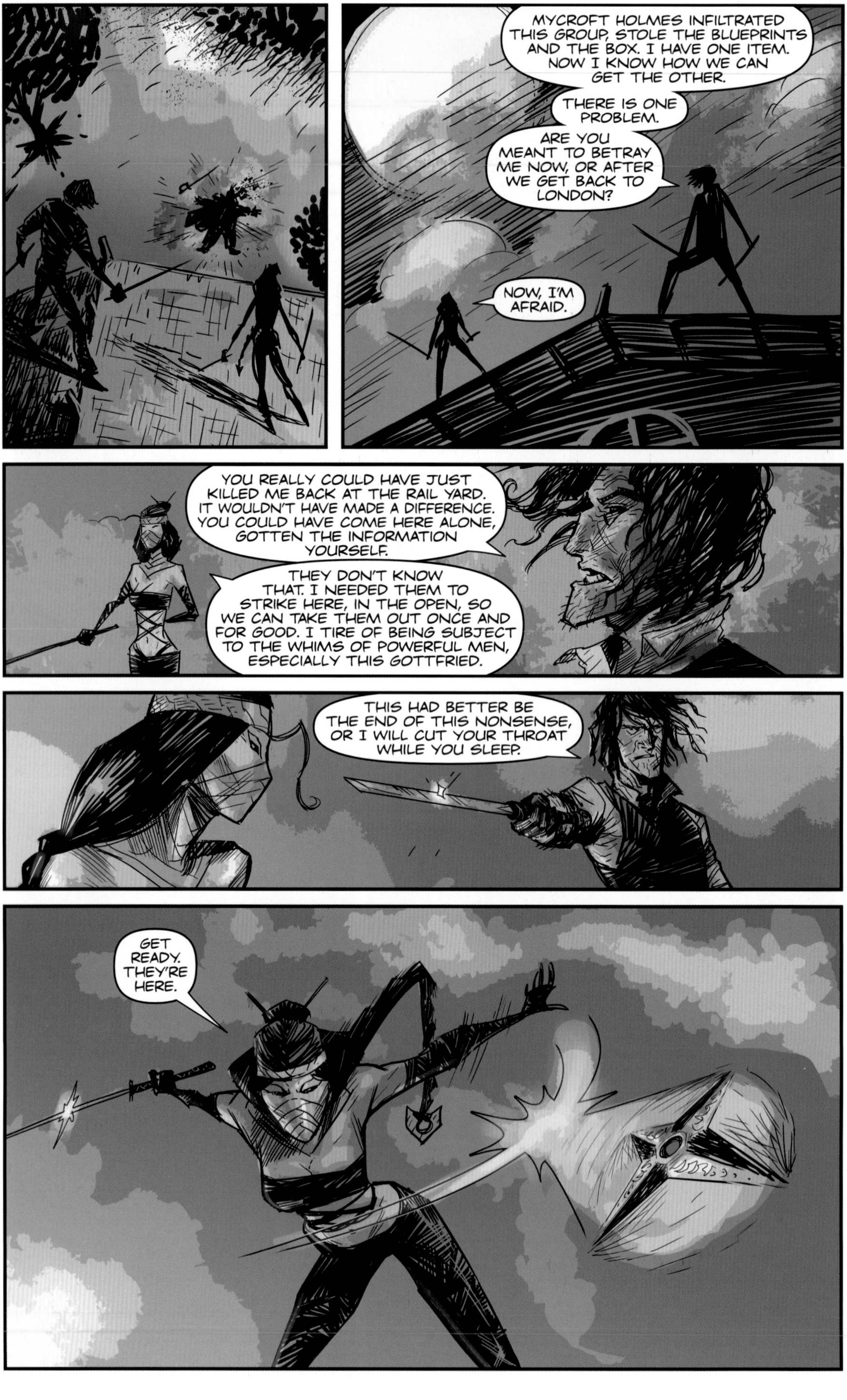
MYCROFT HOLMES INFILTRATED THIS GROUP, STOLE THE BLUEPRINTS AND THE BOX. I HAVE ONE ITEM. NOW I KNOW HOW WE CAN GET THE OTHER.
THERE IS ONE PROBLEM.
ARE YOU MEANT TO BETRAY ME NOW, OR AFTER WE GET BACK TO LONDON?
NOW, I'M AFRAID.
YOU REALLY COULD HAVE JUST KILLED ME BACK AT THE RAIL YARD. IT WOULDN'T HAVE MADE A DIFFERENCE. YOU COULD HAVE COME HERE ALONE, GOTTEN THE INFORMATION YOURSELF.
THEY DON'T KNOW THAT. I NEEDED THEM TO STRIKE HERE, IN THE OPEN, SO WE CAN TAKE THEM OUT ONCE AND FOR GOOD. I TIRE OF BEING SUBJECT TO THE WHIMS OF POWERFUL MEN, ESPECIALLY THIS GOTTFRIED.
THIS HAD BETTER BE THE END OF THIS NONSENSE, OR I WILL CUT YOUR THROAT WHILE YOU SLEEP.
GET READY. THEY'RE HERE.

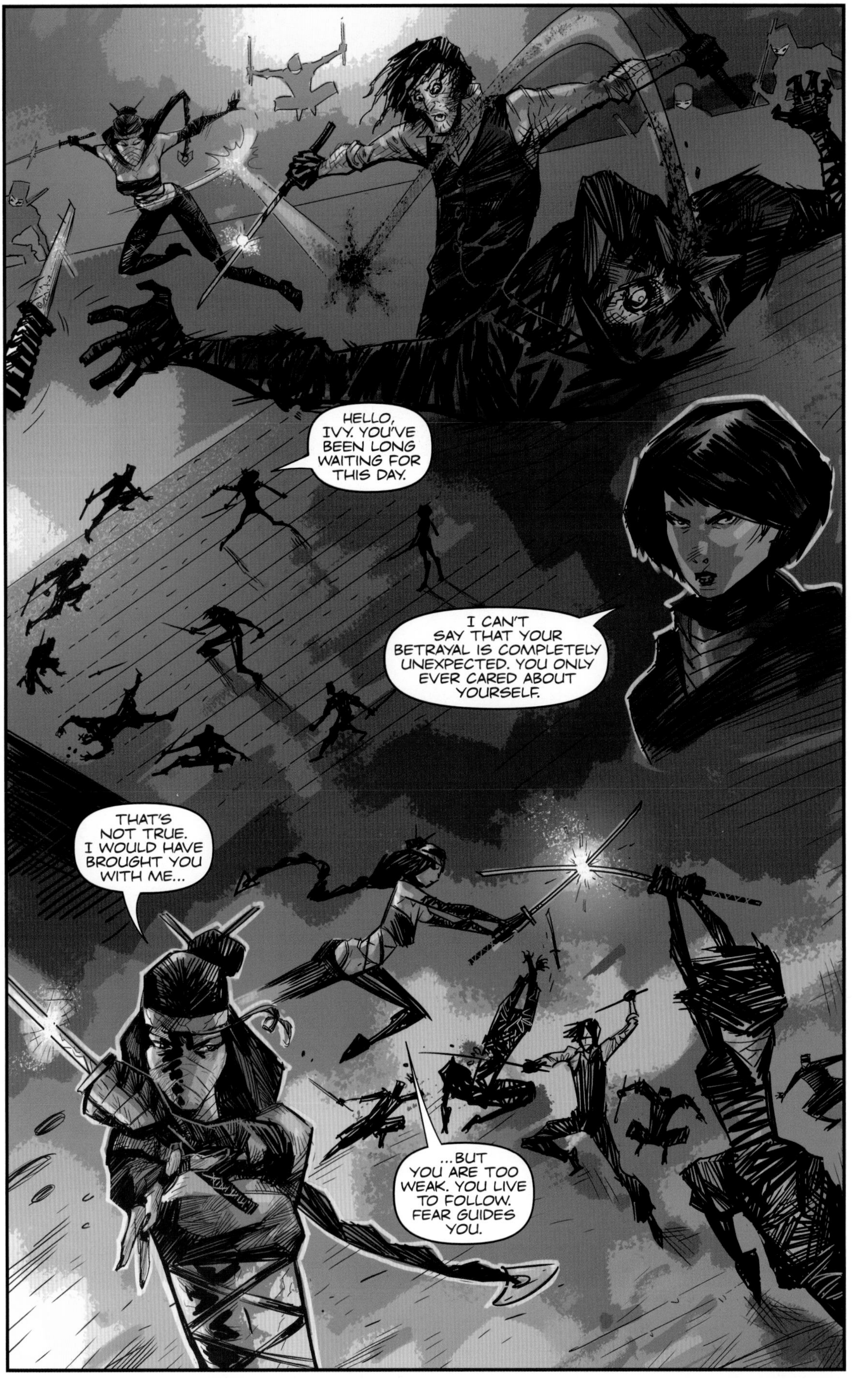
HELLO, IVY. YOU'VE BEEN LONG WAITING FOR THIS DAY.
I CAN'T SAY THAT YOUR BETRAYAL IS COMPLETELY UNEXPECTED. YOU ONLY EVER CARED ABOUT YOURSELF.
THAT'S NOT TRUE. I WOULD HAVE BROUGHT YOU WITH ME...
...BUT YOU ARE TOO WEAK. YOU LIVE TO FOLLOW. FEAR GUIDES YOU.

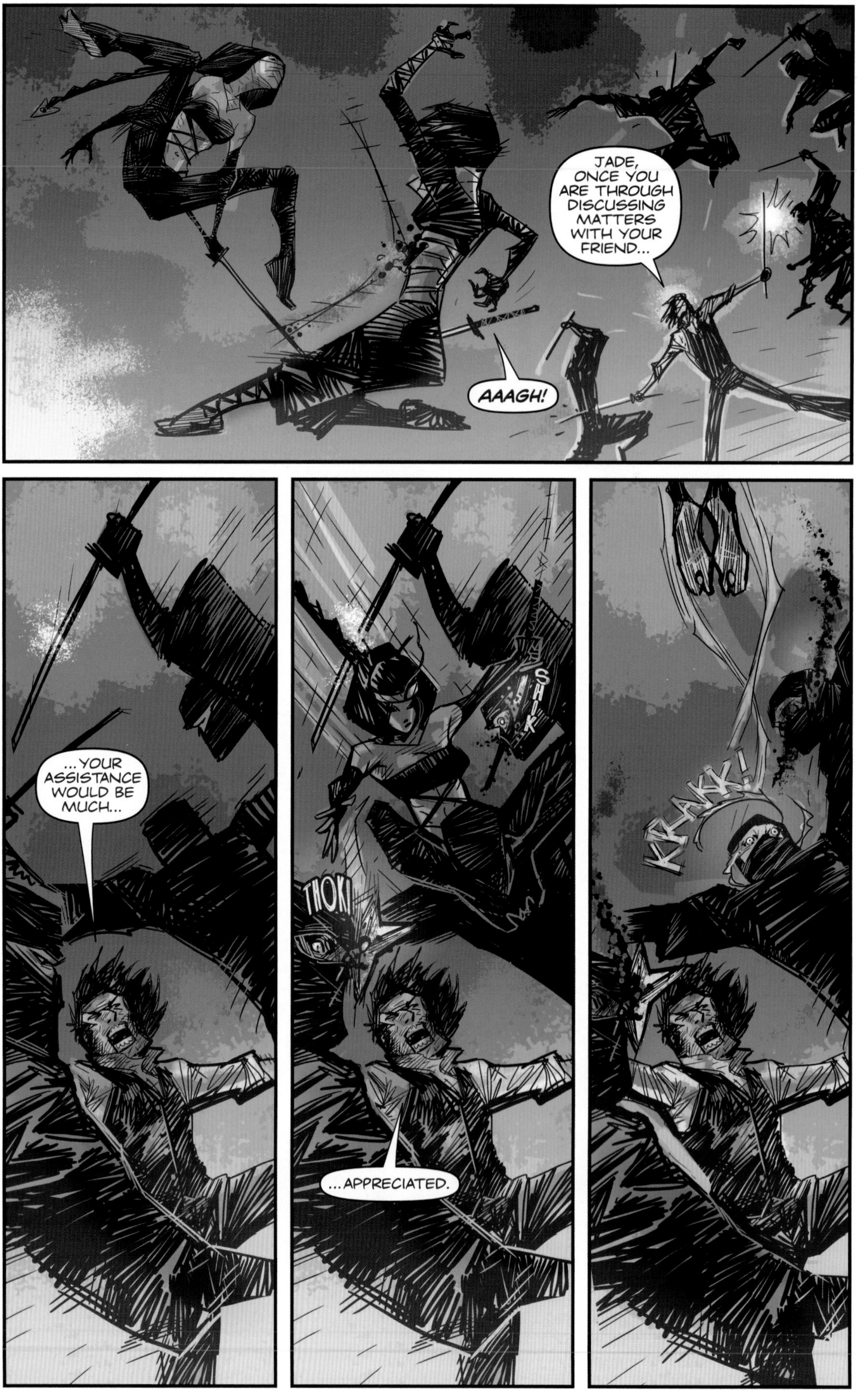
JADE, ONCE YOU ARE THROUGH DISCUSSING MATTERS WITH YOUR FRIEND...
AAAGH!
...YOUR ASSISTANCE WOULD BE MUCH...
SHIK
THOK!
...APPRECIATED.
KRAKK!

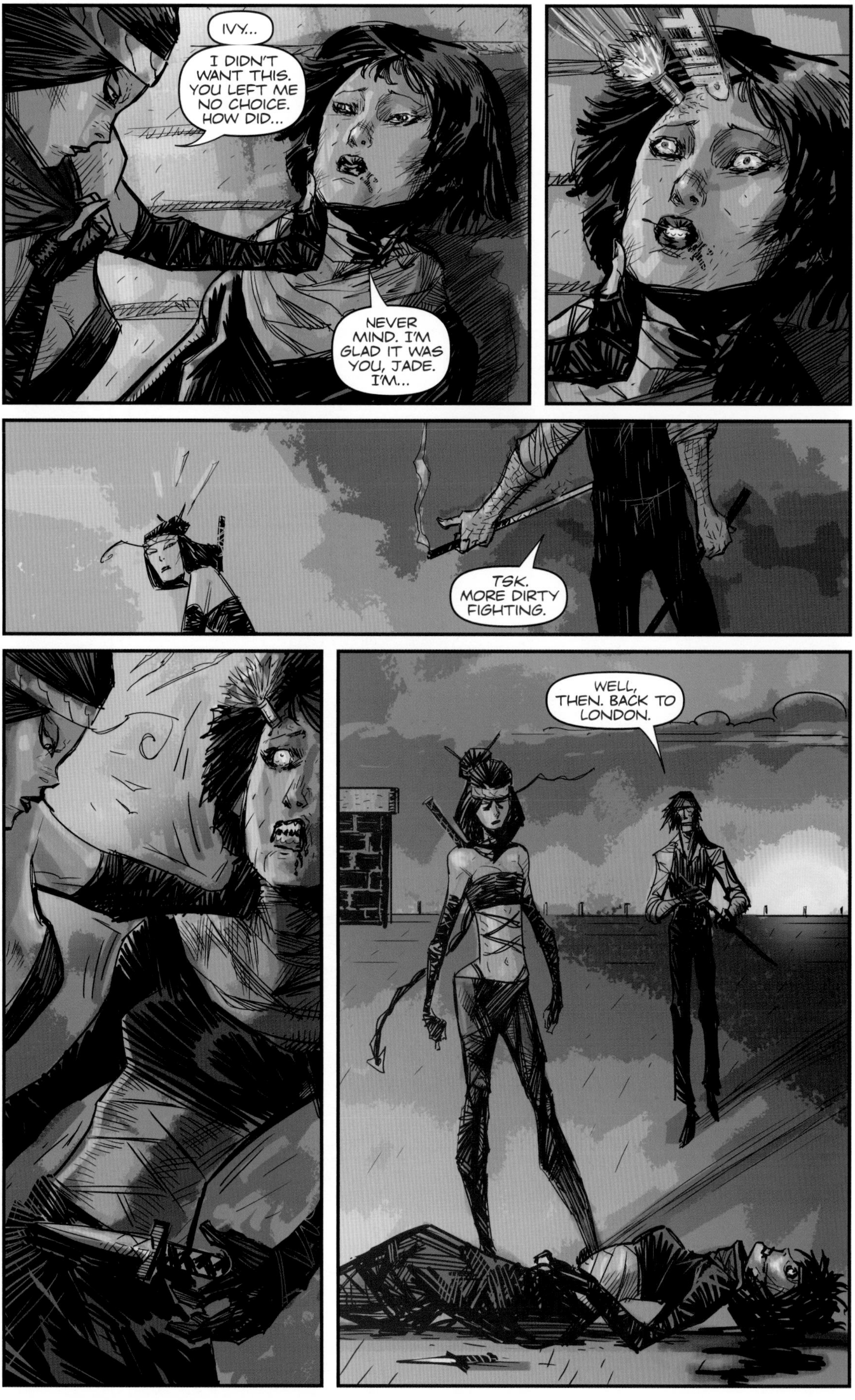
IVY...
I DIDN'T WANT THIS. YOU LEFT ME NO CHOICE. HOW DID...
NEVER MIND. I'M GLAD IT WAS YOU, JADE. I'M...
TSK. MORE DIRTY FIGHTING.
WELL, THEN. BACK TO LONDON.

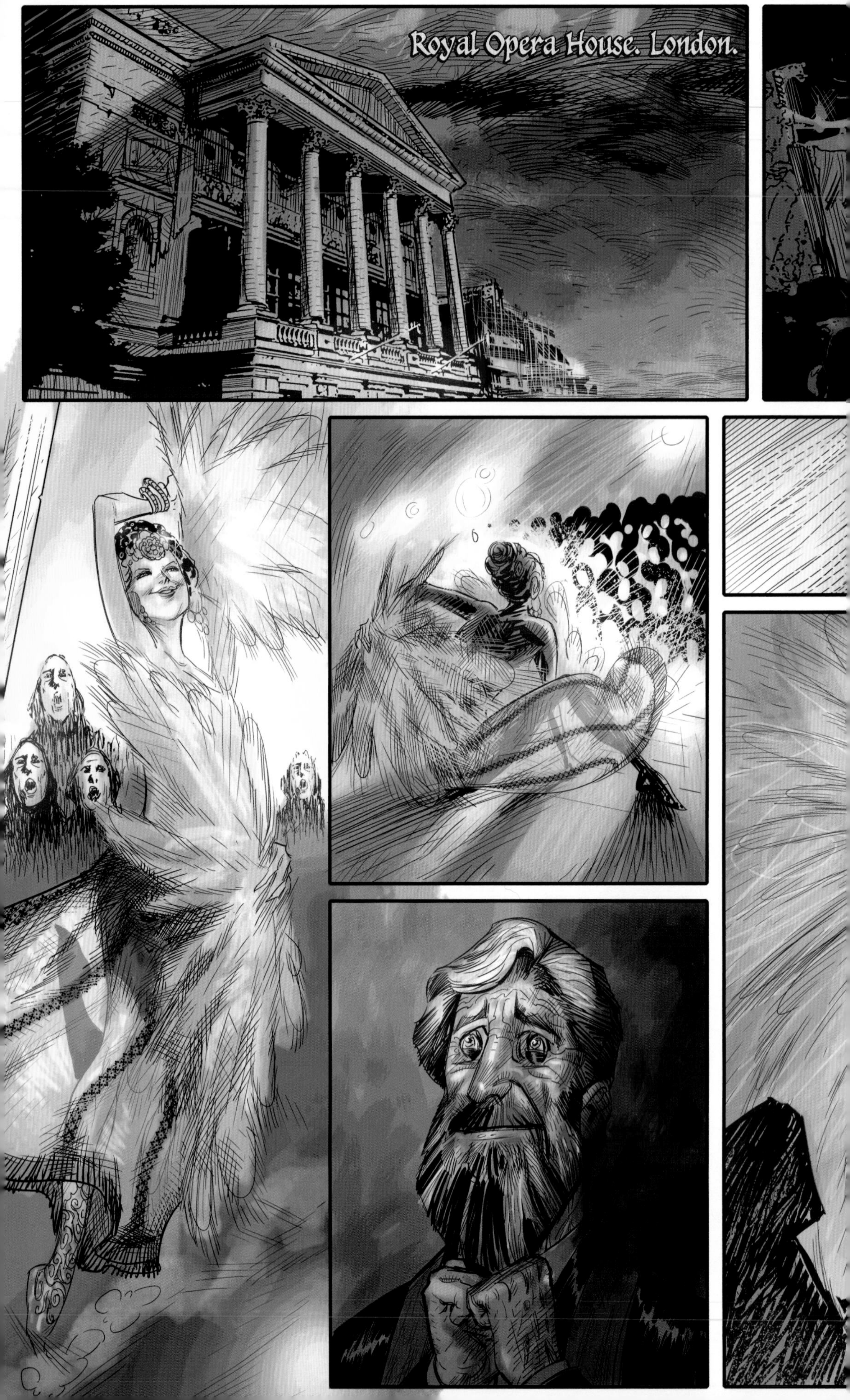
Royal Opera House. London.

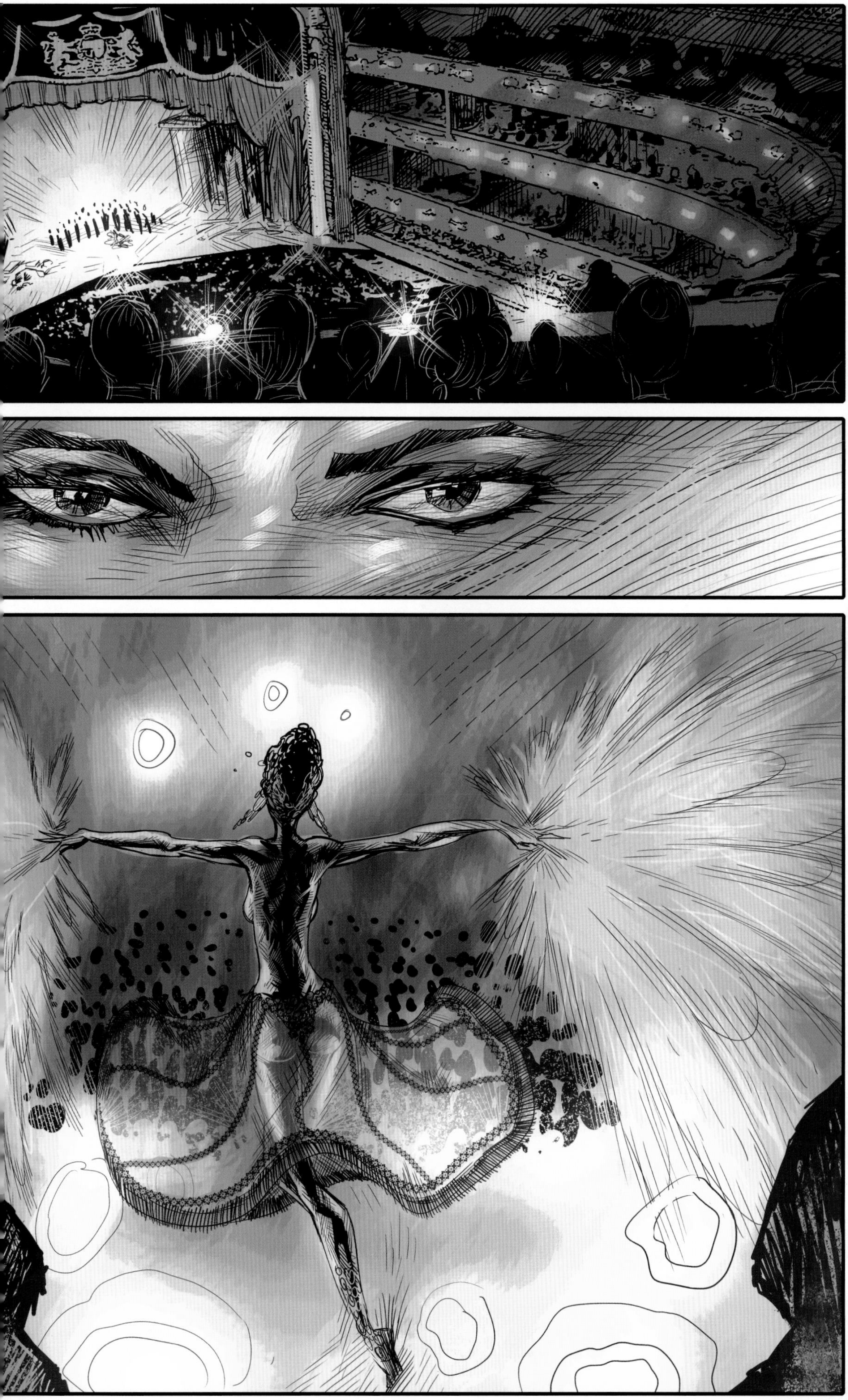

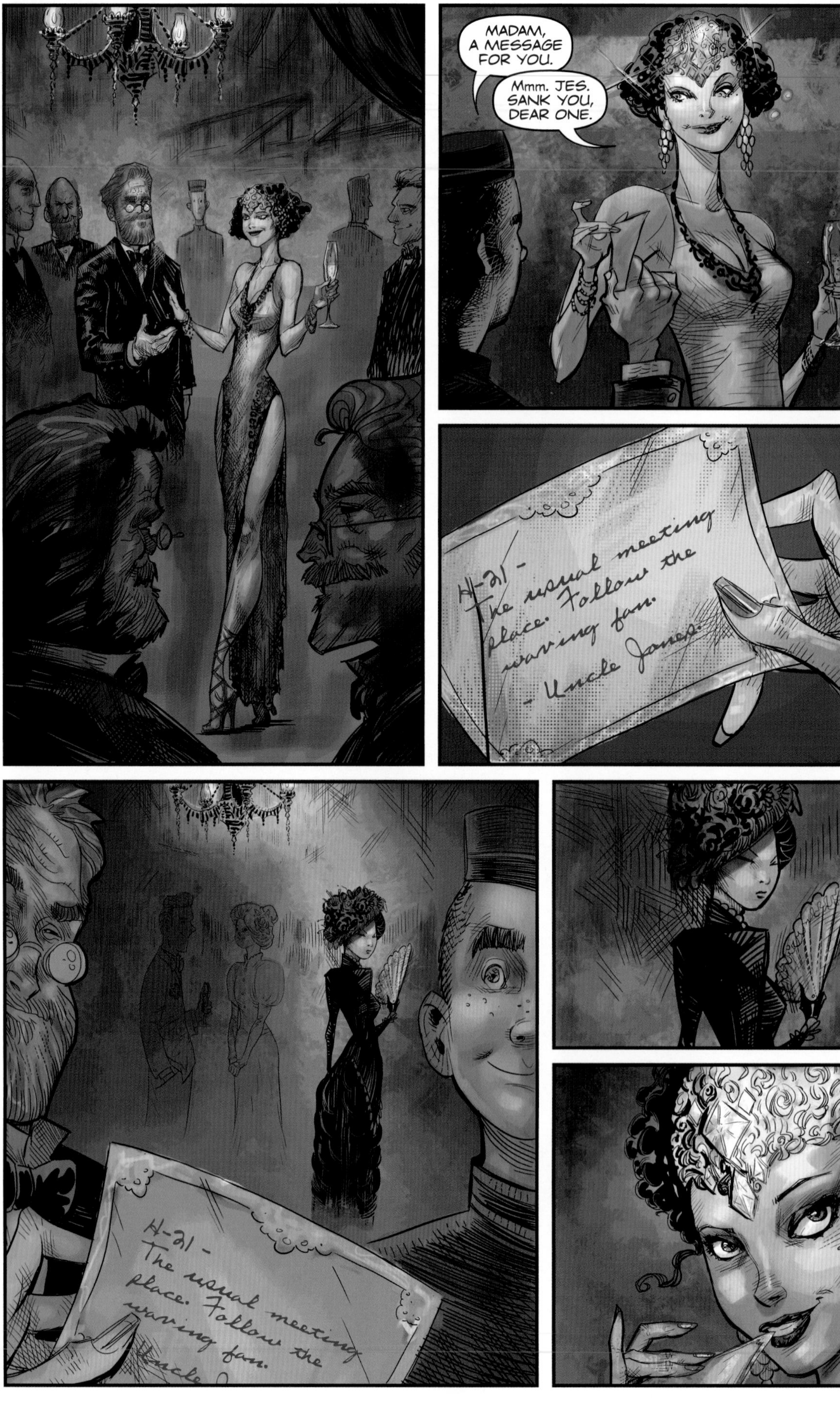
MADAM, A MESSAGE FOR YOU.
Mmm. JES. SANK YOU, DEAR ONE.
H-21 - The usual meeting place. Follow the waving fan. - Uncle James
H-21 - The usual meeting place. Follow the waving fan.

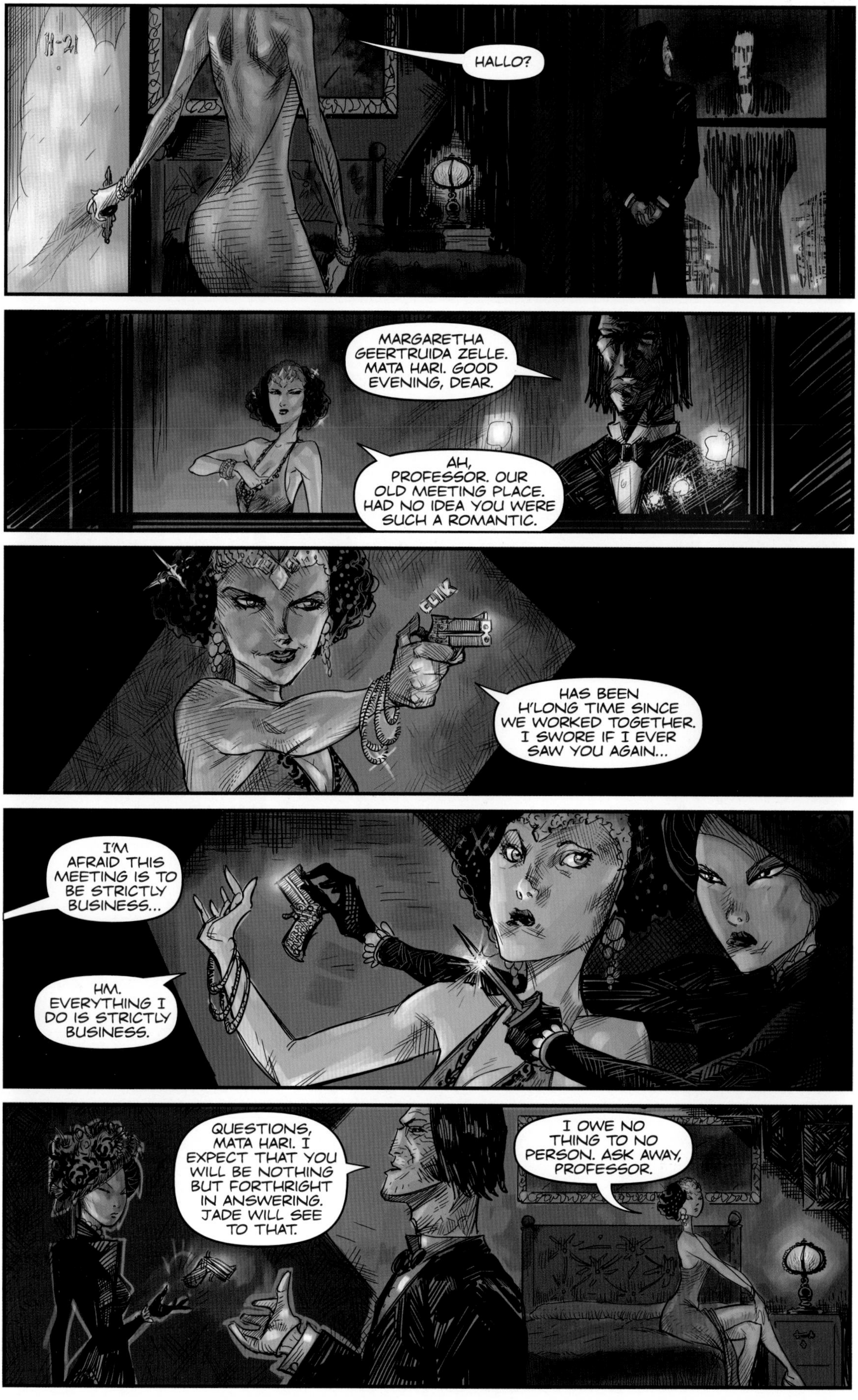
HALLO?
MARGARETHA GEERTRUIDA ZELLE. MATA HARI. GOOD EVENING, DEAR.
AH, PROFESSOR. OUR OLD MEETING PLACE. HAD NO IDEA YOU WERE SUCH A ROMANTIC.
CLIK
HAS BEEN H'LONG TIME SINCE WE WORKED TOGETHER. I SWORE IF I EVER SAW YOU AGAIN...
I'M AFRAID THIS MEETING IS TO BE STRICTLY BUSINESS...
HM. EVERYTHING I DO IS STRICTLY BUSINESS.
QUESTIONS, MATA HARI. I EXPECT THAT YOU WILL BE NOTHING BUT FORTHRIGHT IN ANSWERING. JADE WILL SEE TO THAT.
I OWE NO THING TO NO PERSON. ASK AWAY, PROFESSOR.

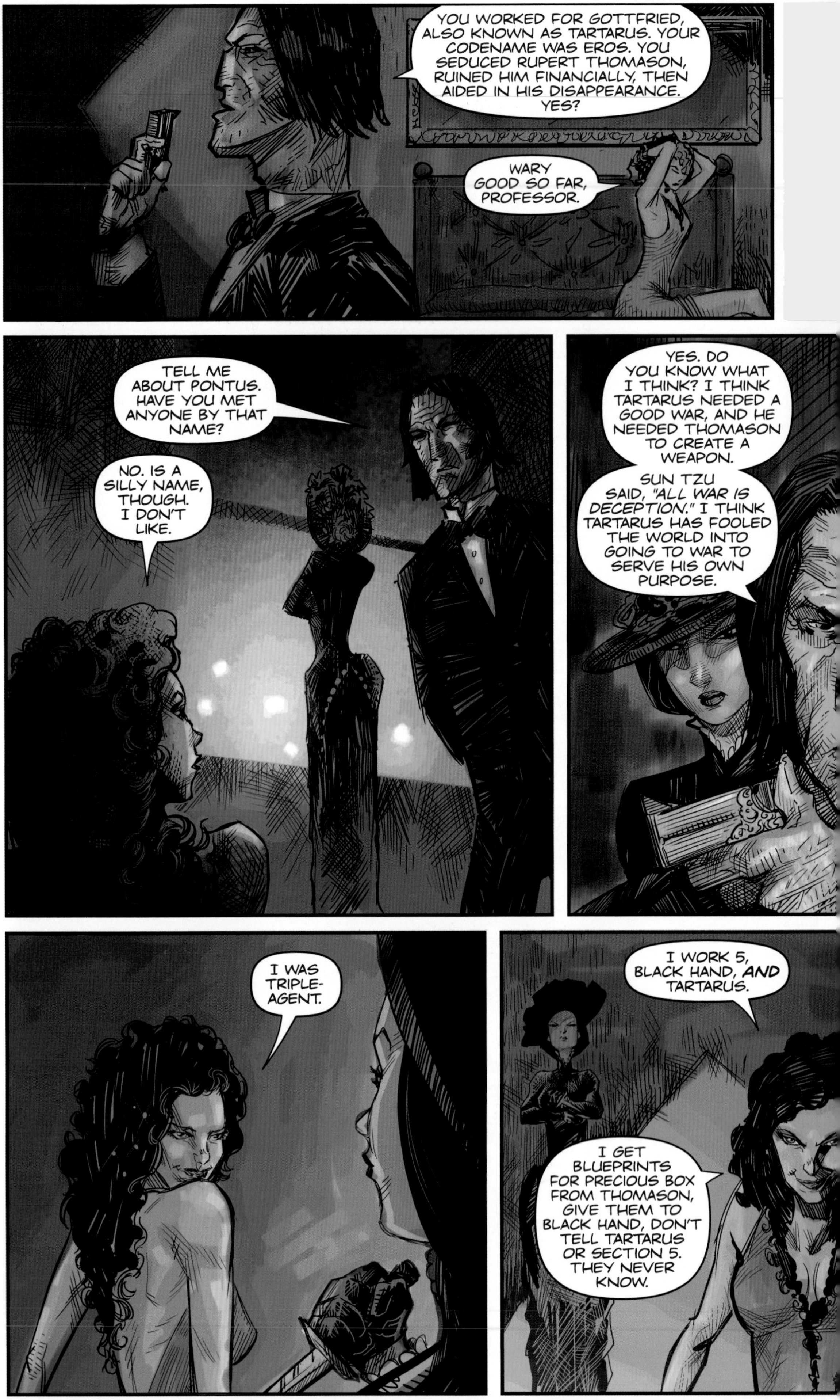
YOU WORKED FOR GOTTFRIED, ALSO KNOWN AS TARTARUS. YOUR CODENAME WAS EROS. YOU SEDUCED RUPERT THOMASON, RUINED HIM FINANCIALLY, THEN AIDED IN HIS DISAPPEARANCE. YES?
WARY GOOD SO FAR, PROFESSOR.
TELL ME ABOUT PONTUS. HAVE YOU MET ANYONE BY THAT NAME?
NO. IS A SILLY NAME, THOUGH. I DON'T LIKE.
YES. DO YOU KNOW WHAT I THINK? I THINK TARTARUS NEEDED A GOOD WAR, AND HE NEEDED THOMASON TO CREATE A WEAPON.
SUN TZU SAID, *"ALL WAR IS DECEPTION."* I THINK TARTARUS HAS FOOLED THE WORLD INTO GOING TO WAR TO SERVE HIS OWN PURPOSE.
I WAS TRIPLE-AGENT.
I WORK 5, BLACK HAND, **AND** TARTARUS.
I GET BLUEPRINTS FOR PRECIOUS BOX FROM THOMASON, GIVE THEM TO BLACK HAND, DON'T TELL TARTARUS OR SECTION 5. THEY NEVER KNOW.

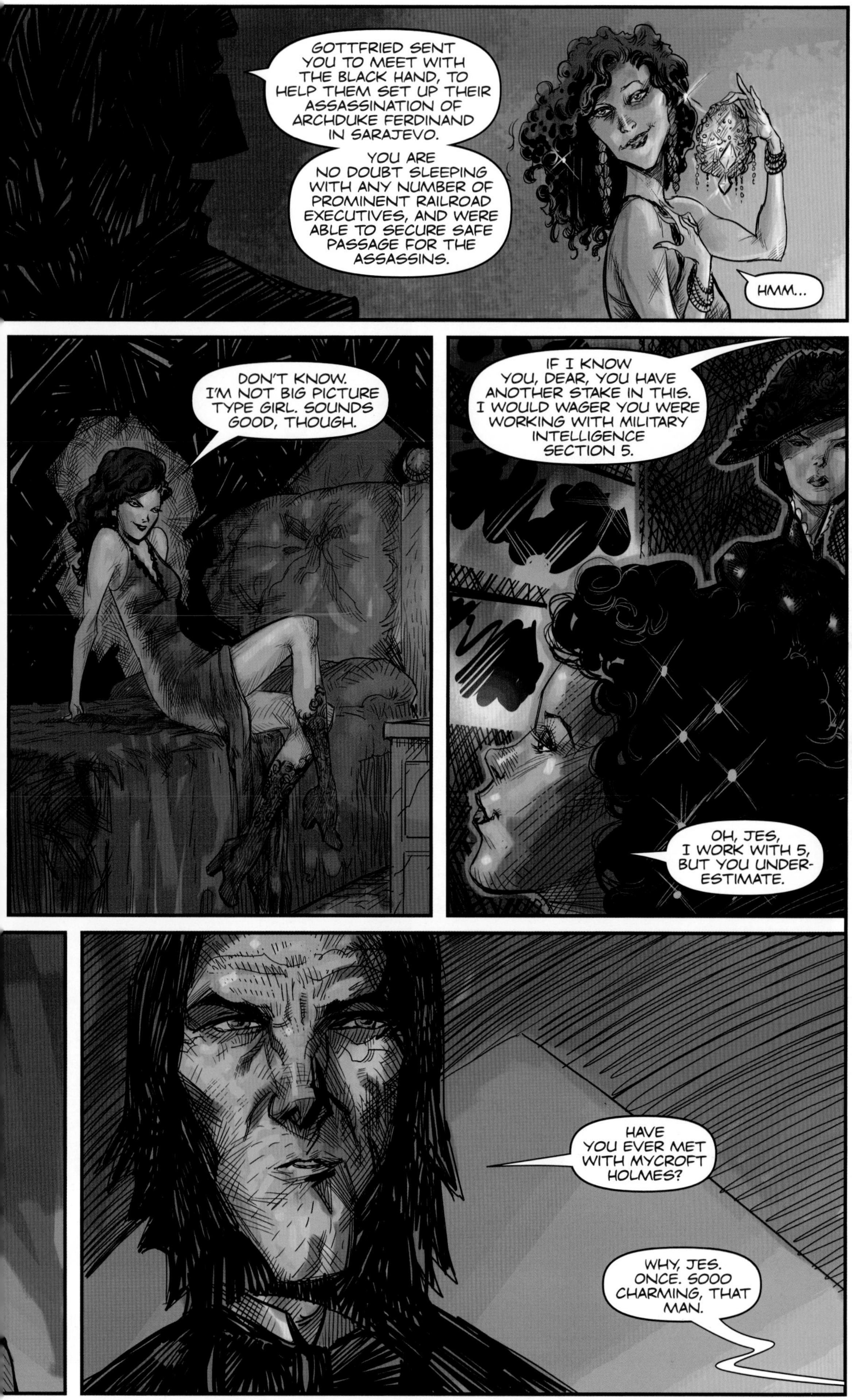
GOTTFRIED SENT YOU TO MEET WITH THE BLACK HAND, TO HELP THEM SET UP THEIR ASSASSINATION OF ARCHDUKE FERDINAND IN SARAJEVO.
YOU ARE NO DOUBT SLEEPING WITH ANY NUMBER OF PROMINENT RAILROAD EXECUTIVES, AND WERE ABLE TO SECURE SAFE PASSAGE FOR THE ASSASSINS.
HMM...
DON'T KNOW. I'M NOT BIG PICTURE TYPE GIRL. SOUNDS GOOD, THOUGH.
IF I KNOW YOU, DEAR, YOU HAVE ANOTHER STAKE IN THIS. I WOULD WAGER YOU WERE WORKING WITH MILITARY INTELLIGENCE SECTION 5.
OH, JES, I WORK WITH 5, BUT YOU UNDER-ESTIMATE.
HAVE YOU EVER MET WITH MYCROFT HOLMES?
WHY, JES. ONCE. SOOO CHARMING, THAT MAN.

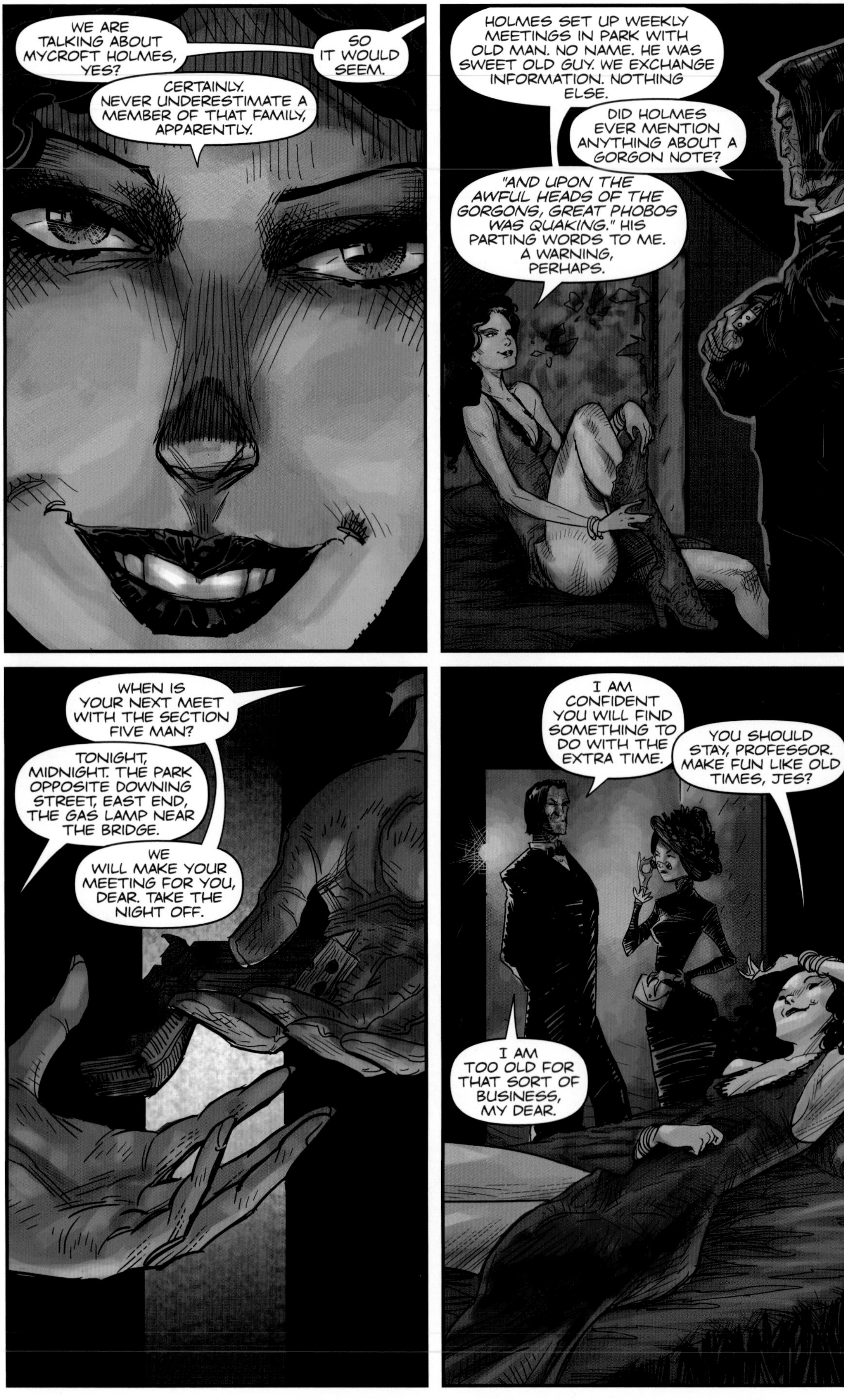
WE ARE TALKING ABOUT MYCROFT HOLMES, YES?
SO IT WOULD SEEM.
CERTAINLY. NEVER UNDERESTIMATE A MEMBER OF THAT FAMILY, APPARENTLY.
HOLMES SET UP WEEKLY MEETINGS IN PARK WITH OLD MAN. NO NAME. HE WAS SWEET OLD GUY. WE EXCHANGE INFORMATION. NOTHING ELSE.
DID HOLMES EVER MENTION ANYTHING ABOUT A GORGON NOTE?
"AND UPON THE AWFUL HEADS OF THE GORGONS, GREAT PHOBOS WAS QUAKING." HIS PARTING WORDS TO ME. A WARNING, PERHAPS.
WHEN IS YOUR NEXT MEET WITH THE SECTION FIVE MAN?
TONIGHT, MIDNIGHT. THE PARK OPPOSITE DOWNING STREET, EAST END, THE GAS LAMP NEAR THE BRIDGE.
WE WILL MAKE YOUR MEETING FOR YOU, DEAR. TAKE THE NIGHT OFF.
I AM CONFIDENT YOU WILL FIND SOMETHING TO DO WITH THE EXTRA TIME.
YOU SHOULD STAY, PROFESSOR. MAKE FUN LIKE OLD TIMES, JES?
I AM TOO OLD FOR THAT SORT OF BUSINESS, MY DEAR.

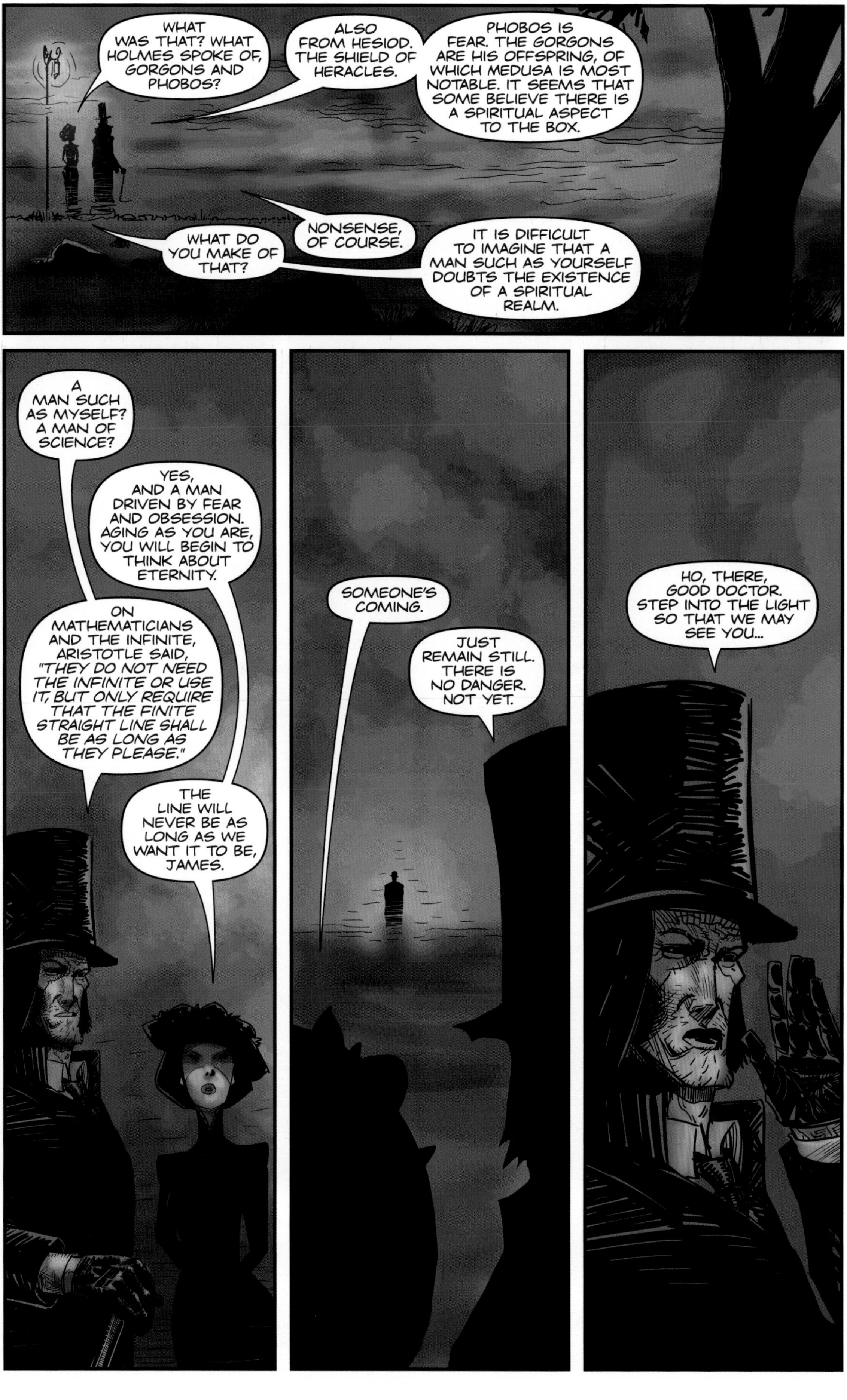
WHAT WAS THAT? WHAT HOLMES SPOKE OF, GORGONS AND PHOBOS?
ALSO FROM HESIOD. THE SHIELD OF HERACLES.
PHOBOS IS FEAR. THE GORGONS ARE HIS OFFSPRING, OF WHICH MEDUSA IS MOST NOTABLE. IT SEEMS THAT SOME BELIEVE THERE IS A SPIRITUAL ASPECT TO THE BOX.
WHAT DO YOU MAKE OF THAT?
NONSENSE, OF COURSE.
IT IS DIFFICULT TO IMAGINE THAT A MAN SUCH AS YOURSELF DOUBTS THE EXISTENCE OF A SPIRITUAL REALM.
A MAN SUCH AS MYSELF? A MAN OF SCIENCE?
YES, AND A MAN DRIVEN BY FEAR AND OBSESSION. AGING AS YOU ARE, YOU WILL BEGIN TO THINK ABOUT ETERNITY.
ON MATHEMATICIANS AND THE INFINITE, ARISTOTLE SAID, *"THEY DO NOT NEED THE INFINITE OR USE IT, BUT ONLY REQUIRE THAT THE FINITE STRAIGHT LINE SHALL BE AS LONG AS THEY PLEASE."*
THE LINE WILL NEVER BE AS LONG AS WE WANT IT TO BE, JAMES.
SOMEONE'S COMING.
JUST REMAIN STILL. THERE IS NO DANGER. NOT YET.
HO, THERE, GOOD DOCTOR. STEP INTO THE LIGHT SO THAT WE MAY SEE YOU...

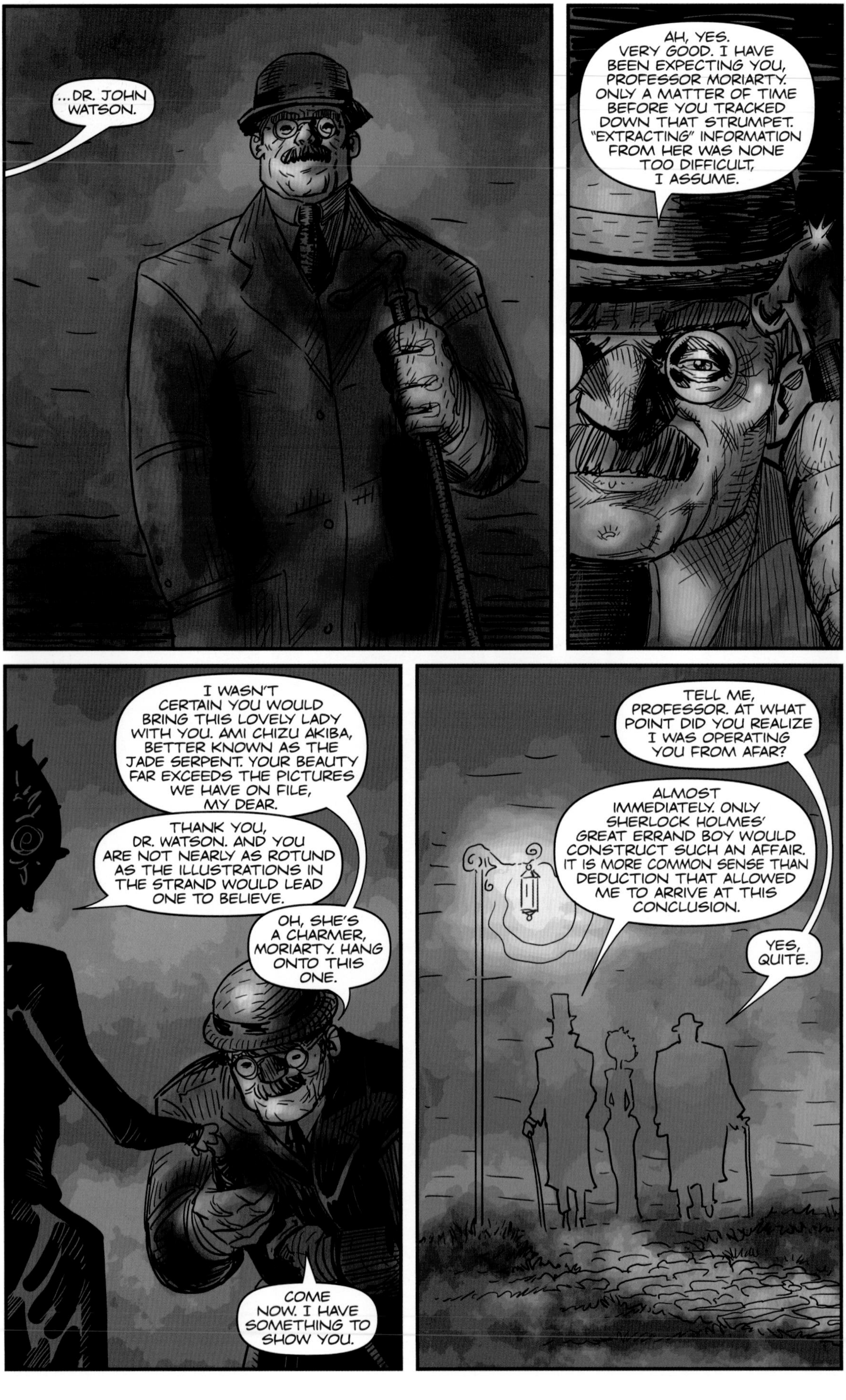
...DR. JOHN WATSON.
AH, YES. VERY GOOD. I HAVE BEEN EXPECTING YOU, PROFESSOR MORIARTY. ONLY A MATTER OF TIME BEFORE YOU TRACKED DOWN THAT STRUMPET. "EXTRACTING" INFORMATION FROM HER WAS NONE TOO DIFFICULT, I ASSUME.
I WASN'T CERTAIN YOU WOULD BRING THIS LOVELY LADY WITH YOU. AMI CHIZU AKIBA, BETTER KNOWN AS THE JADE SERPENT. YOUR BEAUTY FAR EXCEEDS THE PICTURES WE HAVE ON FILE, MY DEAR.
THANK YOU, DR. WATSON. AND YOU ARE NOT NEARLY AS ROTUND AS THE ILLUSTRATIONS IN THE STRAND WOULD LEAD ONE TO BELIEVE.
OH, SHE'S A CHARMER, MORIARTY. HANG ONTO THIS ONE.
COME NOW. I HAVE SOMETHING TO SHOW YOU.
TELL ME, PROFESSOR. AT WHAT POINT DID YOU REALIZE I WAS OPERATING YOU FROM AFAR?
ALMOST IMMEDIATELY. ONLY SHERLOCK HOLMES' GREAT ERRAND BOY WOULD CONSTRUCT SUCH AN AFFAIR. IT IS MORE COMMON SENSE THAN DEDUCTION THAT ALLOWED ME TO ARRIVE AT THIS CONCLUSION.
YES, QUITE.

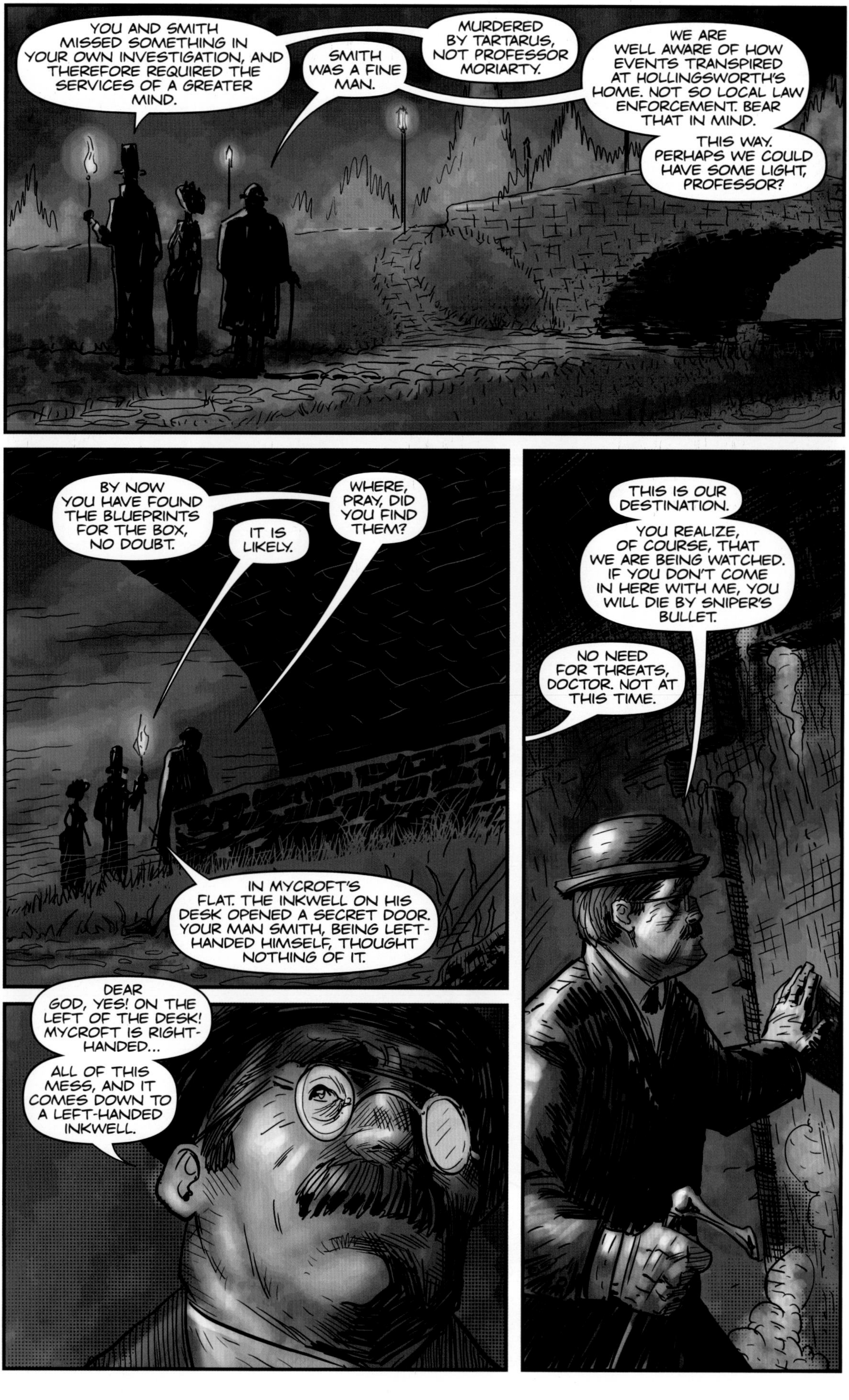
YOU AND SMITH MISSED SOMETHING IN YOUR OWN INVESTIGATION, AND THEREFORE REQUIRED THE SERVICES OF A GREATER MIND.
MURDERED BY TARTARUS, NOT PROFESSOR MORIARTY.
SMITH WAS A FINE MAN.
WE ARE WELL AWARE OF HOW EVENTS TRANSPIRED AT HOLLINGSWORTH'S HOME. NOT SO LOCAL LAW ENFORCEMENT. BEAR THAT IN MIND.
THIS WAY. PERHAPS WE COULD HAVE SOME LIGHT, PROFESSOR?
BY NOW YOU HAVE FOUND THE BLUEPRINTS FOR THE BOX, NO DOUBT.
WHERE, PRAY, DID YOU FIND THEM?
IT IS LIKELY.
IN MYCROFT'S FLAT. THE INKWELL ON HIS DESK OPENED A SECRET DOOR. YOUR MAN SMITH, BEING LEFT-HANDED HIMSELF, THOUGHT NOTHING OF IT.
DEAR GOD, YES! ON THE LEFT OF THE DESK! MYCROFT IS RIGHT-HANDED...
ALL OF THIS MESS, AND IT COMES DOWN TO A LEFT-HANDED INKWELL.
THIS IS OUR DESTINATION.
YOU REALIZE, OF COURSE, THAT WE ARE BEING WATCHED. IF YOU DON'T COME IN HERE WITH ME, YOU WILL DIE BY SNIPER'S BULLET.
NO NEED FOR THREATS, DOCTOR. NOT AT THIS TIME.

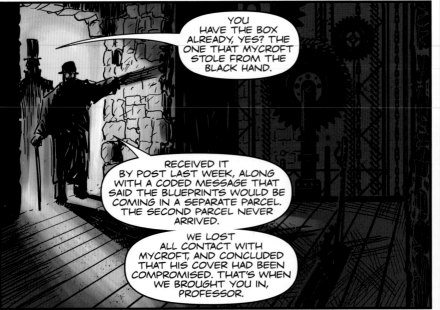

YOU HAVE THE BOX ALREADY, YES? THE ONE THAT MYCROFT STOLE FROM THE BLACK HAND.

RECEIVED IT BY POST LAST WEEK, ALONG WITH A CODED MESSAGE THAT SAID THE BLUEPRINTS WOULD BE COMING IN A SEPARATE PARCEL. THE SECOND PARCEL NEVER ARRIVED.

WE LOST ALL CONTACT WITH MYCROFT, AND CONCLUDED THAT HIS COVER HAD BEEN COMPROMISED. THAT'S WHEN WE BROUGHT YOU IN, PROFESSOR.

DO HOLD ONTO YOURSELVES, PLEASE.

TALLY HO!

SHOOM

KLAK!

MYCROFT HAS BEEN AN AGENT OF SECURITY SERVICES FOR AS LONG AS HIS BROTHER HAS BEEN KNOWN FOR HIS DETECTIVE WORK, YOU SEE. ONE BROTHER WAS THE PUBLIC FACE OF CRIME FIGHTING, THE OTHER STAYED IN SHADOW.

FOLLOW ME...

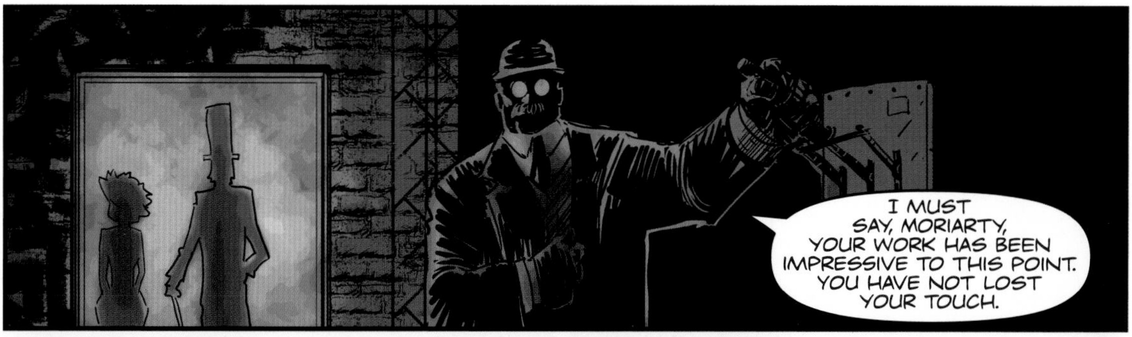
I MUST SAY, MORIARTY, YOUR WORK HAS BEEN IMPRESSIVE TO THIS POINT. YOU HAVE NOT LOST YOUR TOUCH.

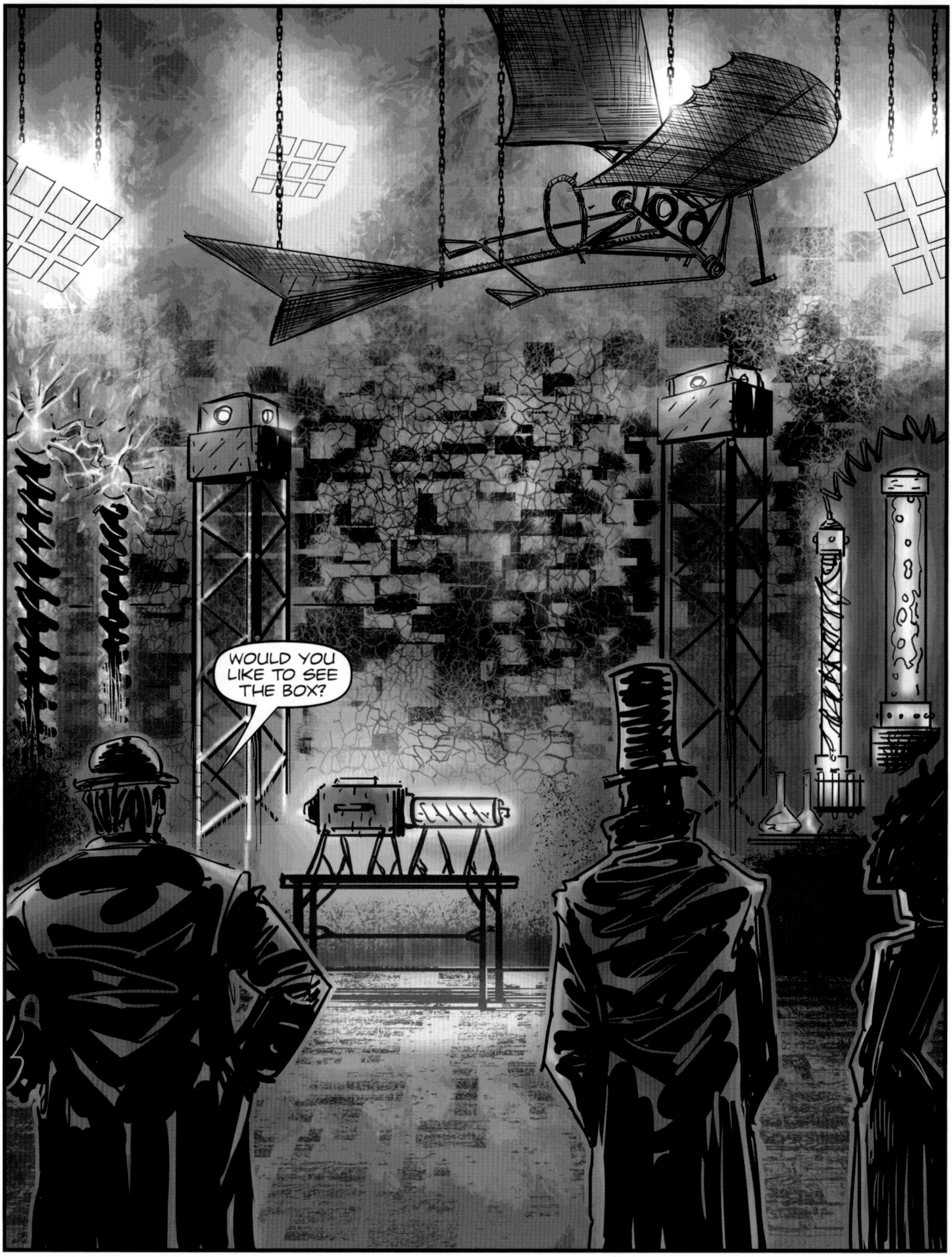
WOULD YOU LIKE TO SEE THE BOX?

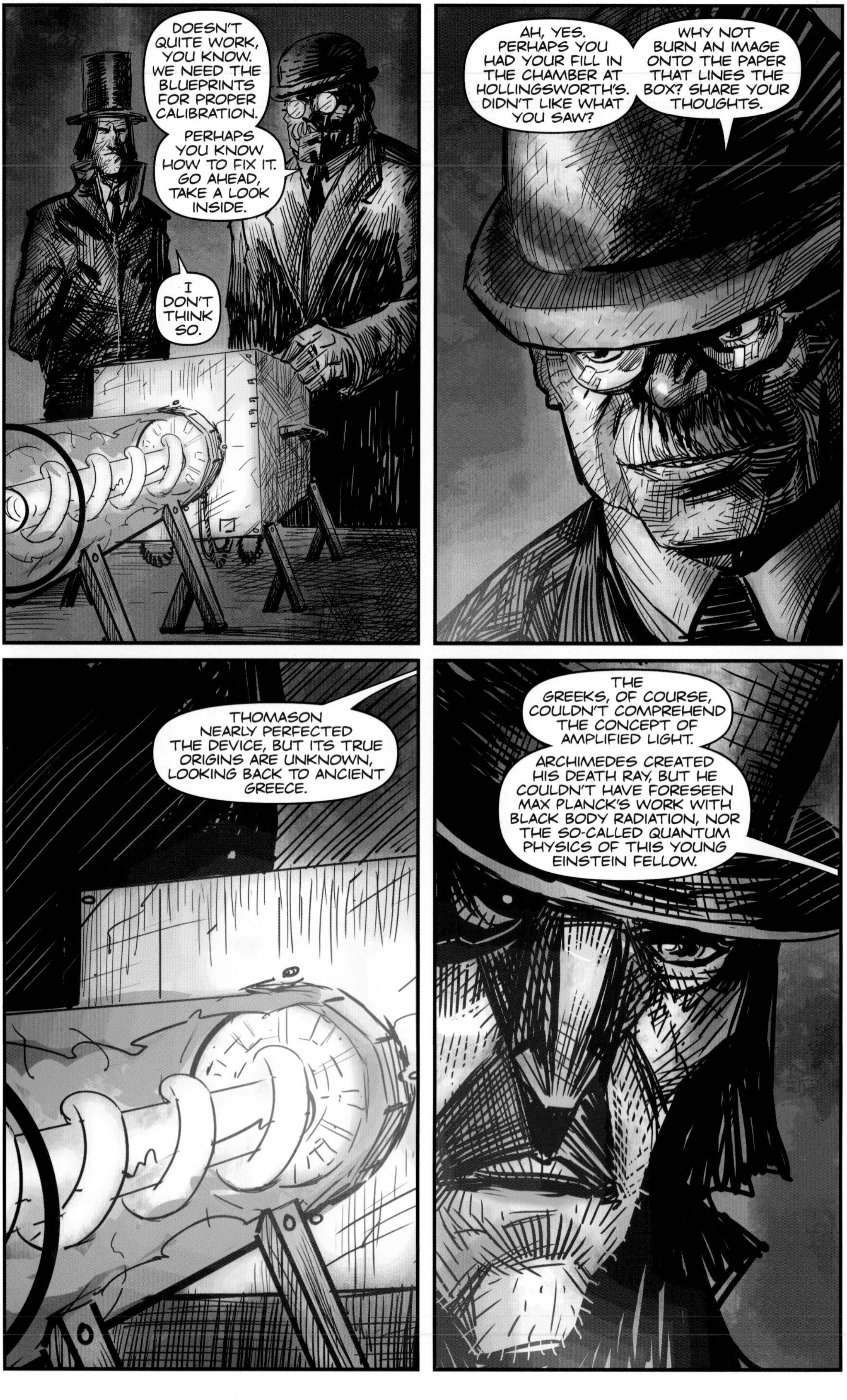
DOESN'T QUITE WORK, YOU KNOW. WE NEED THE BLUEPRINTS FOR PROPER CALIBRATION.
PERHAPS YOU KNOW HOW TO FIX IT. GO AHEAD, TAKE A LOOK INSIDE.
I DON'T THINK SO.
AH, YES. PERHAPS YOU HAD YOUR FILL IN THE CHAMBER AT HOLLINGSWORTH'S. DIDN'T LIKE WHAT YOU SAW?
WHY NOT BURN AN IMAGE ONTO THE PAPER THAT LINES THE BOX? SHARE YOUR THOUGHTS.
THOMASON NEARLY PERFECTED THE DEVICE, BUT ITS TRUE ORIGINS ARE UNKNOWN, LOOKING BACK TO ANCIENT GREECE.
THE GREEKS, OF COURSE, COULDN'T COMPREHEND THE CONCEPT OF AMPLIFIED LIGHT.
ARCHIMEDES CREATED HIS DEATH RAY, BUT HE COULDN'T HAVE FORESEEN MAX PLANCK'S WORK WITH BLACK BODY RADIATION, NOR THE SO-CALLED QUANTUM PHYSICS OF THIS YOUNG EINSTEIN FELLOW.

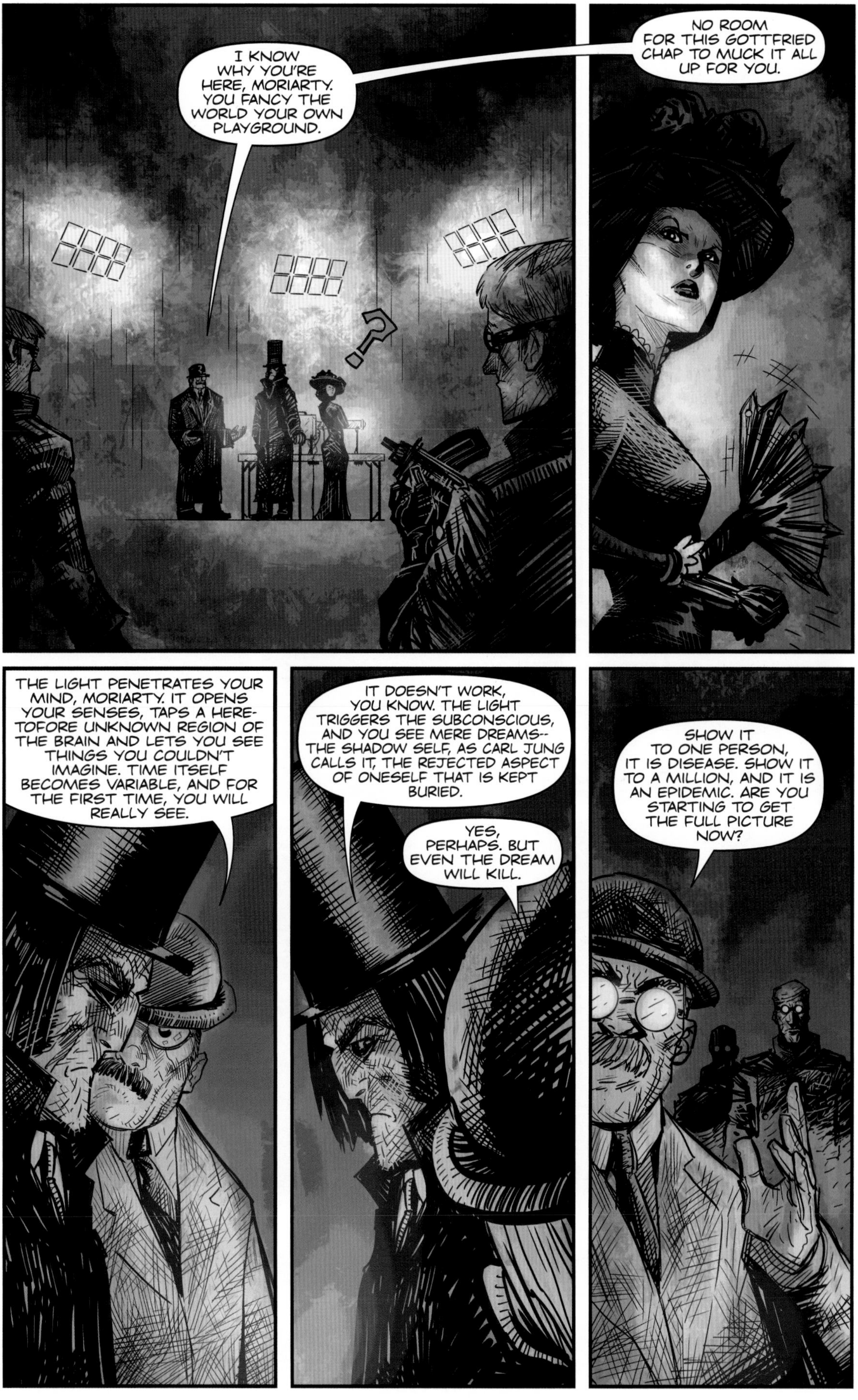
I KNOW WHY YOU'RE HERE, MORIARTY. YOU FANCY THE WORLD YOUR OWN PLAYGROUND.
NO ROOM FOR THIS GOTTFRIED CHAP TO MUCK IT ALL UP FOR YOU.
?
THE LIGHT PENETRATES YOUR MIND, MORIARTY. IT OPENS YOUR SENSES, TAPS A HERETOFORE UNKNOWN REGION OF THE BRAIN AND LETS YOU SEE THINGS YOU COULDN'T IMAGINE. TIME ITSELF BECOMES VARIABLE, AND FOR THE FIRST TIME, YOU WILL REALLY SEE.
IT DOESN'T WORK, YOU KNOW. THE LIGHT TRIGGERS THE SUBCONSCIOUS, AND YOU SEE MERE DREAMS-- THE SHADOW SELF, AS CARL JUNG CALLS IT, THE REJECTED ASPECT OF ONESELF THAT IS KEPT BURIED.
YES, PERHAPS. BUT EVEN THE DREAM WILL KILL.
SHOW IT TO ONE PERSON, IT IS DISEASE. SHOW IT TO A MILLION, AND IT IS AN EPIDEMIC. ARE YOU STARTING TO GET THE FULL PICTURE NOW?

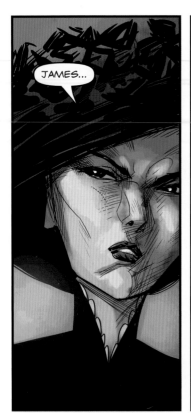

JAMES...

HE'S GOING TO UNLEASH THIS THING ON LONDON AND DRIVE US ALL MAD WITH VISIONS OF DEATH-- WHETHER REAL OR IMAGINED IS OF NO CONSEQUENCE.

THEN HE'S GOING TO GIVE IT AWAY TO EVERY SIDE CAUGHT UP IN THIS RIDICULOUS WAR...

CAUSING THE WORLD TO SINK INTO UTTER CHAOS, THE ASHES OF WHICH HE SHALL FANCY HIMSELF RULER AND GOD.

A CLEVER PLAN. BUT NOT MY PLAN. I PREFER TO RULE THE LIVING, NOT THE DEAD.

ENOUGH TALKING...

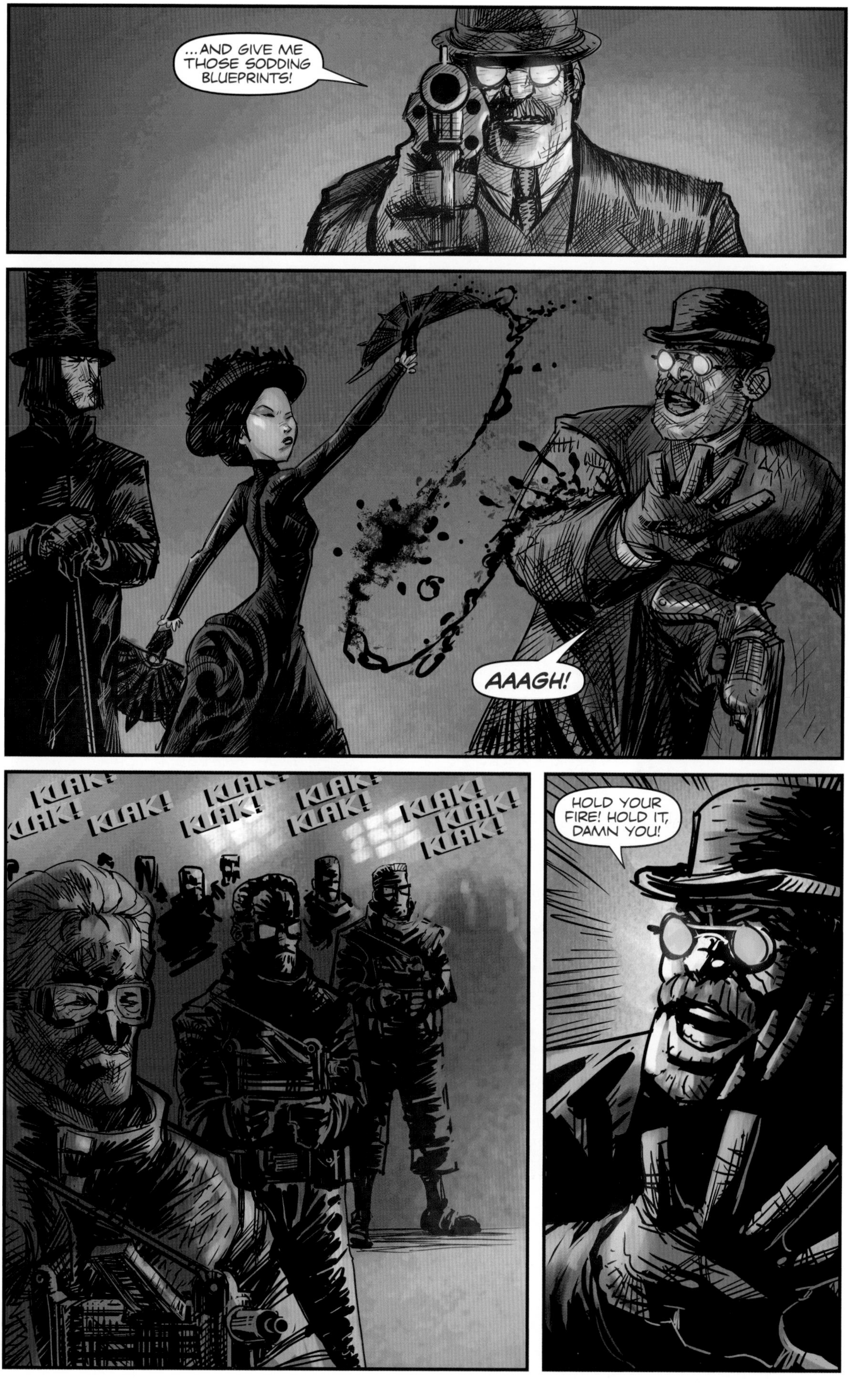
...AND GIVE ME THOSE SODDING BLUEPRINTS!
AAAGH!
KLAK! KLAK! KLAK! KLAK! KLAK! KLAK! KLAK! KLAK! KLAK!
HOLD YOUR FIRE! HOLD IT, DAMN YOU!

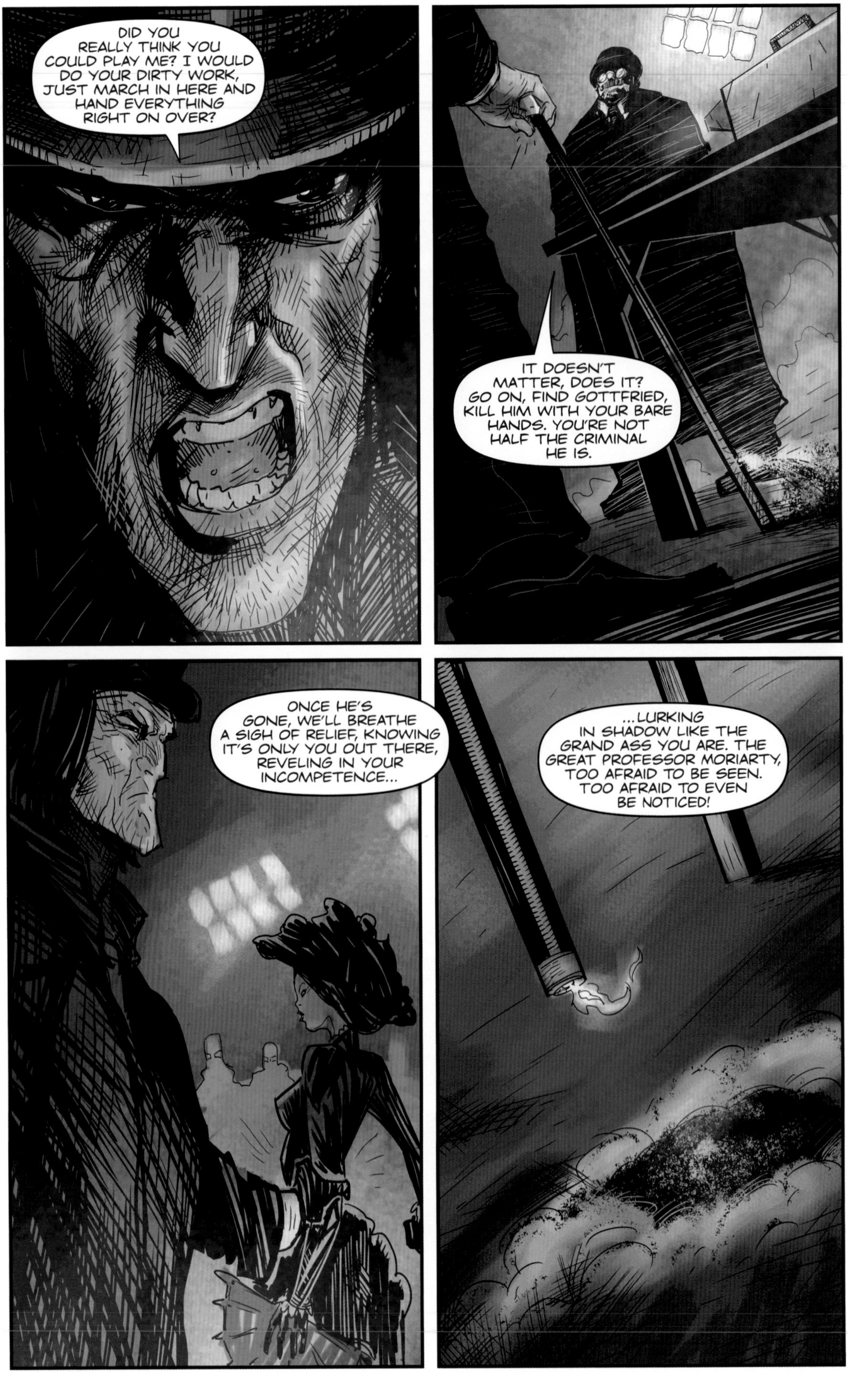
DID YOU REALLY THINK YOU COULD PLAY ME? I WOULD DO YOUR DIRTY WORK, JUST MARCH IN HERE AND HAND EVERYTHING RIGHT ON OVER?
IT DOESN'T MATTER, DOES IT? GO ON, FIND GOTTFRIED, KILL HIM WITH YOUR BARE HANDS. YOU'RE NOT HALF THE CRIMINAL HE IS.
ONCE HE'S GONE, WE'LL BREATHE A SIGH OF RELIEF, KNOWING IT'S ONLY YOU OUT THERE, REVELING IN YOUR INCOMPETENCE...
...LURKING IN SHADOW LIKE THE GRAND ASS YOU ARE. THE GREAT PROFESSOR MORIARTY, TOO AFRAID TO BE SEEN. TOO AFRAID TO EVEN BE NOTICED!

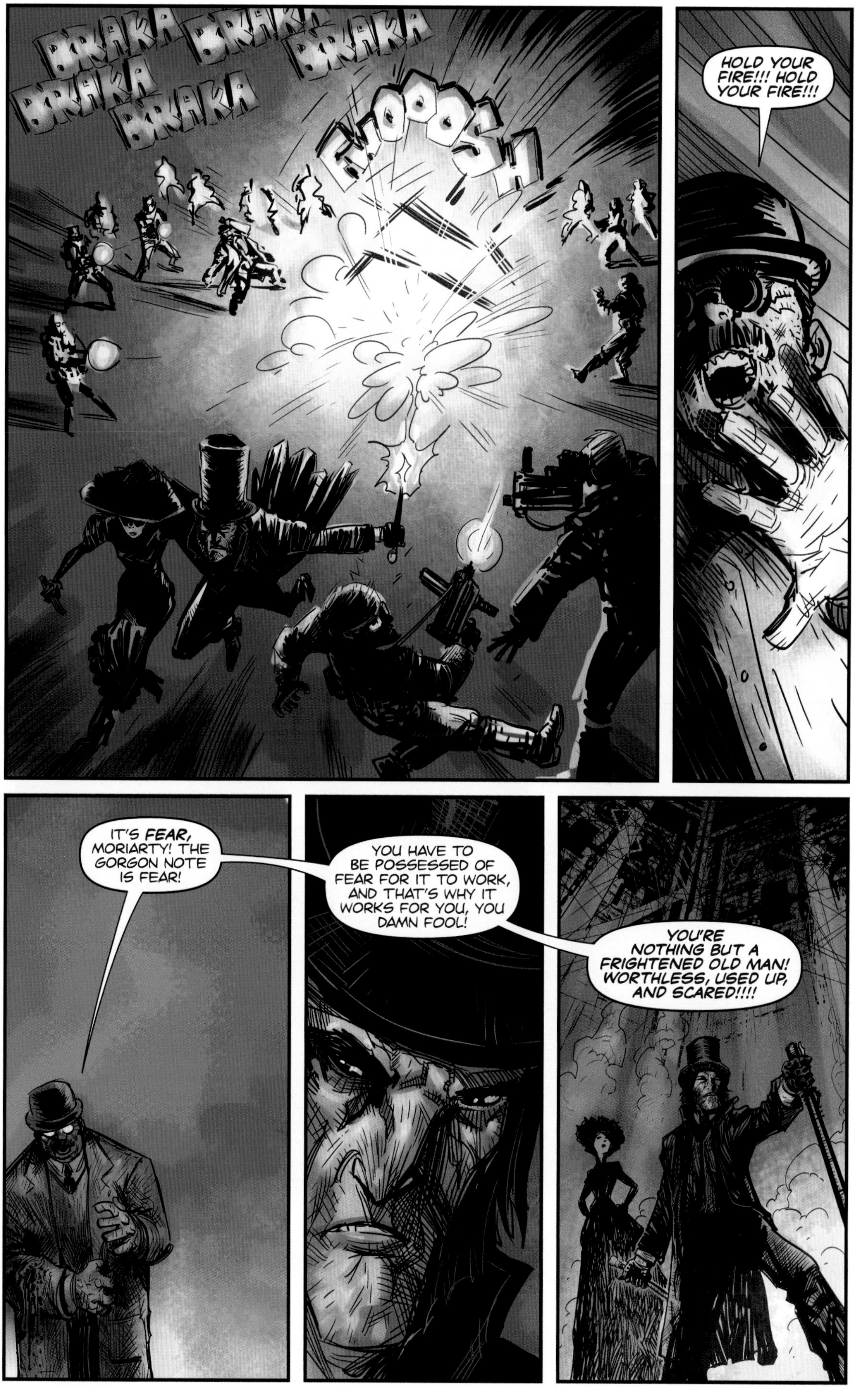
BRAKA BRAKA BRAKA BRAKA BRAKA
FWOOOSH
HOLD YOUR FIRE!!! HOLD YOUR FIRE!!!
IT'S FEAR, MORIARTY! THE GORGON NOTE IS FEAR!
YOU HAVE TO BE POSSESSED OF FEAR FOR IT TO WORK, AND THAT'S WHY IT WORKS FOR YOU, YOU DAMN FOOL!
YOU'RE NOTHING BUT A FRIGHTENED OLD MAN! WORTHLESS, USED UP, AND SCARED!!!!

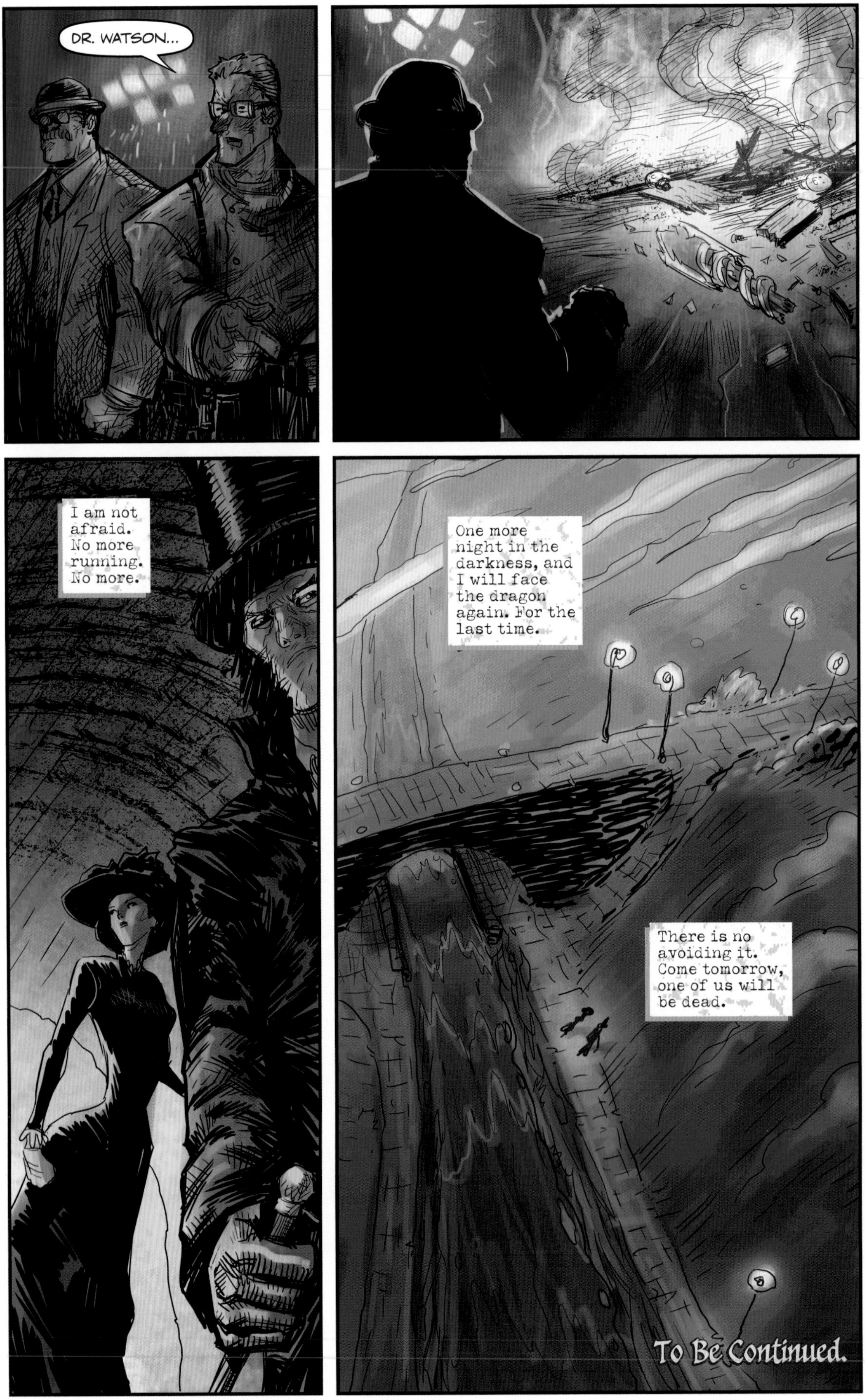
DR. WATSON...
I am not afraid. No more running. No more.
One more night in the darkness, and I will face the dragon again. For the last time.
There is no avoiding it. Come tomorrow, one of us will be dead.
To Be Continued.

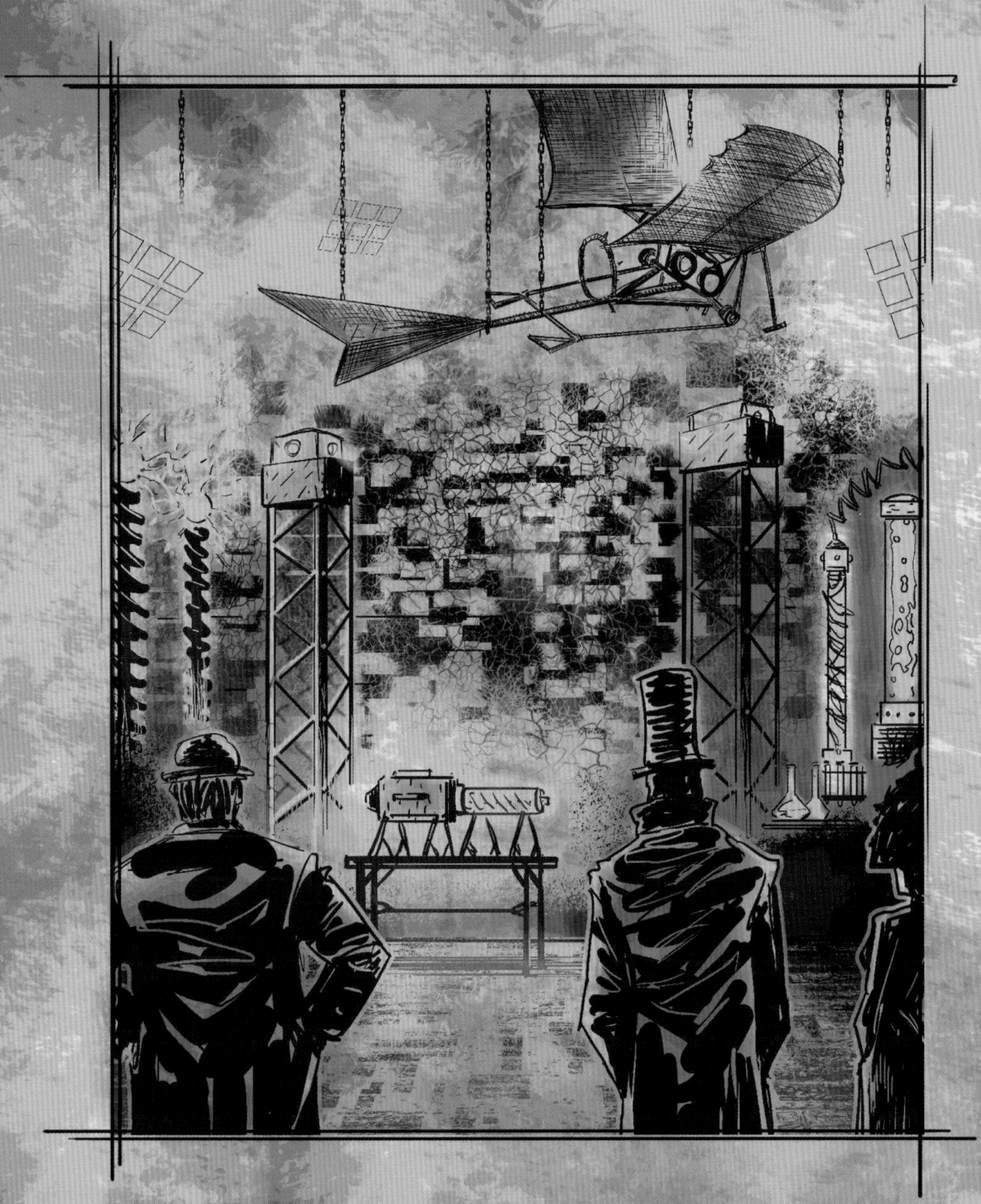

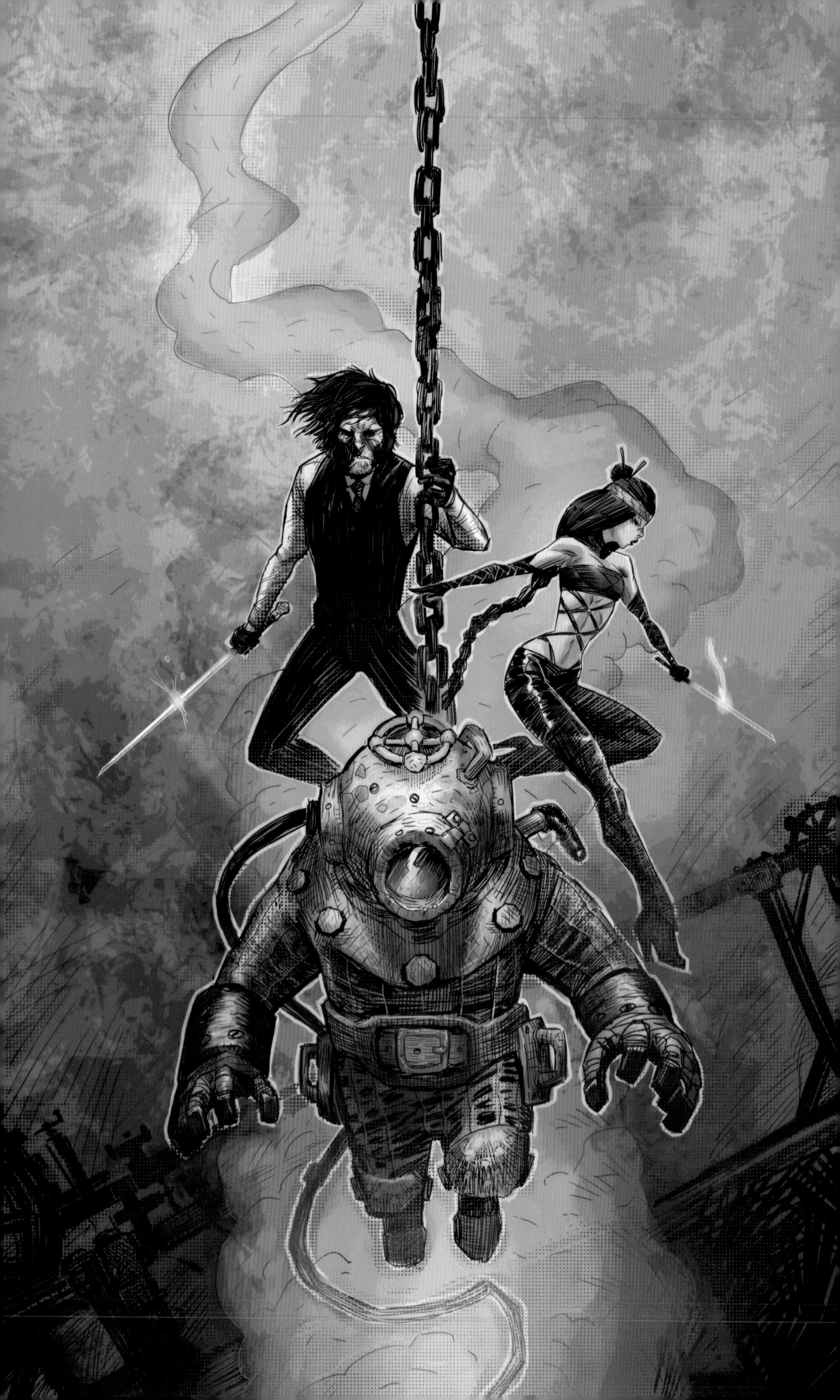

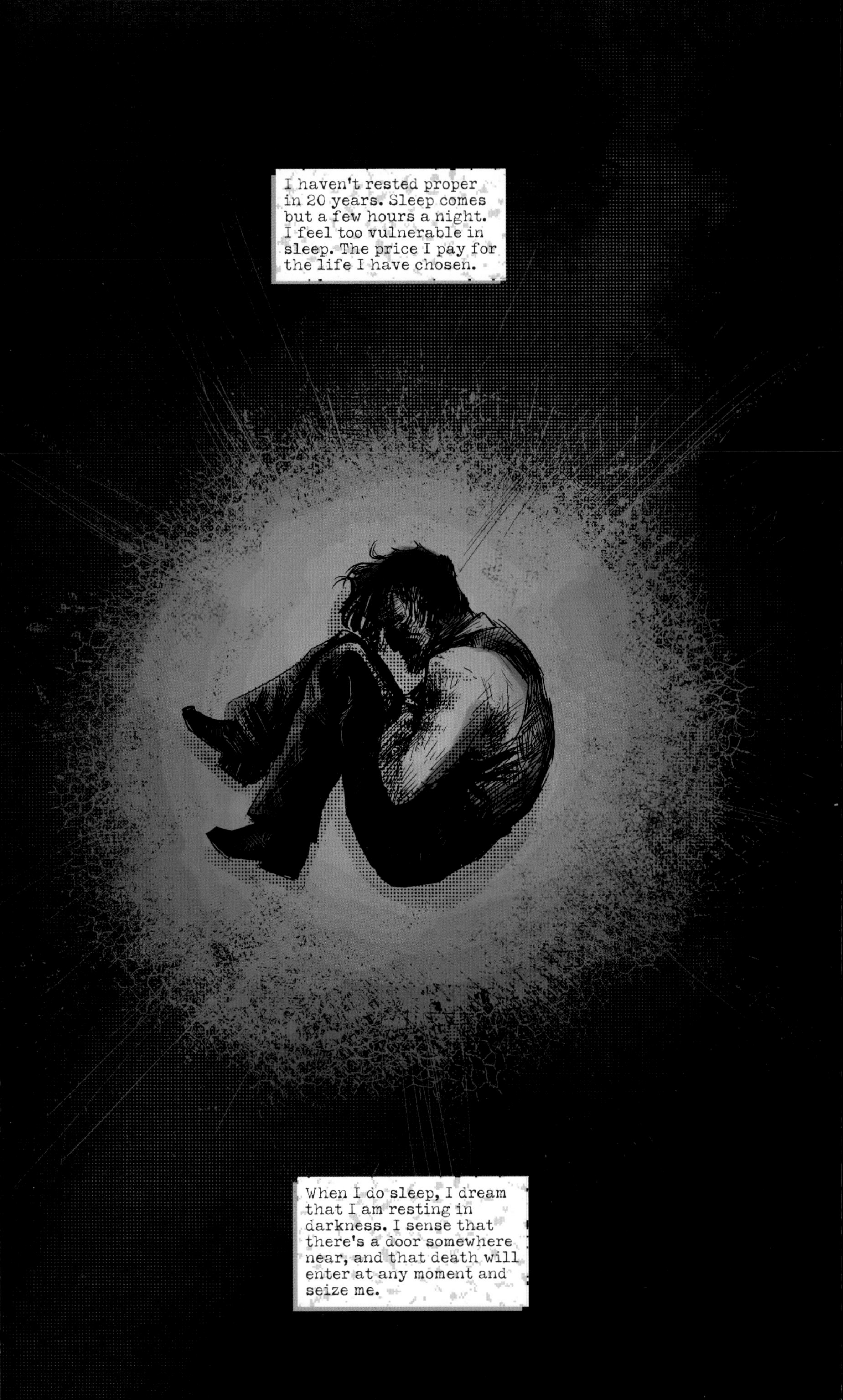
I haven't rested proper in 20 years. Sleep comes but a few hours a night. I feel too vulnerable in sleep. The price I pay for the life I have chosen.
When I do sleep, I dream that I am resting in darkness. I sense that there's a door somewhere near, and that death will enter at any moment and seize me.

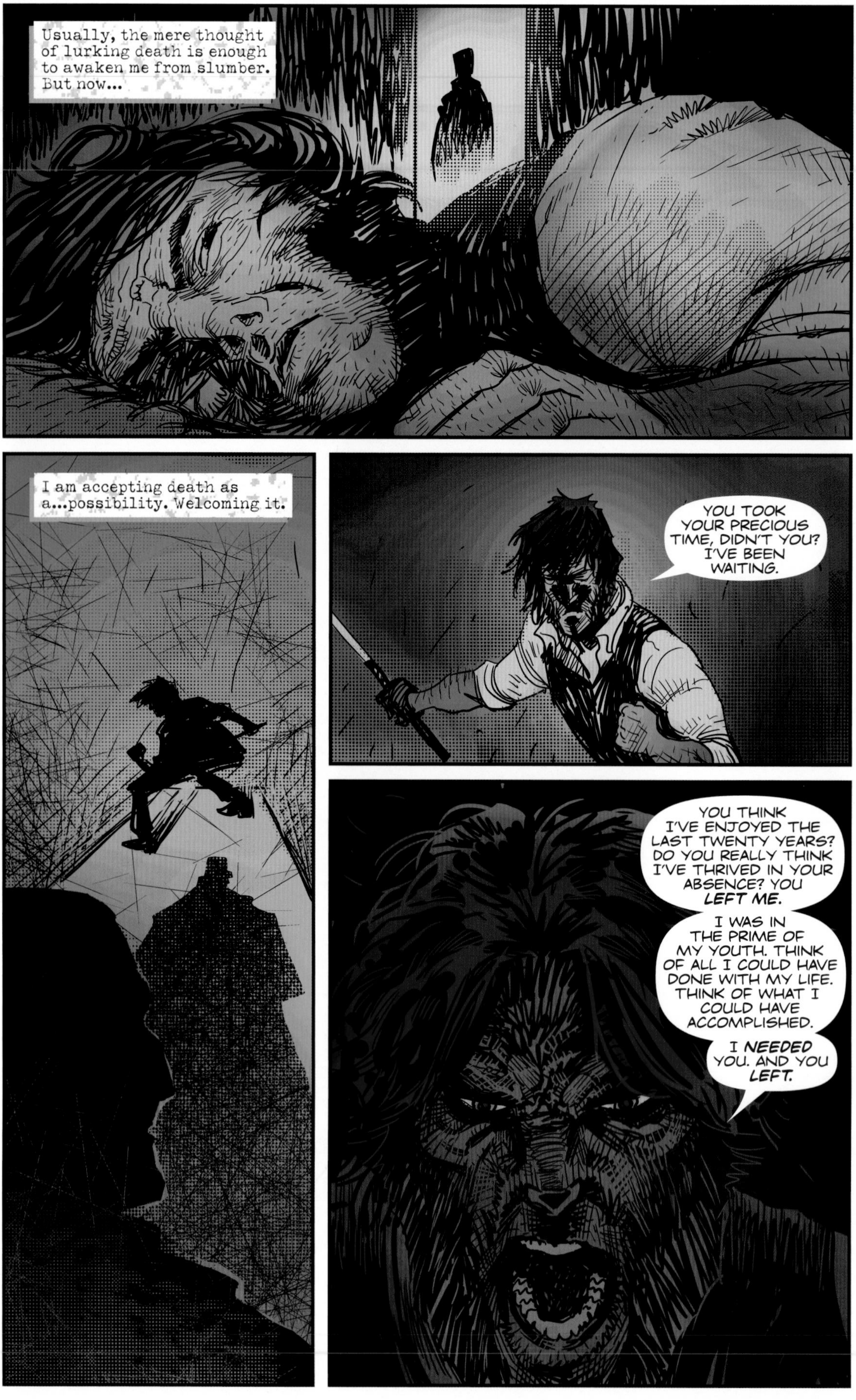
Usually, the mere thought of lurking death is enough to awaken me from slumber. But now...
I am accepting death as a...possibility. Welcoming it.
YOU TOOK YOUR PRECIOUS TIME, DIDN'T YOU? I'VE BEEN WAITING.
YOU THINK I'VE ENJOYED THE LAST TWENTY YEARS? DO YOU REALLY THINK I'VE THRIVED IN YOUR ABSENCE? YOU LEFT ME.
I WAS IN THE PRIME OF MY YOUTH. THINK OF ALL I COULD HAVE DONE WITH MY LIFE. THINK OF WHAT I COULD HAVE ACCOMPLISHED.
I NEEDED YOU. AND YOU LEFT.

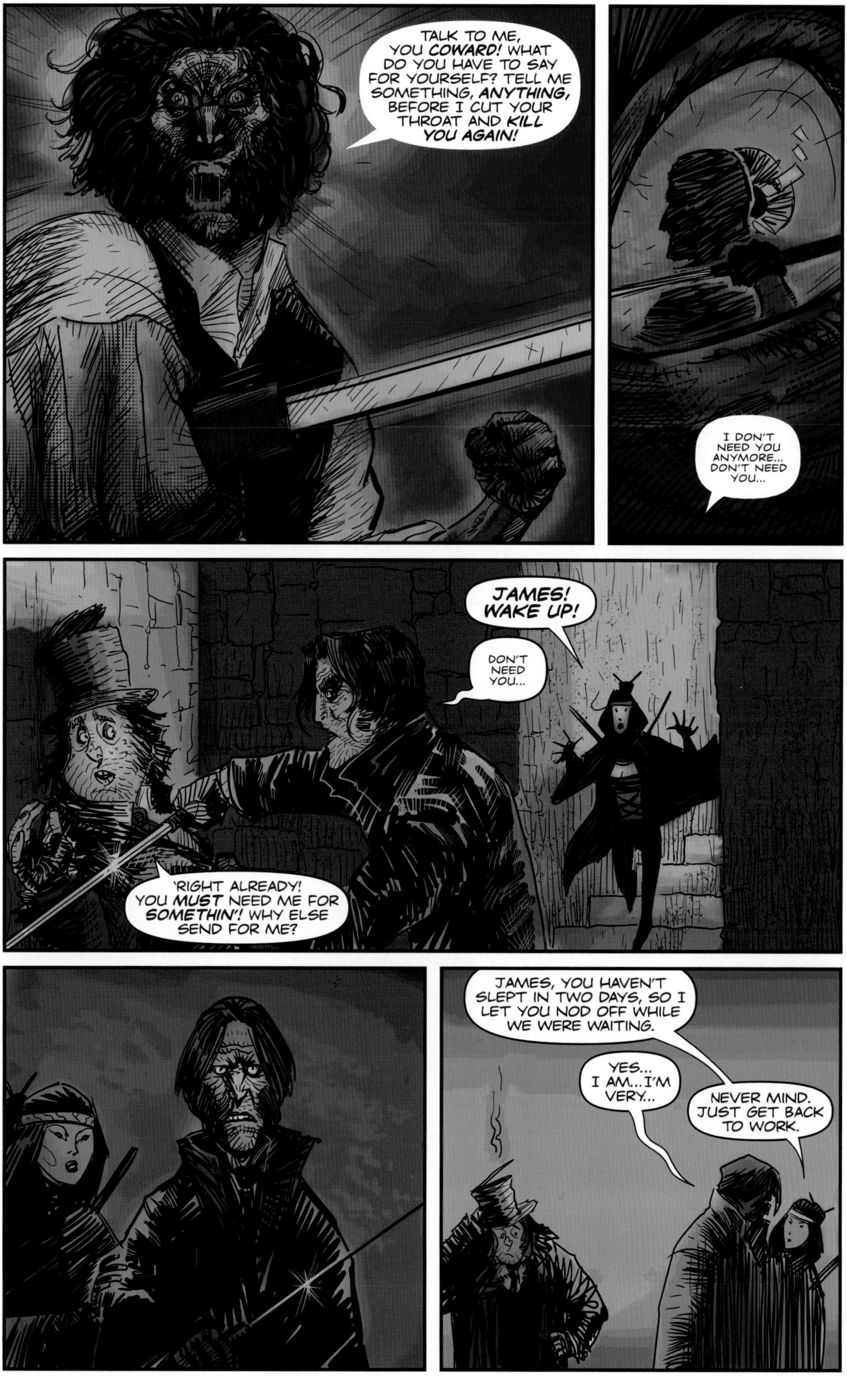
TALK TO ME, YOU COWARD! WHAT DO YOU HAVE TO SAY FOR YOURSELF? TELL ME SOMETHING, ANYTHING, BEFORE I CUT YOUR THROAT AND KILL YOU AGAIN!
I DON'T NEED YOU ANYMORE... DON'T NEED YOU...
JAMES! WAKE UP!
DON'T NEED YOU...
'RIGHT ALREADY! YOU MUST NEED ME FOR SOMETHIN'! WHY ELSE SEND FOR ME?
JAMES, YOU HAVEN'T SLEPT IN TWO DAYS, SO I LET YOU NOD OFF WHILE WE WERE WAITING.
YES... I AM...I'M VERY...
NEVER MIND. JUST GET BACK TO WORK.

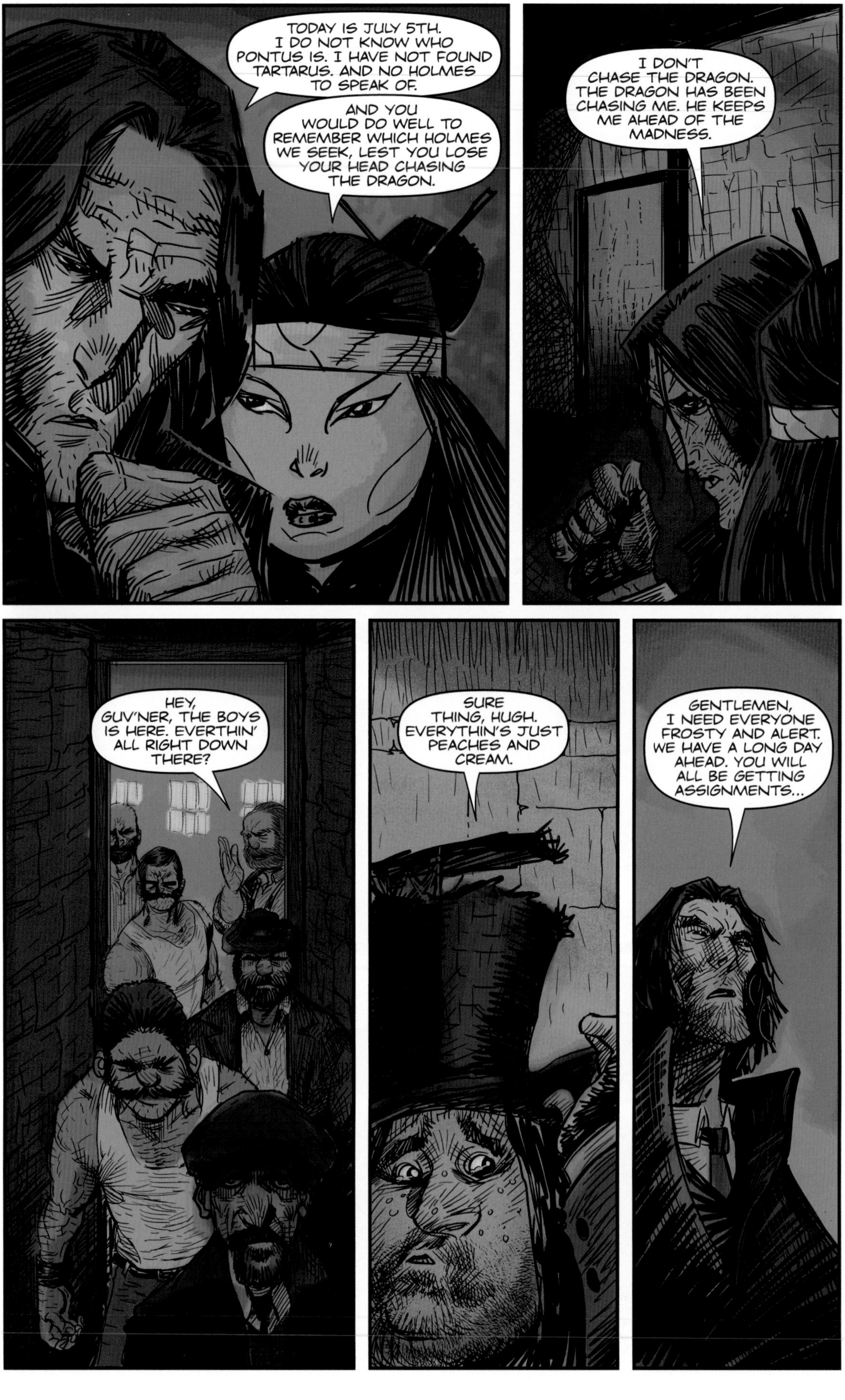
TODAY IS JULY 5TH. I DO NOT KNOW WHO PONTUS IS. I HAVE NOT FOUND TARTARUS. AND NO HOLMES TO SPEAK OF.
AND YOU WOULD DO WELL TO REMEMBER WHICH HOLMES WE SEEK, LEST YOU LOSE YOUR HEAD CHASING THE DRAGON.
I DON'T CHASE THE DRAGON. THE DRAGON HAS BEEN CHASING ME. HE KEEPS ME AHEAD OF THE MADNESS.
HEY, GUV'NER, THE BOYS IS HERE. EVERTHIN' ALL RIGHT DOWN THERE?
SURE THING, HUGH. EVERYTHIN'S JUST PEACHES AND CREAM.
GENTLEMEN, I NEED EVERYONE FROSTY AND ALERT. WE HAVE A LONG DAY AHEAD. YOU WILL ALL BE GETTING ASSIGNMENTS...

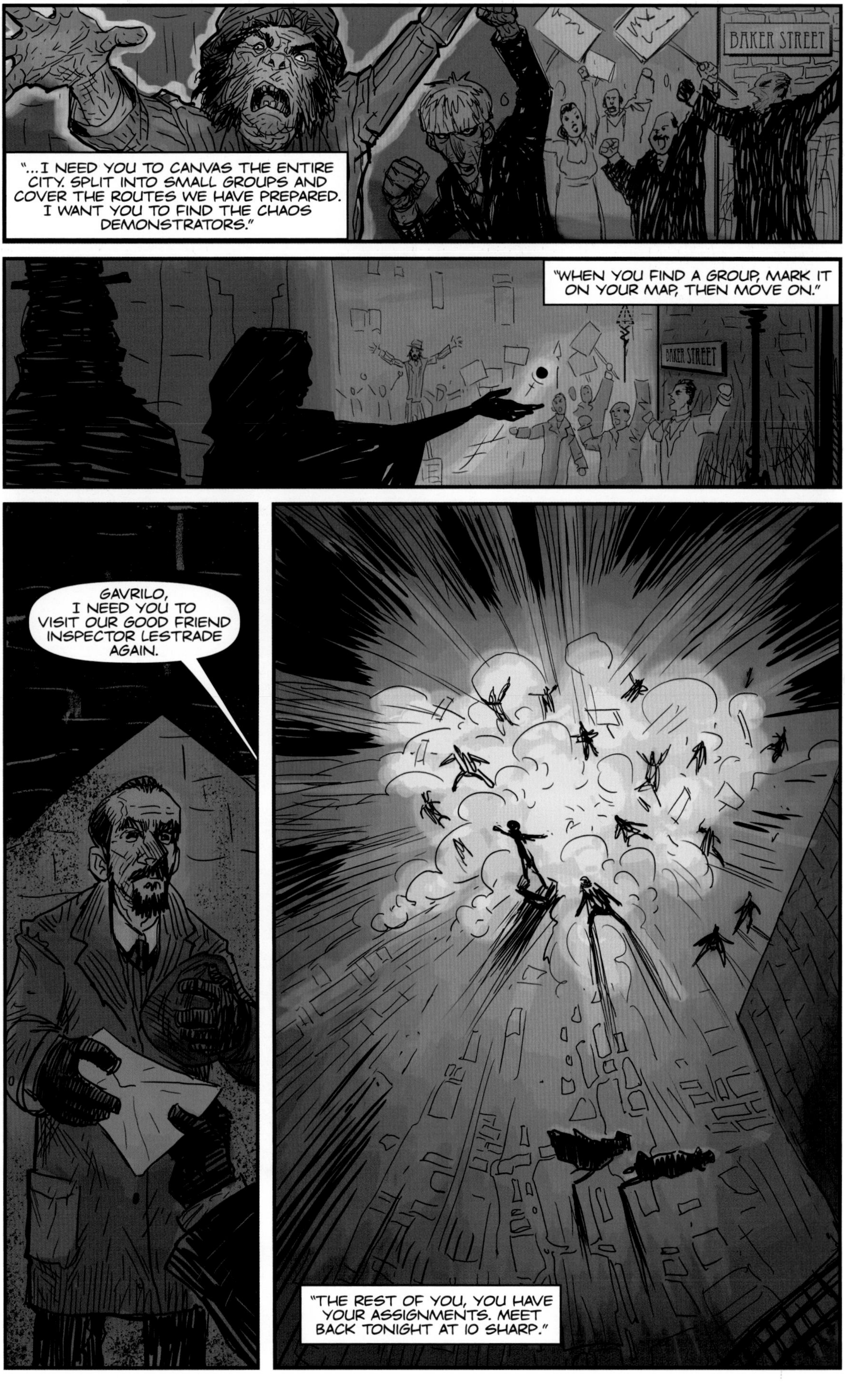
"...I NEED YOU TO CANVAS THE ENTIRE CITY. SPLIT INTO SMALL GROUPS AND COVER THE ROUTES WE HAVE PREPARED. I WANT YOU TO FIND THE CHAOS DEMONSTRATORS."
BAKER STREET
"WHEN YOU FIND A GROUP, MARK IT ON YOUR MAP, THEN MOVE ON."
BAKER STREET
GAVRILO, I NEED YOU TO VISIT OUR GOOD FRIEND INSPECTOR LESTRADE AGAIN.
"THE REST OF YOU, YOU HAVE YOUR ASSIGNMENTS. MEET BACK TONIGHT AT 10 SHARP."

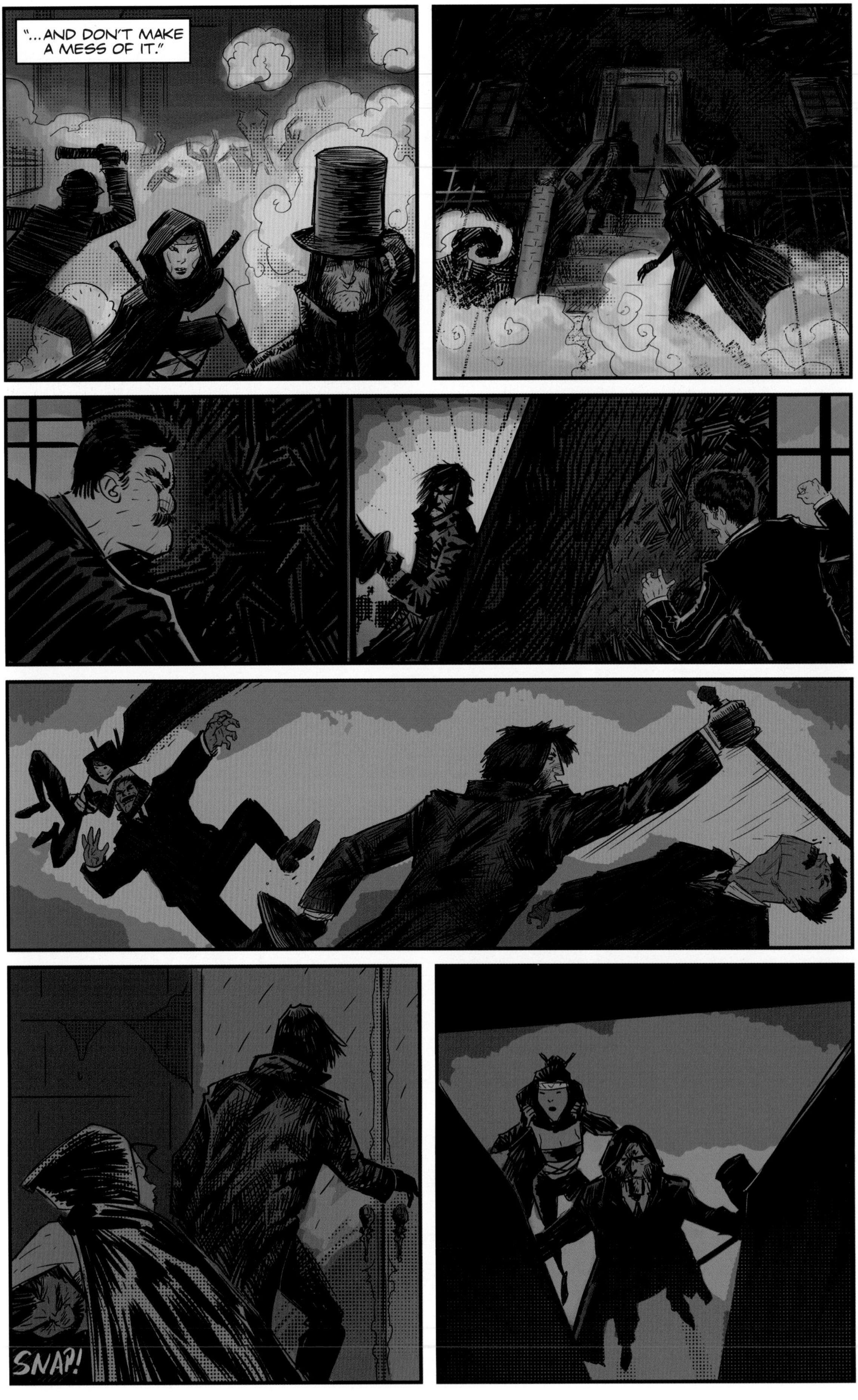
"...AND DON'T MAKE A MESS OF IT."
SNAP!

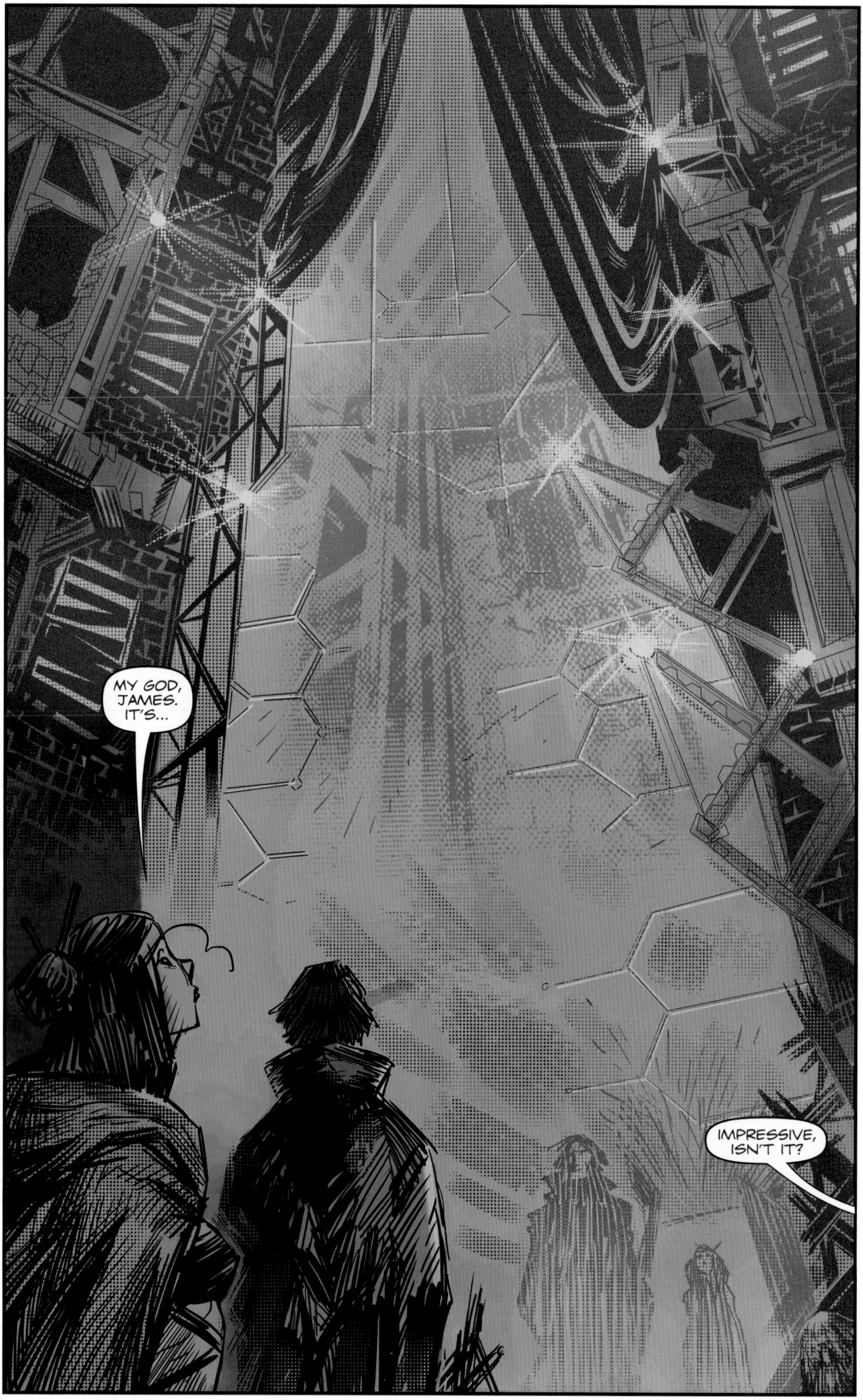
MY GOD, JAMES. IT'S...
IMPRESSIVE, ISN'T IT?

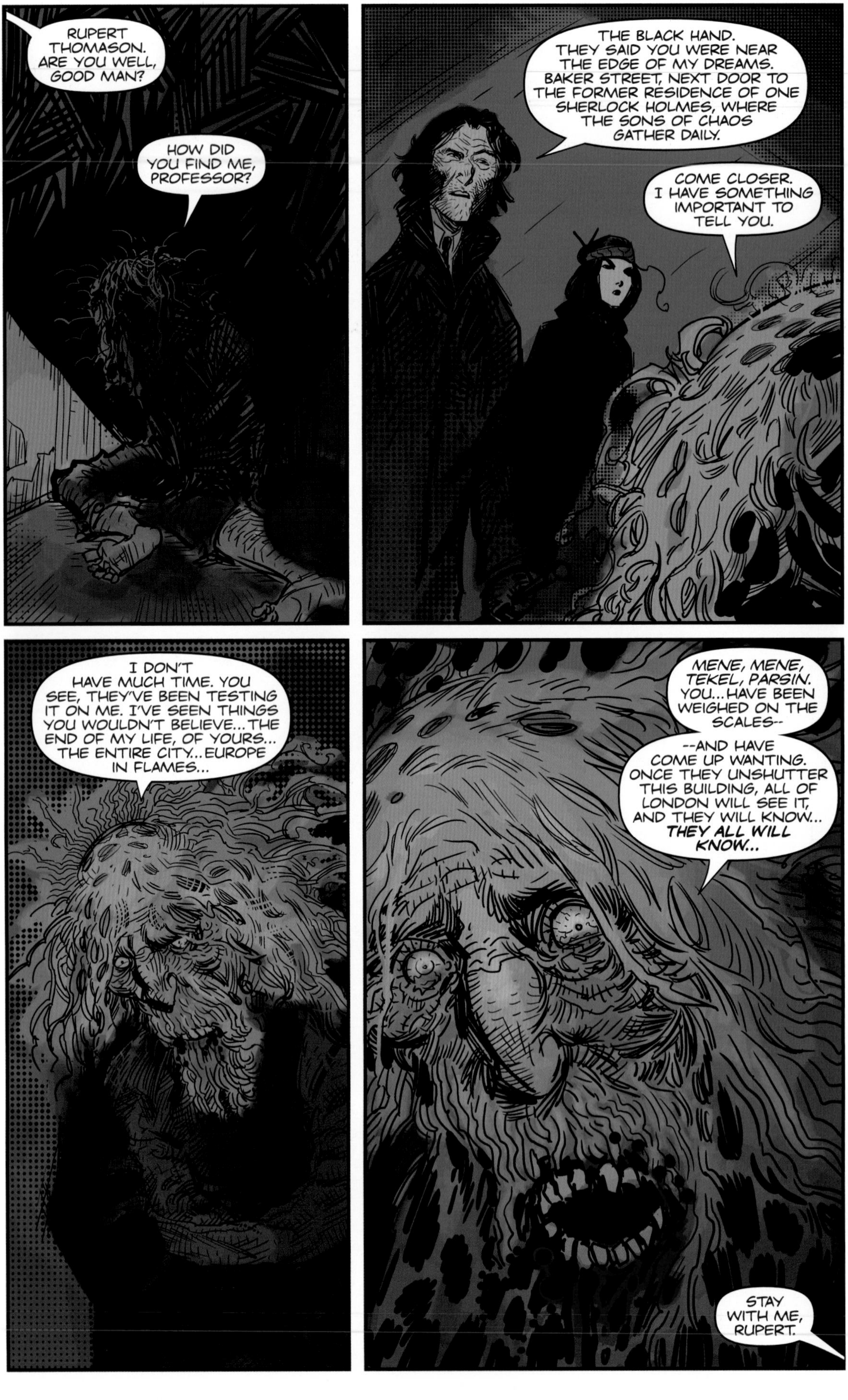
RUPERT THOMASON. ARE YOU WELL, GOOD MAN?
HOW DID YOU FIND ME, PROFESSOR?
THE BLACK HAND. THEY SAID YOU WERE NEAR THE EDGE OF MY DREAMS. BAKER STREET, NEXT DOOR TO THE FORMER RESIDENCE OF ONE SHERLOCK HOLMES, WHERE THE SONS OF CHAOS GATHER DAILY.
COME CLOSER. I HAVE SOMETHING IMPORTANT TO TELL YOU.
I DON'T HAVE MUCH TIME. YOU SEE, THEY'VE BEEN TESTING IT ON ME. I'VE SEEN THINGS YOU WOULDN'T BELIEVE... THE END OF MY LIFE, OF YOURS... THE ENTIRE CITY... EUROPE IN FLAMES...
MENE, MENE, TEKEL, PARSIN. YOU... HAVE BEEN WEIGHED ON THE SCALES--
--AND HAVE COME UP WANTING. ONCE THEY UNSHUTTER THIS BUILDING, ALL OF LONDON WILL SEE IT, AND THEY WILL KNOW... ***THEY ALL WILL KNOW...***
STAY WITH ME, RUPERT.

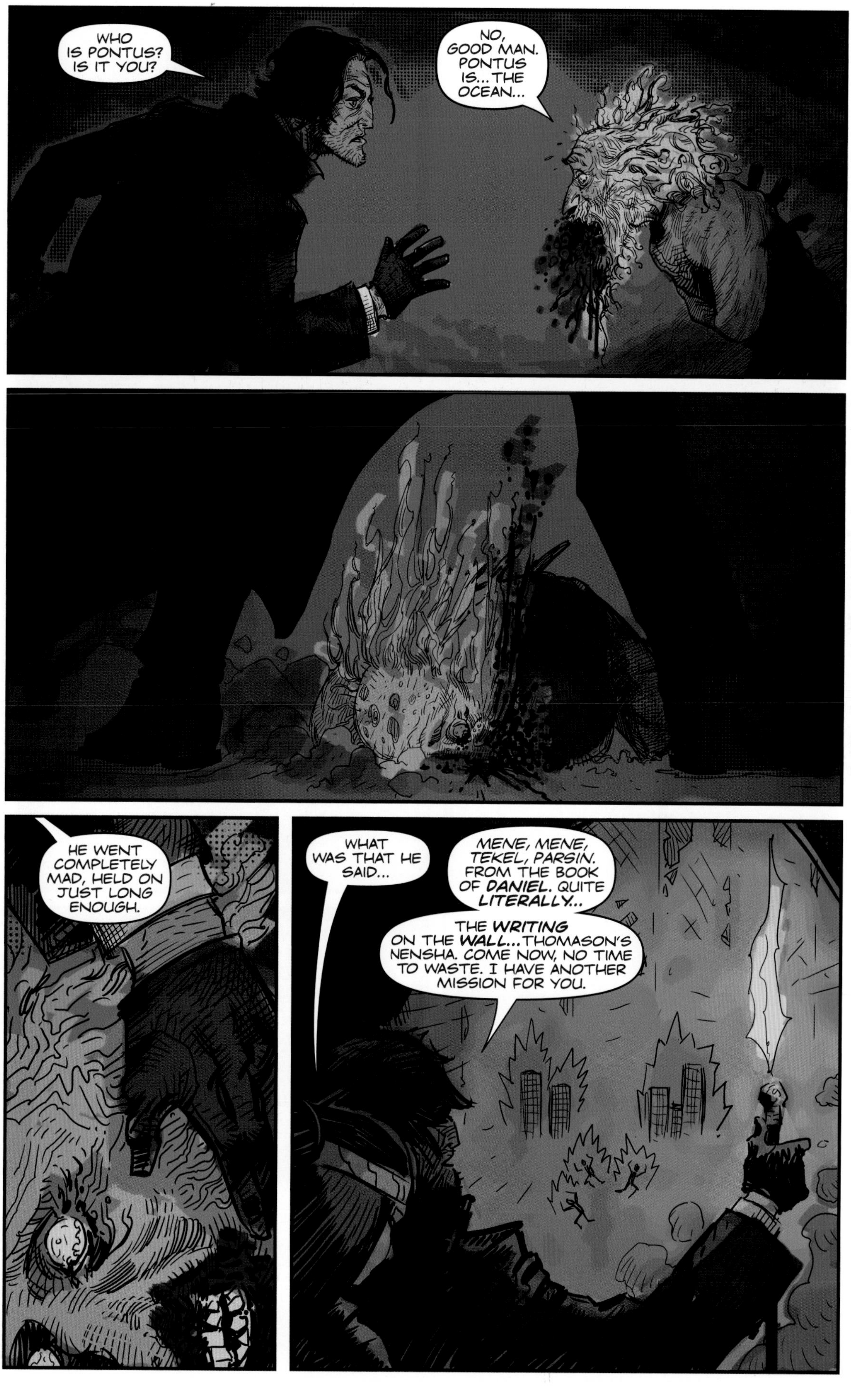
WHO IS PONTUS? IS IT YOU?
NO, GOOD MAN. PONTUS IS...THE OCEAN...
HE WENT COMPLETELY MAD, HELD ON JUST LONG ENOUGH.
WHAT WAS THAT HE SAID...
MENE, MENE, TEKEL, PARSIN. FROM THE BOOK OF DANIEL. QUITE LITERALLY...
THE WRITING ON THE WALL...THOMASON'S NENSHA. COME NOW, NO TIME TO WASTE. I HAVE ANOTHER MISSION FOR YOU.

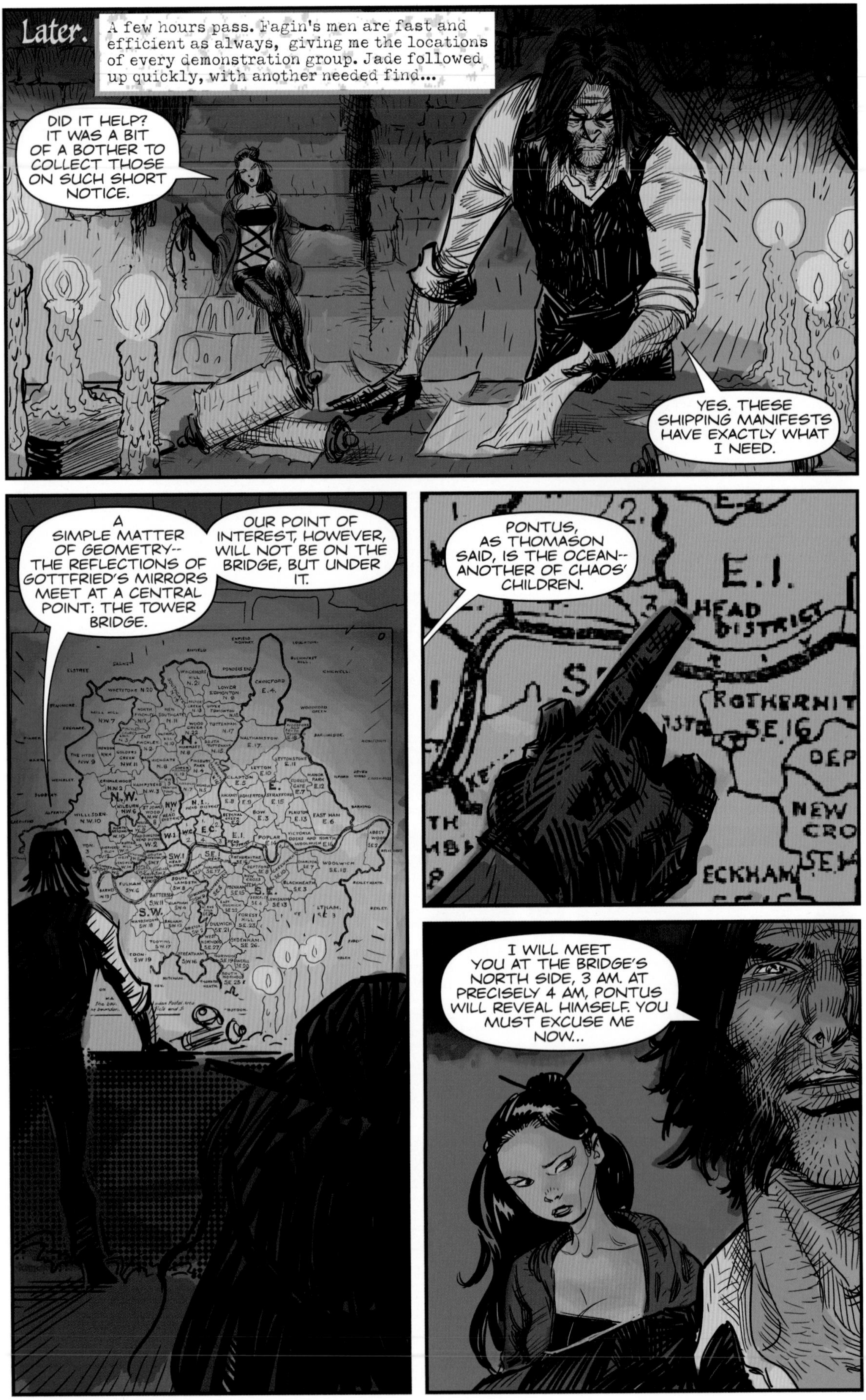
Later.
A few hours pass. Fagin's men are fast and efficient as always, giving me the locations of every demonstration group. Jade followed up quickly, with another needed find...
DID IT HELP? IT WAS A BIT OF A BOTHER TO COLLECT THOSE ON SUCH SHORT NOTICE.
YES. THESE SHIPPING MANIFESTS HAVE EXACTLY WHAT I NEED.
A SIMPLE MATTER OF GEOMETRY-- THE REFLECTIONS OF GOTTFRIED'S MIRRORS MEET AT A CENTRAL POINT: THE TOWER BRIDGE.
OUR POINT OF INTEREST, HOWEVER, WILL NOT BE ON THE BRIDGE, BUT UNDER IT.
PONTUS, AS THOMASON SAID, IS THE OCEAN-- ANOTHER OF CHAOS' CHILDREN.
I WILL MEET YOU AT THE BRIDGE'S NORTH SIDE, 3 AM. AT PRECISELY 4 AM, PONTUS WILL REVEAL HIMSELF. YOU MUST EXCUSE ME NOW...

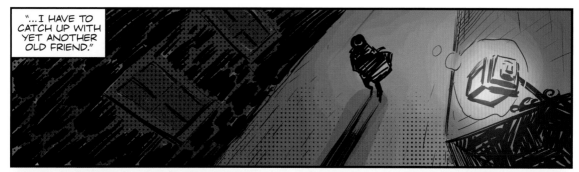

"...I HAVE TO CATCH UP WITH YET ANOTHER OLD FRIEND."

INSPECTOR LESTRADE. SO GOOD TO SEE YOU AGAIN.

I OWE YOU NOTHING, YOU HEAR? I PAID MY LAST DEBT TO YOU. WE'RE DONE.

YOU WILL NEVER BE DONE WITH ME, INSPECTOR. NOT SINCE THE HIGH STREET INCIDENT. YOU ARE MINE.

PEOPLE THOUGHT ME THE LESSER DETECTIVE, BUT HOLMES TREATED ME WITH RESPECT. I ALWAYS DID MY PART TO HELP, AND HE KNEW THAT. BUT YOU, YOU NEVER HAD ANY RESPECT FOR MY SKILL.

RESPECT ME *NOW*, MORIARTY!

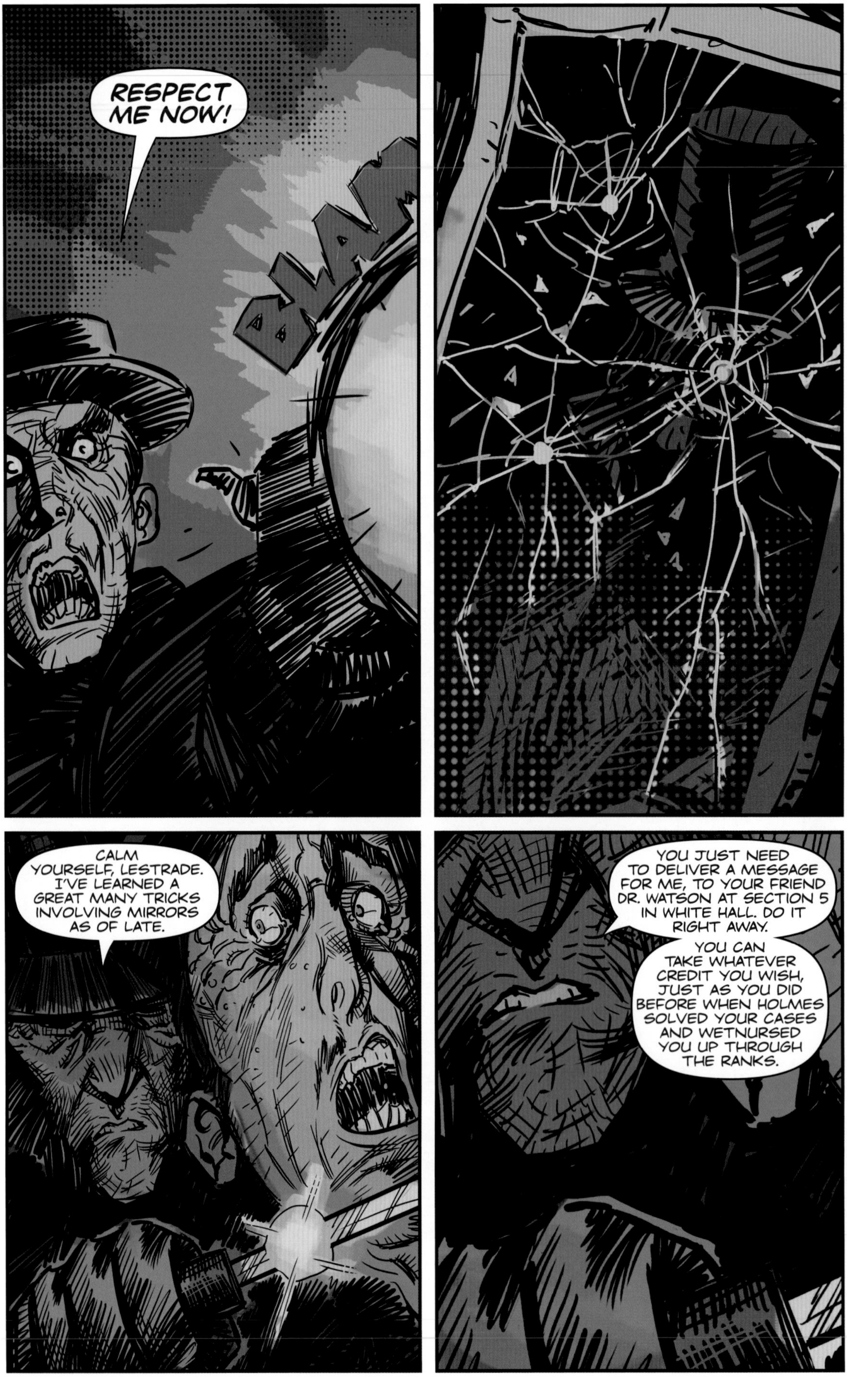
RESPECT ME NOW!
CALM YOURSELF, LESTRADE. I'VE LEARNED A GREAT MANY TRICKS INVOLVING MIRRORS AS OF LATE.
YOU JUST NEED TO DELIVER A MESSAGE FOR ME, TO YOUR FRIEND DR. WATSON AT SECTION 5 IN WHITE HALL. DO IT RIGHT AWAY.
YOU CAN TAKE WHATEVER CREDIT YOU WISH, JUST AS YOU DID BEFORE WHEN HOLMES SOLVED YOUR CASES AND WETNURSED YOU UP THROUGH THE RANKS.

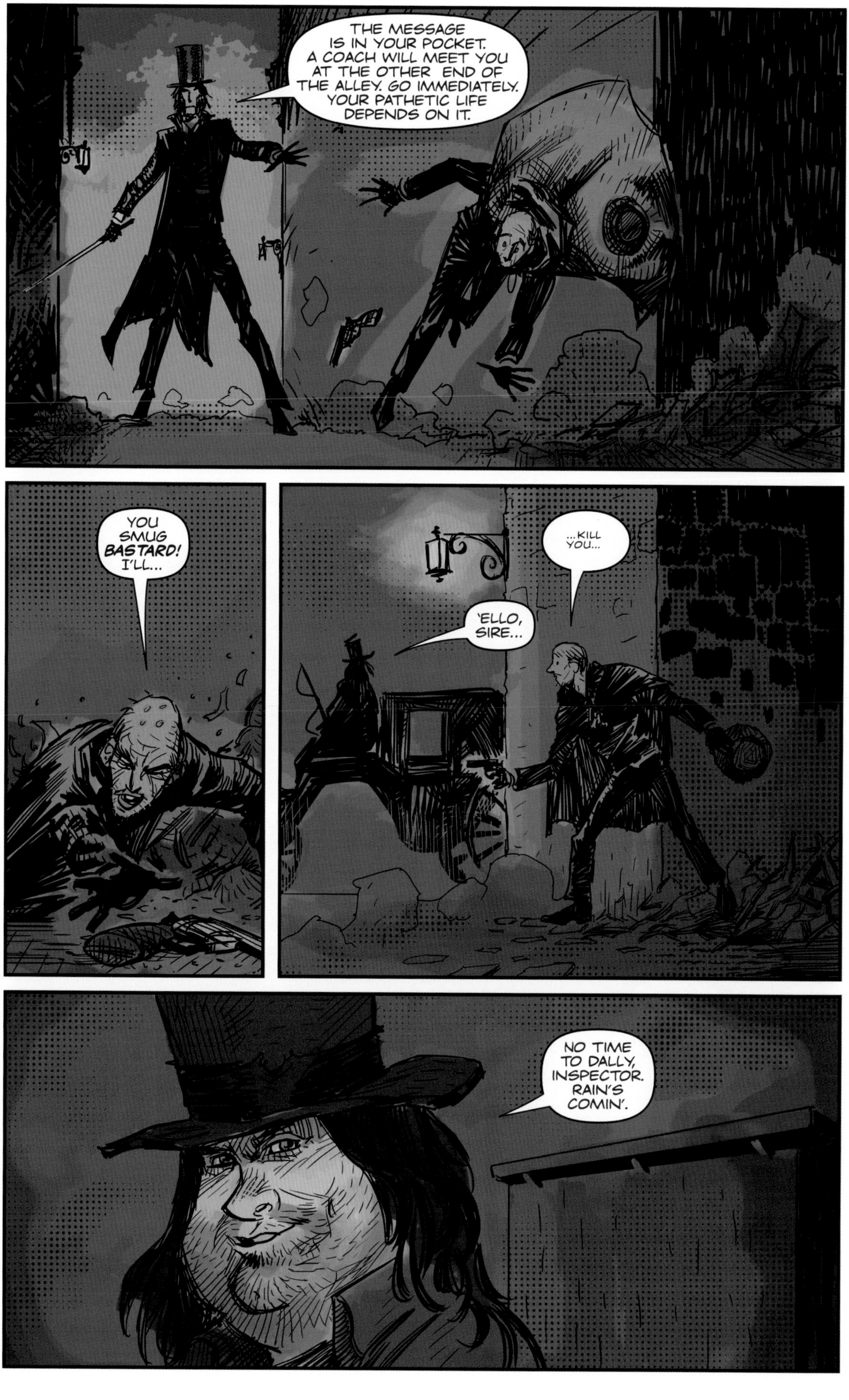
THE MESSAGE IS IN YOUR POCKET. A COACH WILL MEET YOU AT THE OTHER END OF THE ALLEY. GO IMMEDIATELY. YOUR PATHETIC LIFE DEPENDS ON IT.
YOU SMUG **BASTARD!** I'LL...
...KILL YOU...
'ELLO, SIRE...
NO TIME TO DALLY, INSPECTOR. RAIN'S COMIN'.

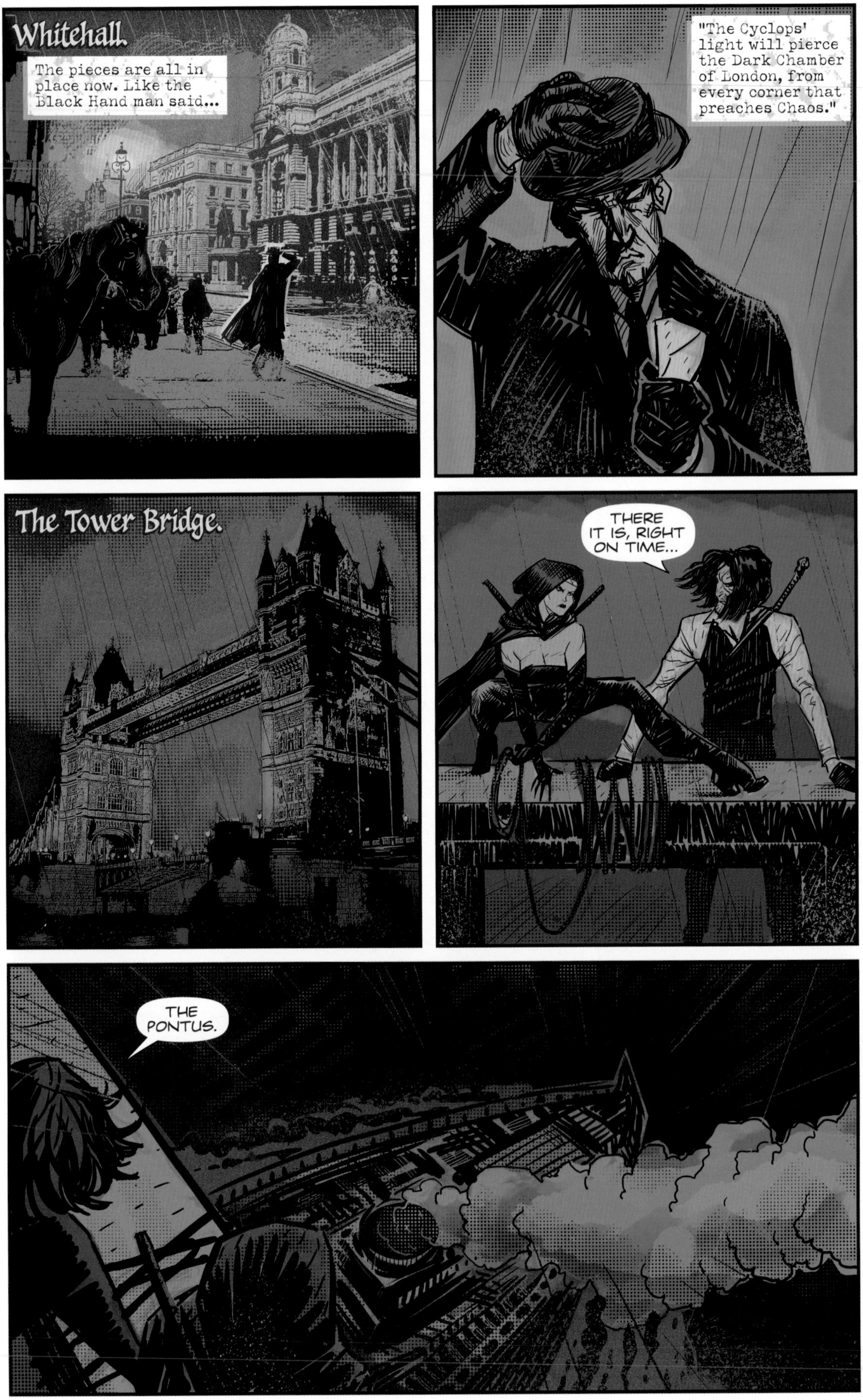
Whitehall.
The pieces are all in place now. Like the Black Hand man said...
"The Cyclops' light will pierce the Dark Chamber of London, from every corner that preaches Chaos."
The Tower Bridge.
THERE IT IS, RIGHT ON TIME...
THE PONTUS.

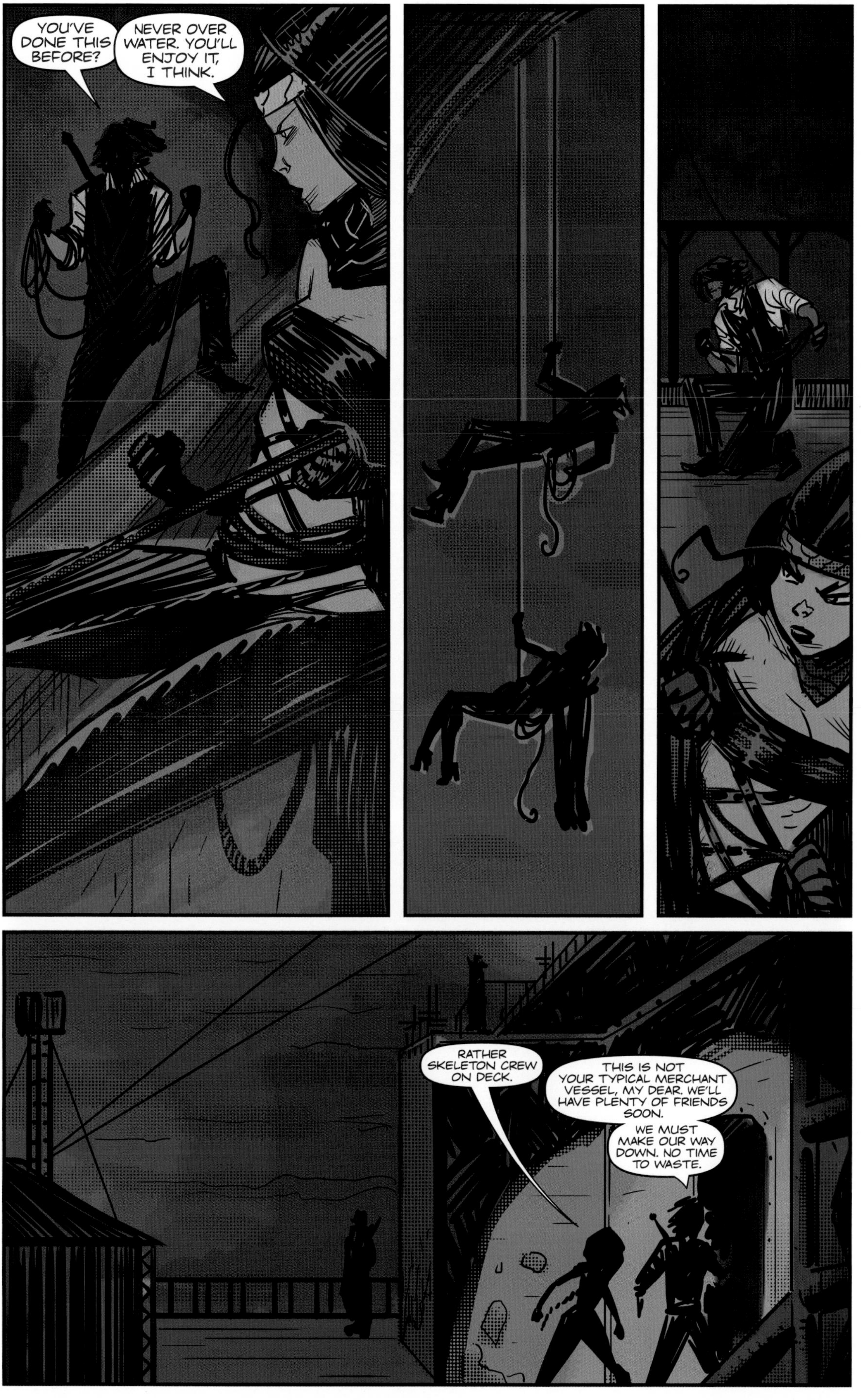
YOU'VE DONE THIS BEFORE?
NEVER OVER WATER. YOU'LL ENJOY IT, I THINK.
RATHER SKELETON CREW ON DECK.
THIS IS NOT YOUR TYPICAL MERCHANT VESSEL, MY DEAR. WE'LL HAVE PLENTY OF FRIENDS SOON.
WE MUST MAKE OUR WAY DOWN. NO TIME TO WASTE.

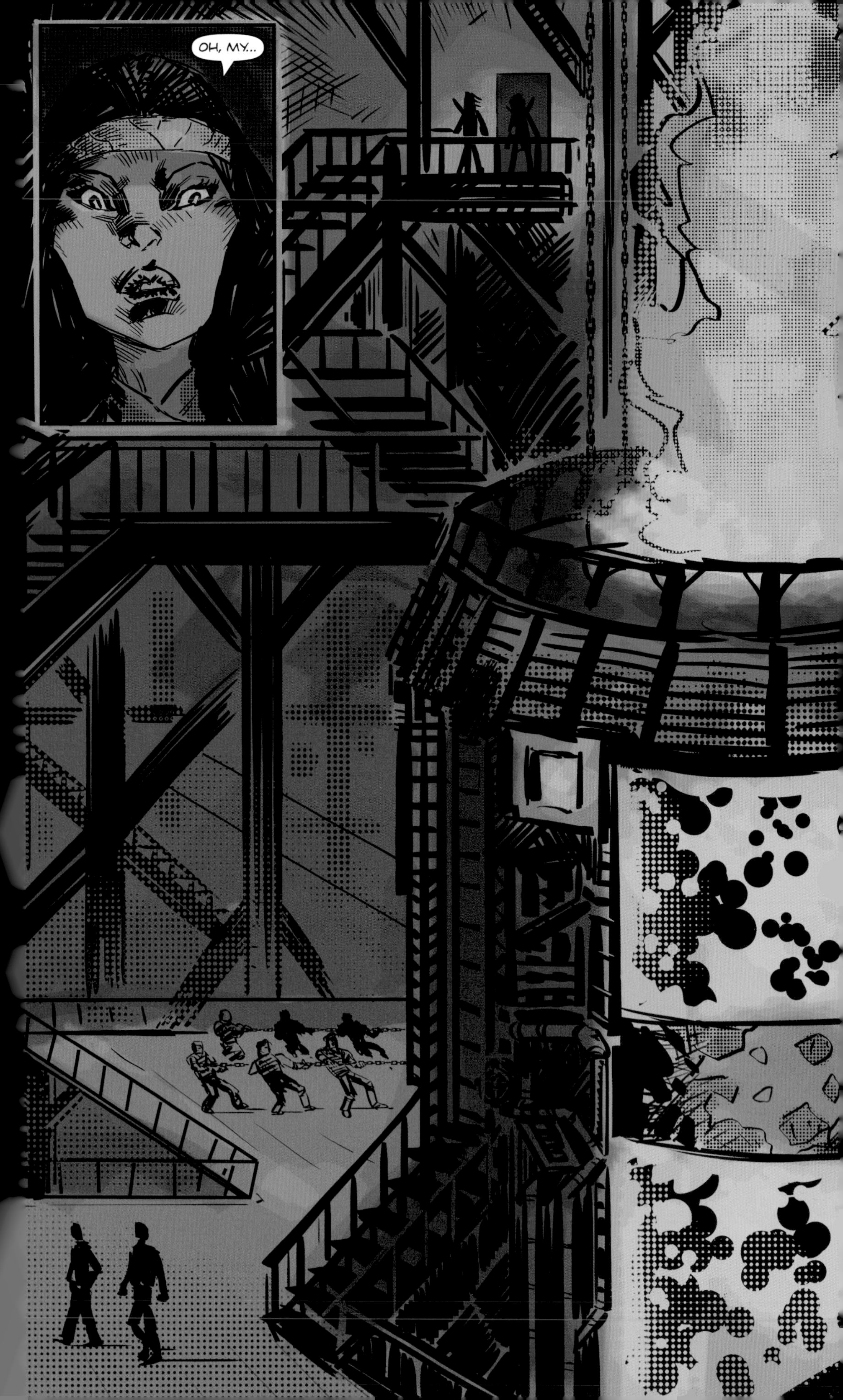
OH, MY...

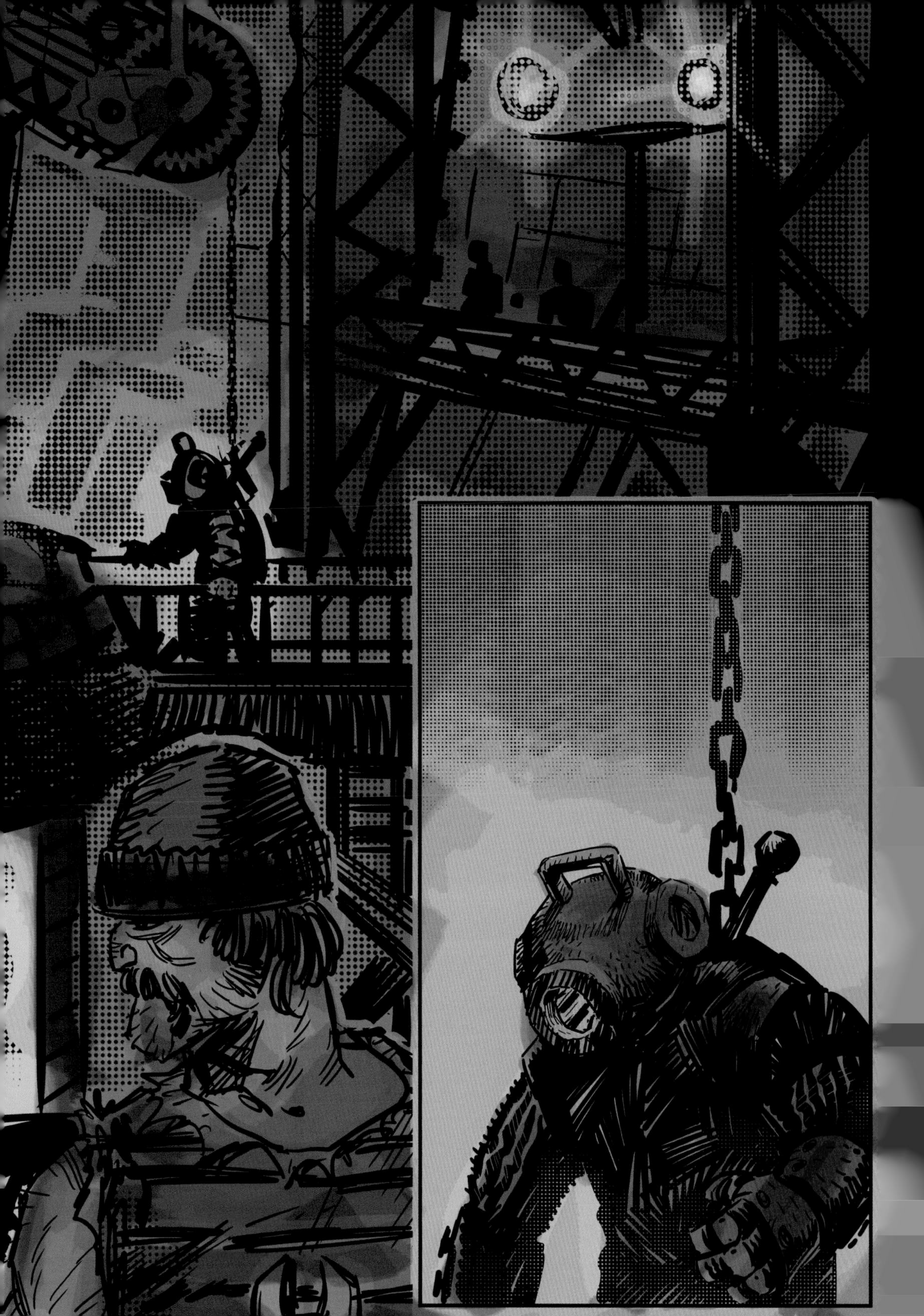

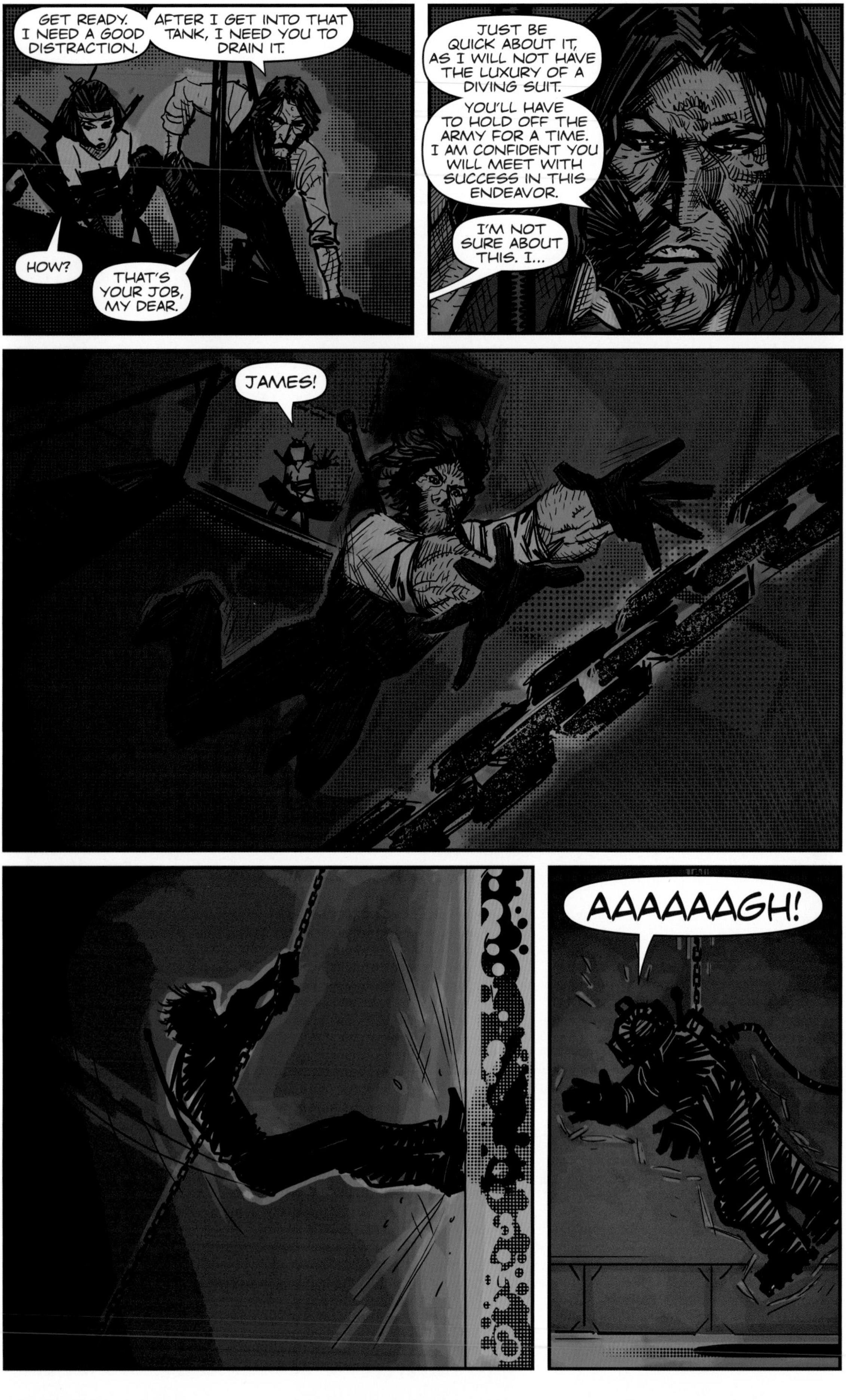
GET READY. I NEED A GOOD DISTRACTION.
AFTER I GET INTO THAT TANK, I NEED YOU TO DRAIN IT.
HOW?
THAT'S YOUR JOB, MY DEAR.
JUST BE QUICK ABOUT IT, AS I WILL NOT HAVE THE LUXURY OF A DIVING SUIT.
YOU'LL HAVE TO HOLD OFF THE ARMY FOR A TIME. I AM CONFIDENT YOU WILL MEET WITH SUCCESS IN THIS ENDEAVOR.
I'M NOT SURE ABOUT THIS. I...
JAMES!
AAAAAAGH!

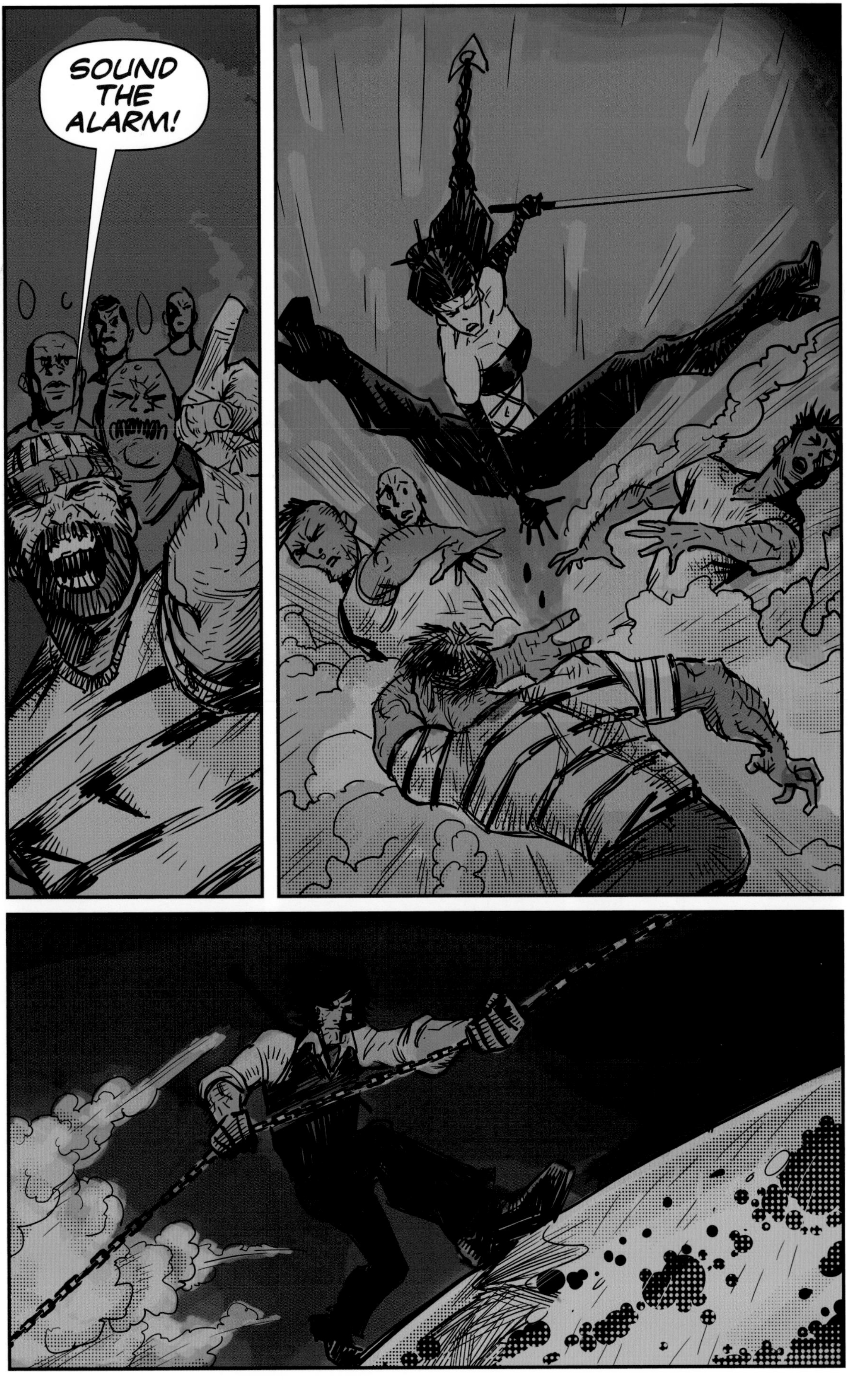
SOUND THE ALARM!

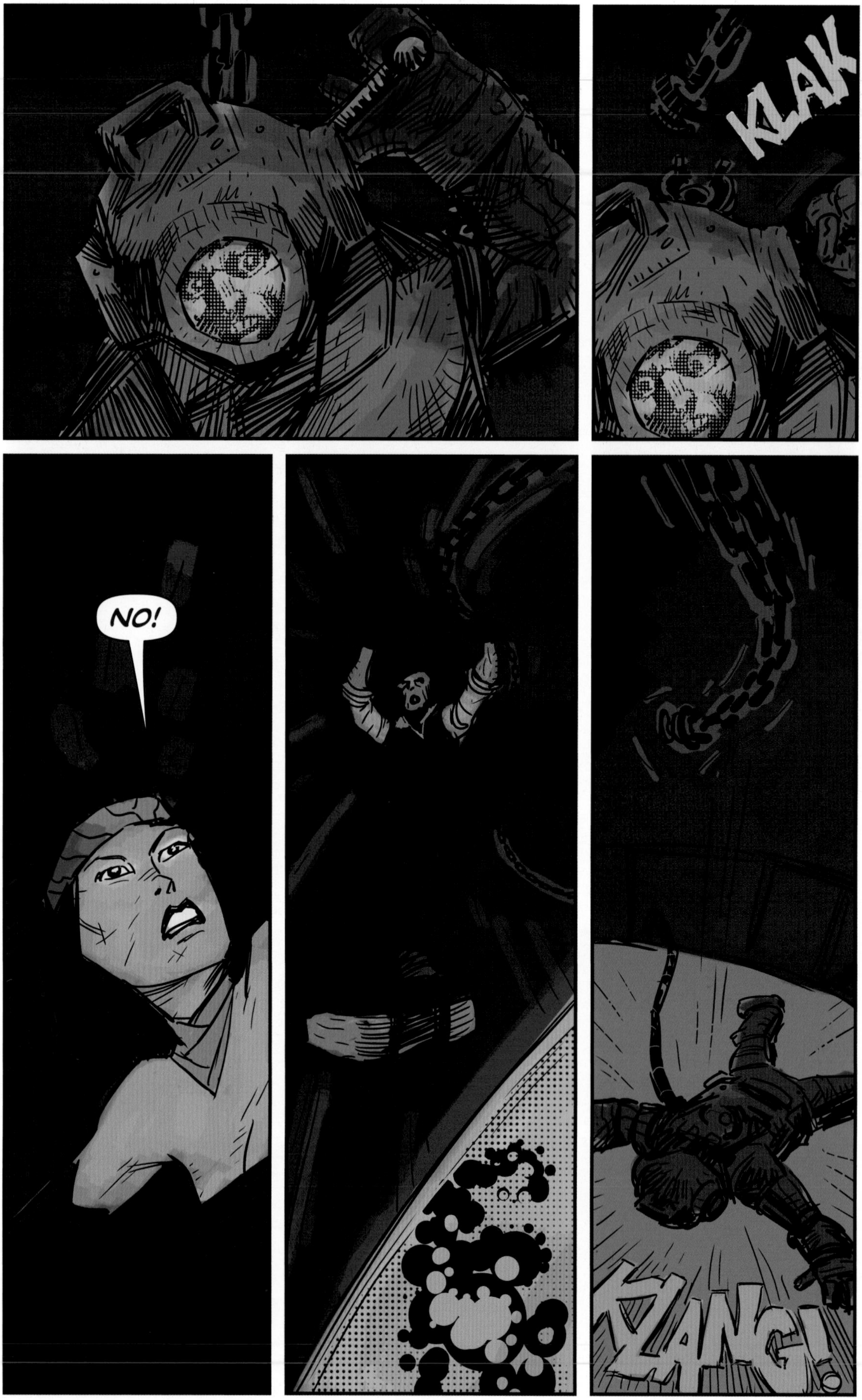

KLAK
NO!
ZANG!

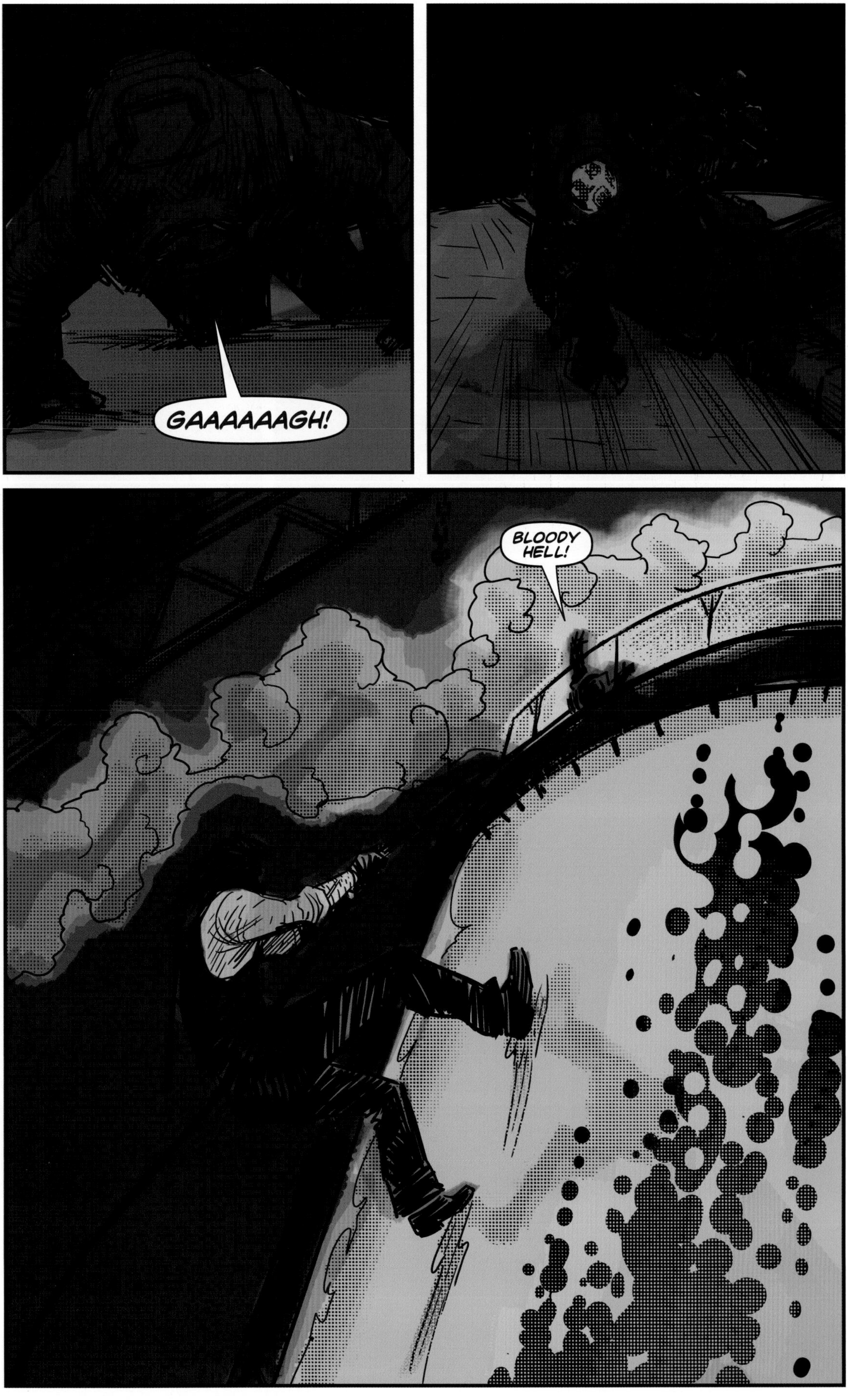
GAAAAAAGH!
BLOODY HELL!

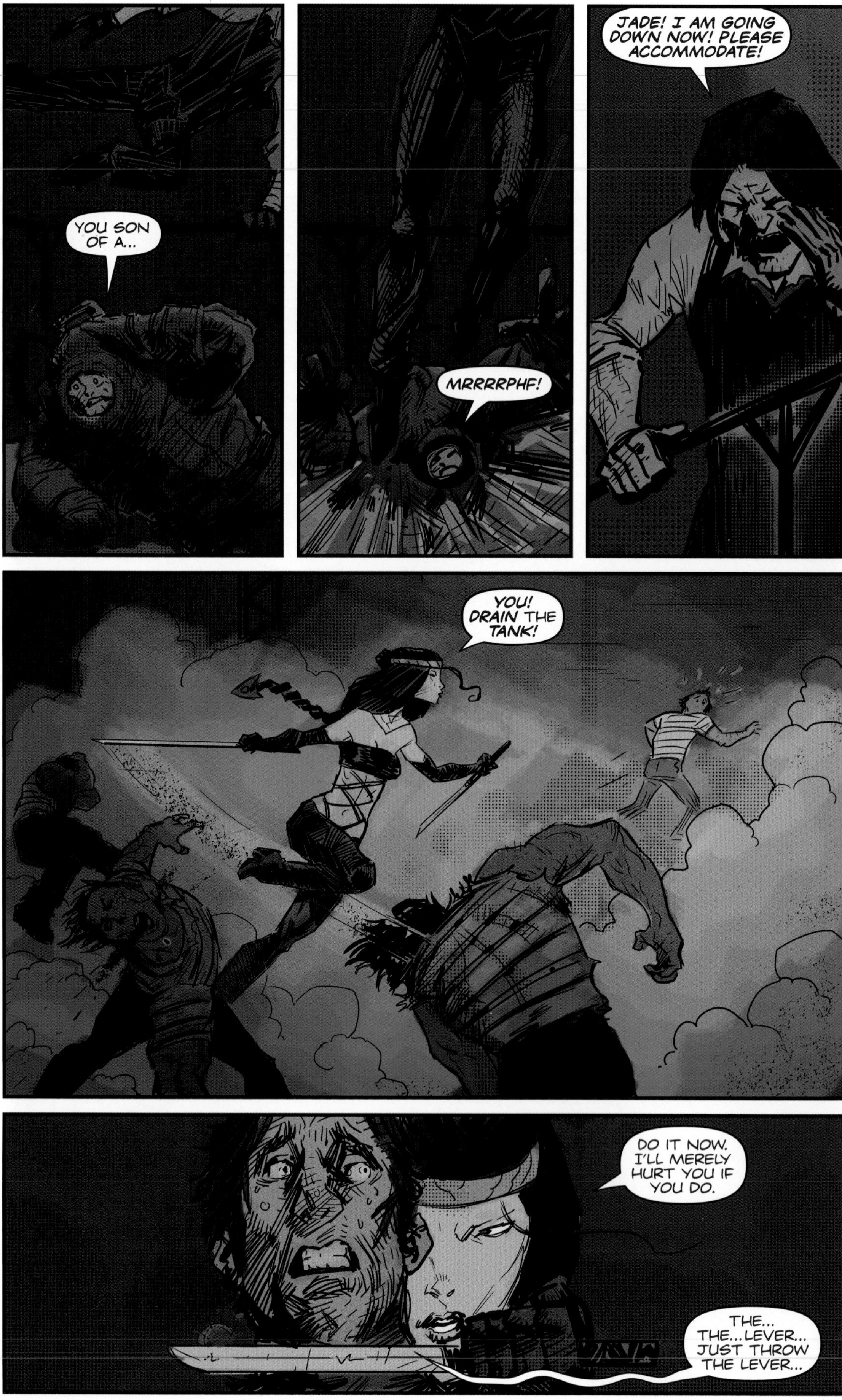
YOU SON OF A...
MRRRRPHF!
JADE! I AM GOING DOWN NOW! PLEASE ACCOMMODATE!
YOU! DRAIN THE TANK!
DO IT NOW. I'LL MERELY HURT YOU IF YOU DO.
THE... THE...LEVER... JUST THROW THE LEVER...

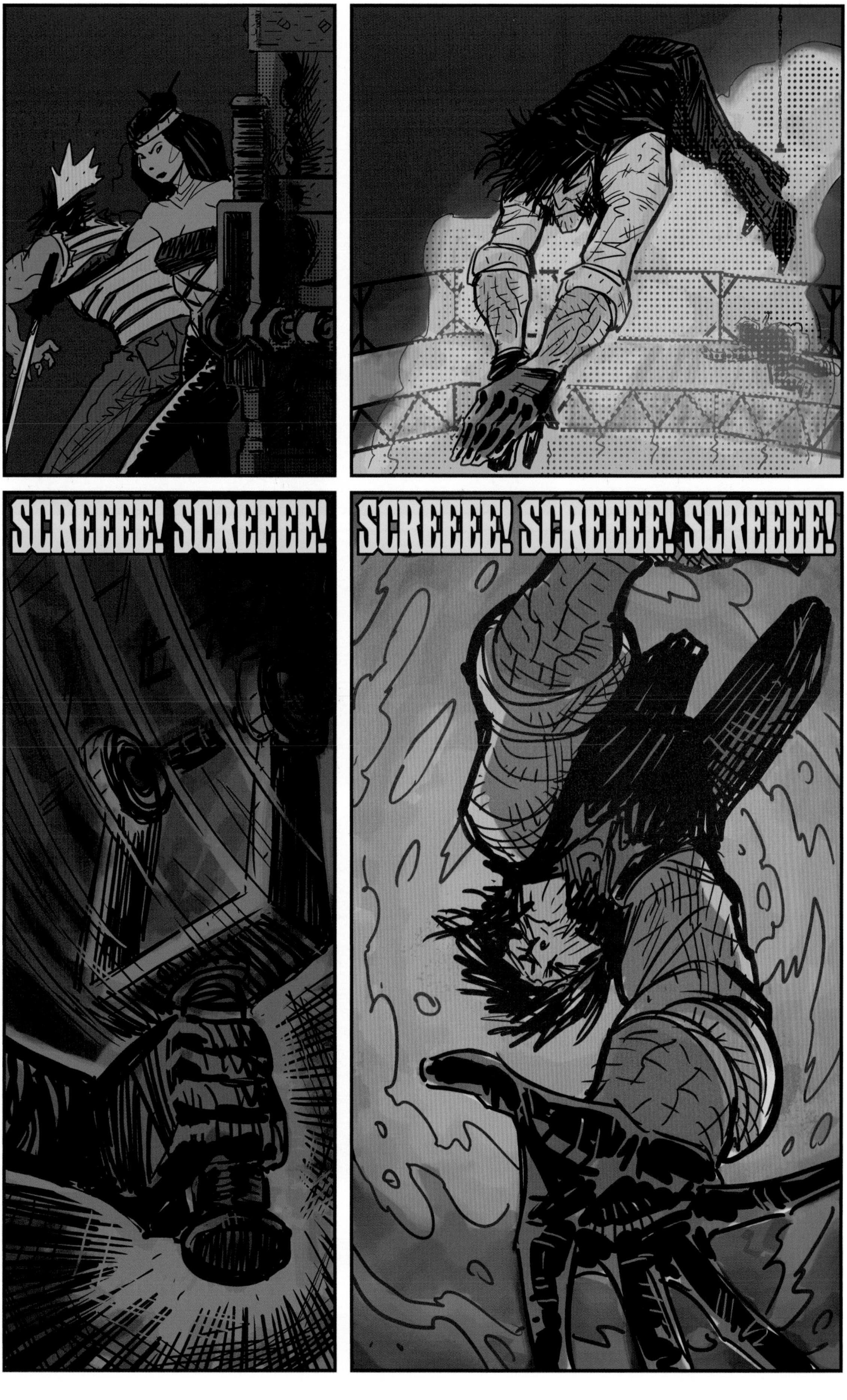
SCREEEE! SCREEEE!
SCREEEE! SCREEEE! SCREEEE!

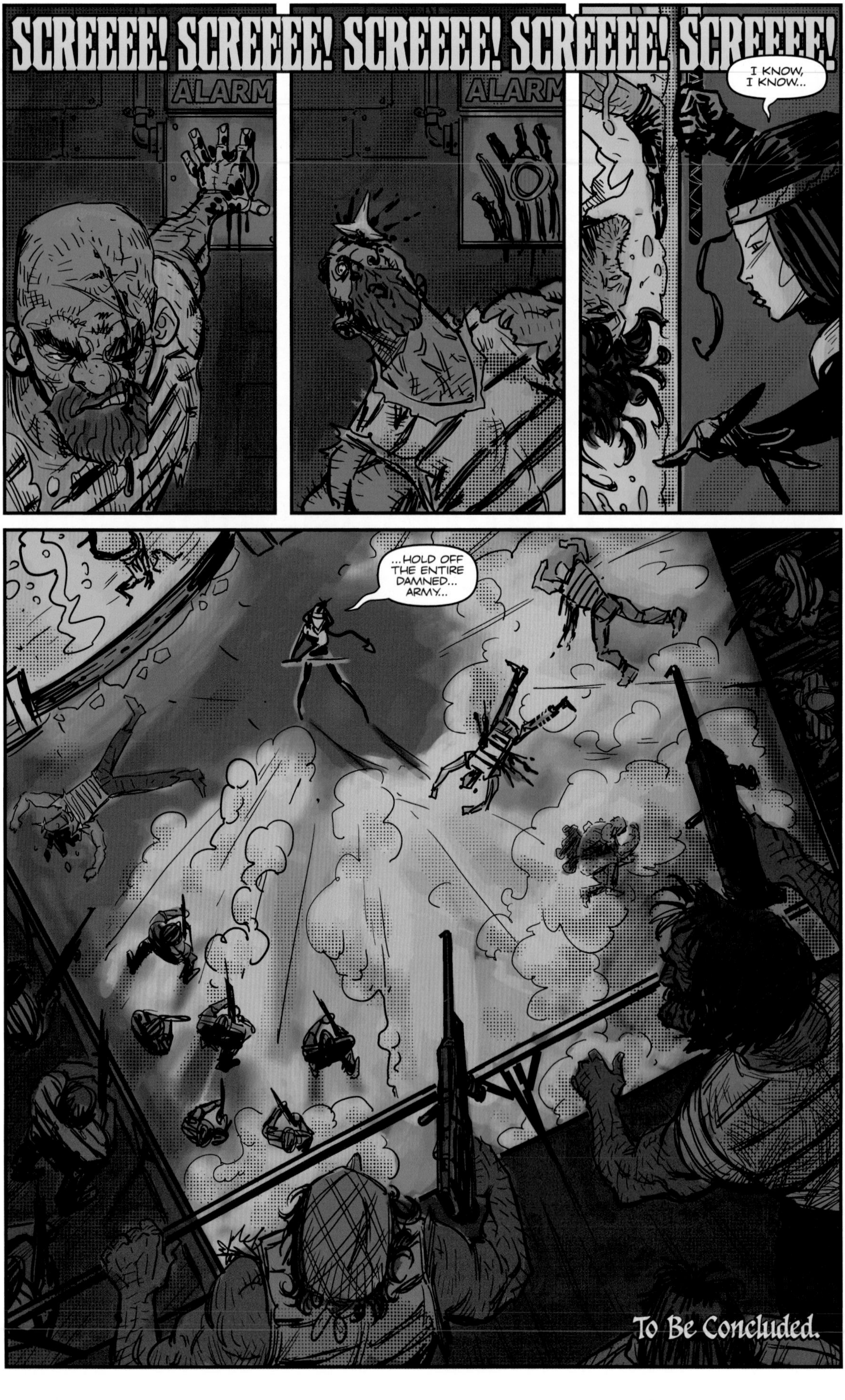
SCREEEE! SCREEEE! SCREEEE! SCREEEE! SCREEEE!
ALARM
ALARM
I KNOW, I KNOW...
...HOLD OFF THE ENTIRE DAMNED... ARMY...
To Be Concluded.

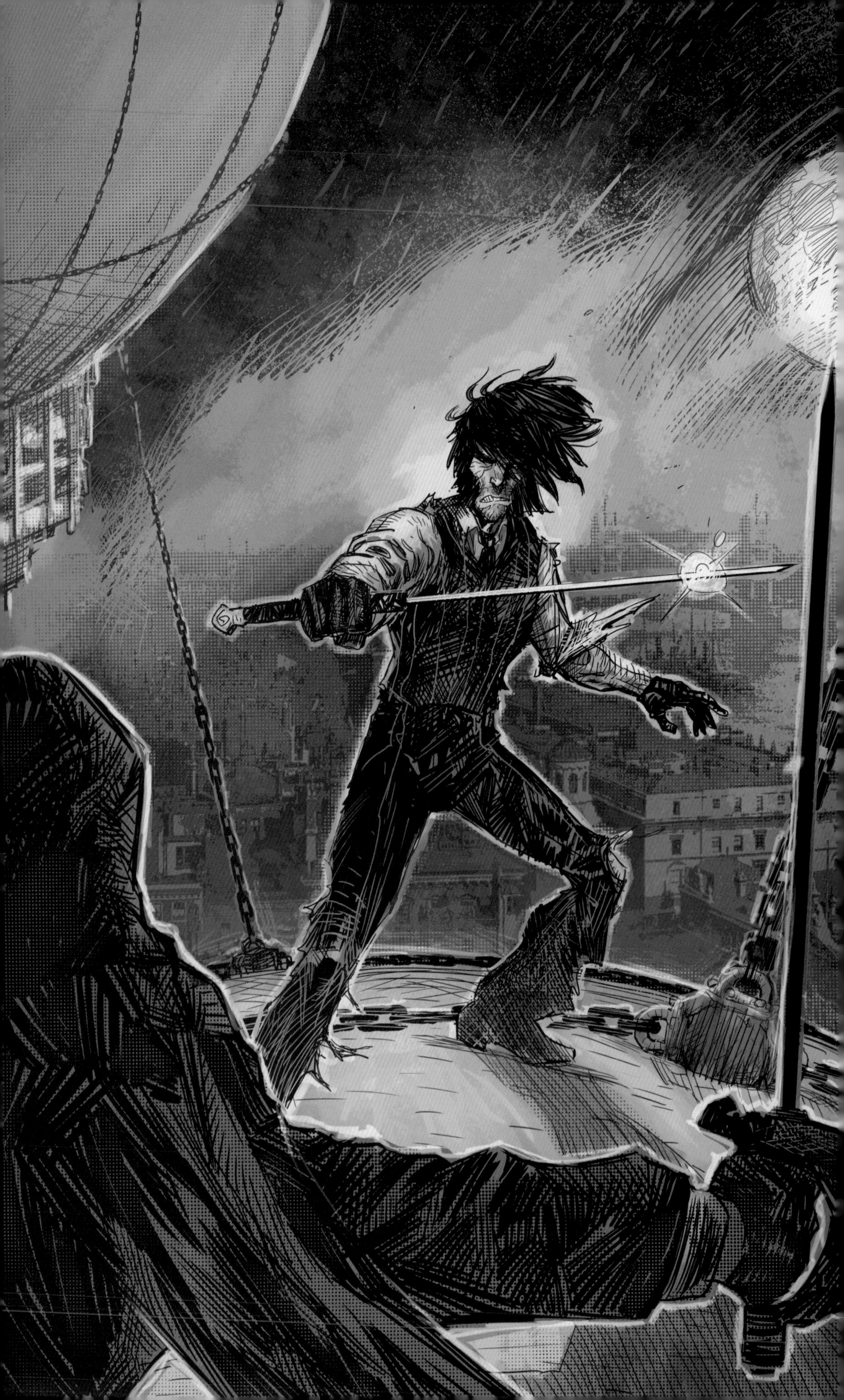

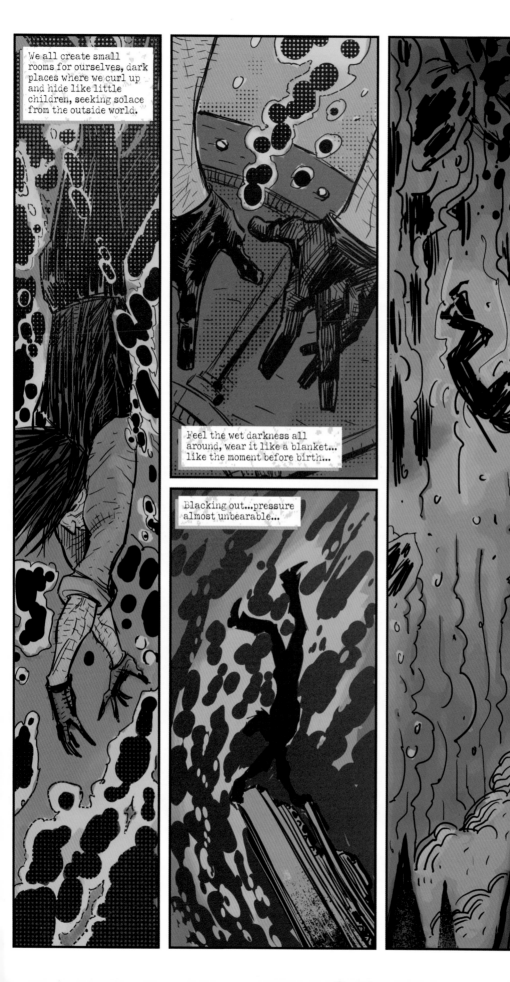

We all create small rooms for ourselves, dark places where we curl up and hide like little children, seeking solace from the outside world.

Feel the wet darkness all around, wear it like a blanket... like the moment before birth...

Blacking out...pressure almost unbearable...

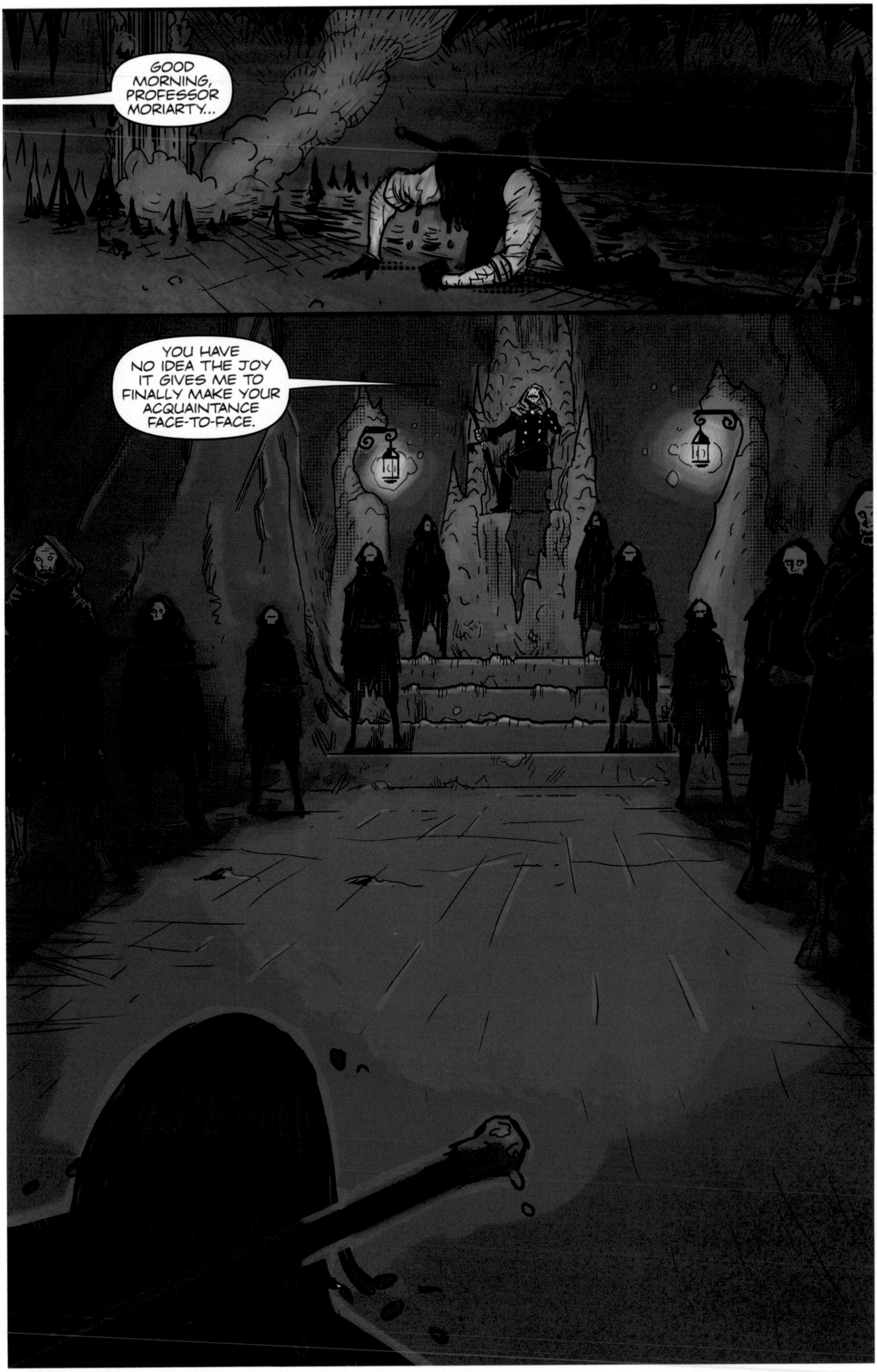
GOOD MORNING, PROFESSOR MORIARTY...
YOU HAVE NO IDEA THE JOY IT GIVES ME TO FINALLY MAKE YOUR ACQUAINTANCE FACE-TO-FACE.

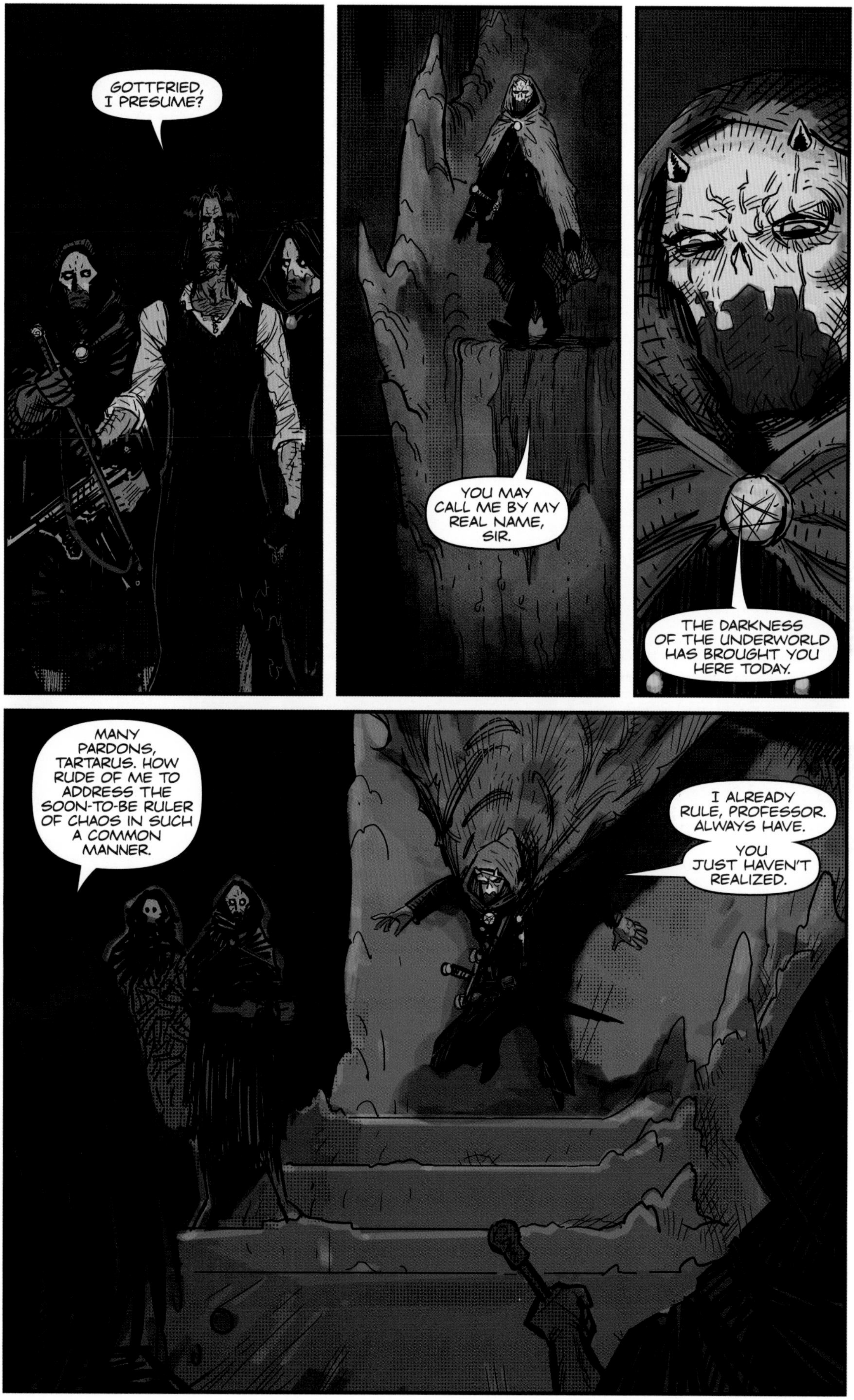
GOTTFRIED, I PRESUME?
YOU MAY CALL ME BY MY REAL NAME, SIR.
THE DARKNESS OF THE UNDERWORLD HAS BROUGHT YOU HERE TODAY.
MANY PARDONS, TARTARUS. HOW RUDE OF ME TO ADDRESS THE SOON-TO-BE RULER OF CHAOS IN SUCH A COMMON MANNER.
I ALREADY RULE, PROFESSOR. ALWAYS HAVE.
YOU JUST HAVEN'T REALIZED.

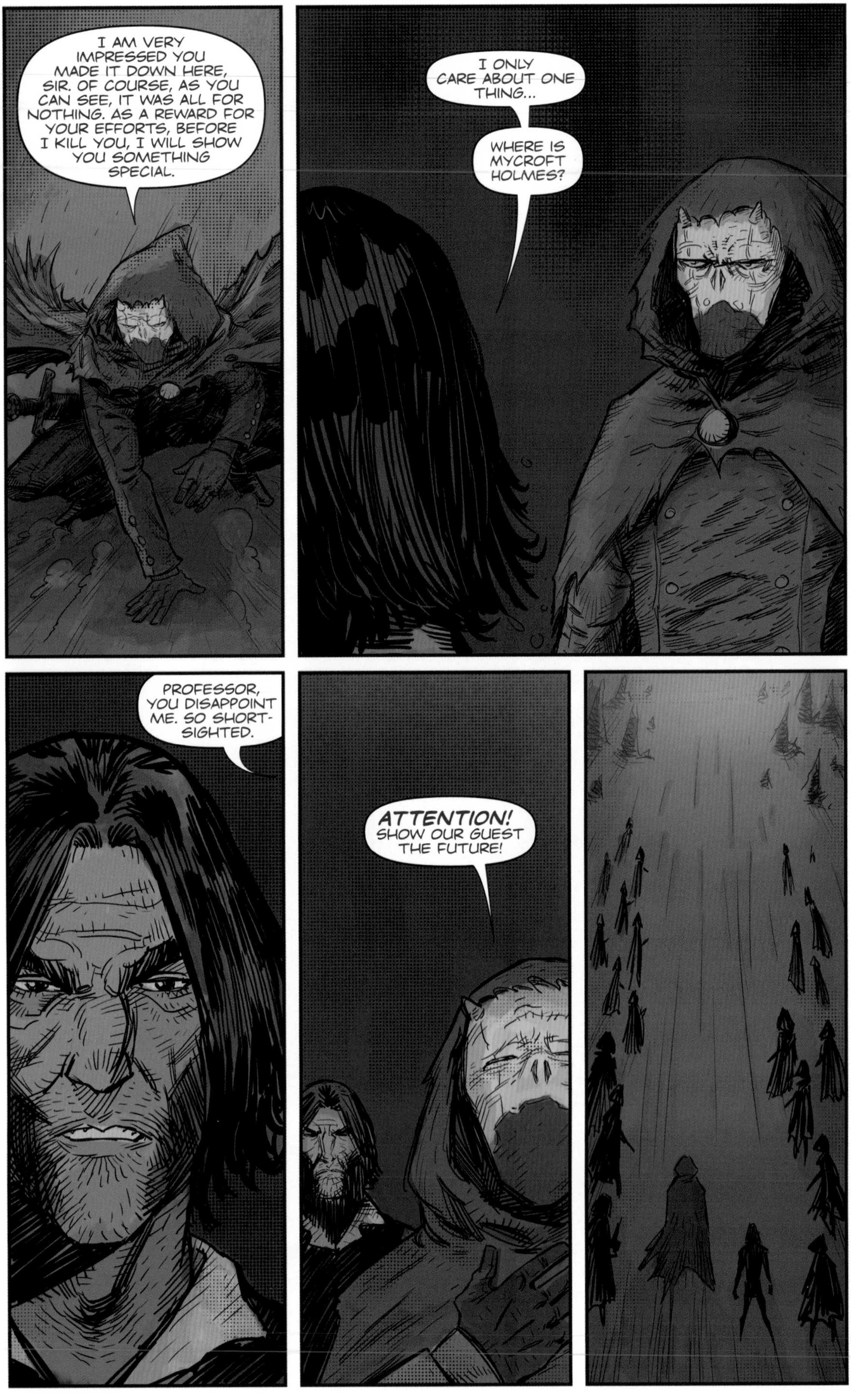
I AM VERY IMPRESSED YOU MADE IT DOWN HERE, SIR. OF COURSE, AS YOU CAN SEE, IT WAS ALL FOR NOTHING. AS A REWARD FOR YOUR EFFORTS, BEFORE I KILL YOU, I WILL SHOW YOU SOMETHING SPECIAL.
I ONLY CARE ABOUT ONE THING...
WHERE IS MYCROFT HOLMES?
PROFESSOR, YOU DISAPPOINT ME. SO SHORT-SIGHTED.
ATTENTION! SHOW OUR GUEST THE FUTURE!

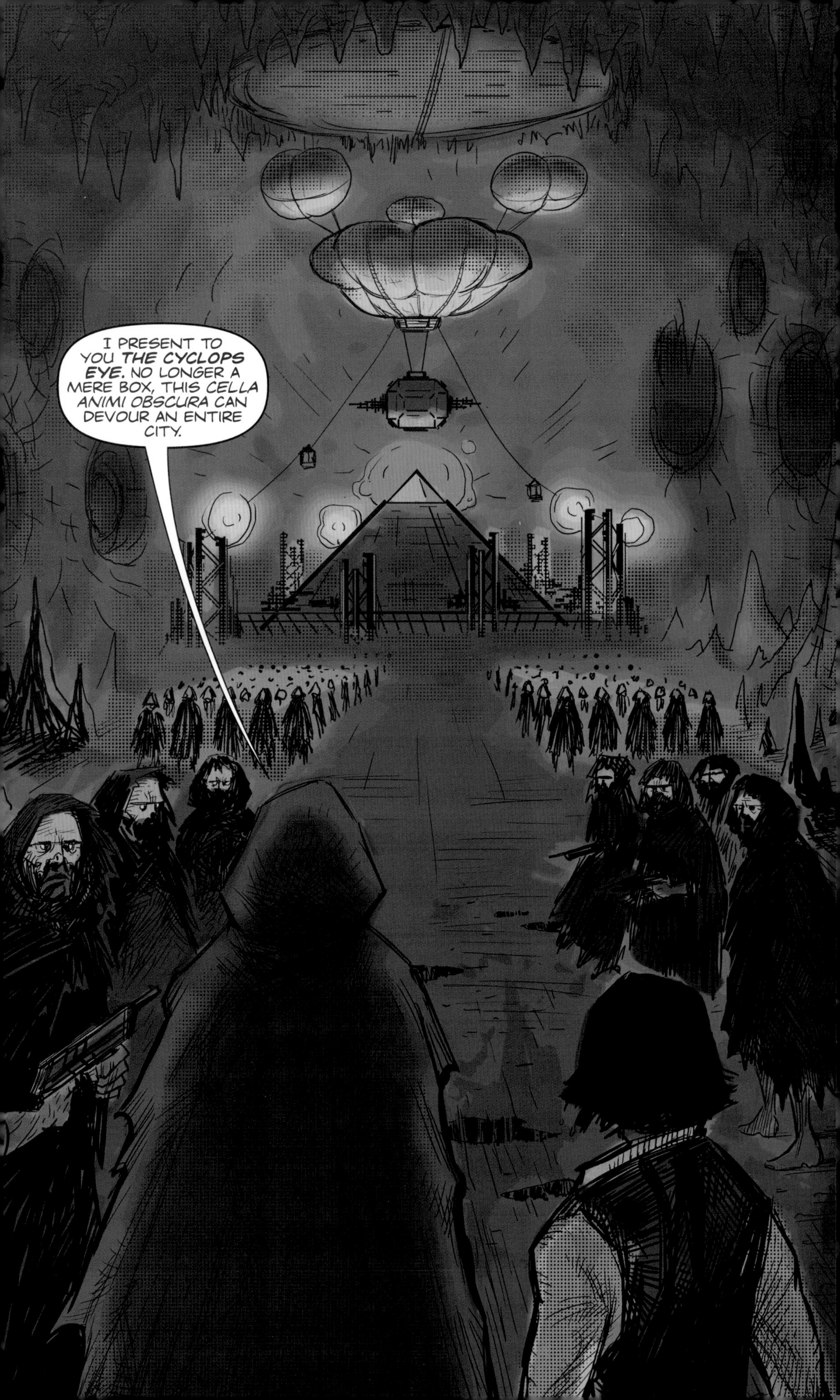
I PRESENT TO YOU **THE CYCLOPS EYE.** NO LONGER A MERE BOX, THIS *CELLA ANIMI OBSCURA* CAN DEVOUR AN ENTIRE CITY.

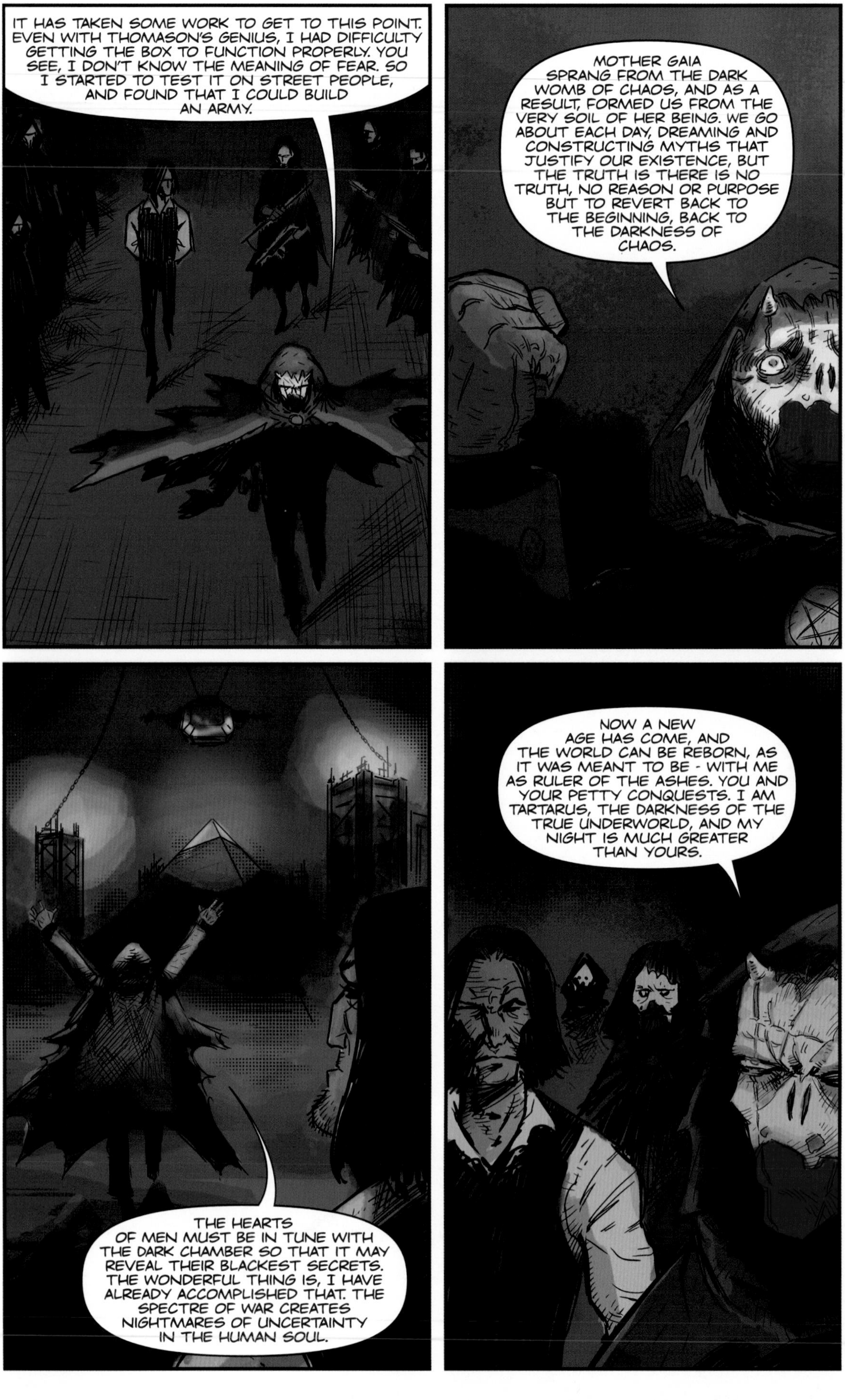

IT HAS TAKEN SOME WORK TO GET TO THIS POINT. EVEN WITH THOMASON'S GENIUS, I HAD DIFFICULTY GETTING THE BOX TO FUNCTION PROPERLY. YOU SEE, I DON'T KNOW THE MEANING OF FEAR. SO I STARTED TO TEST IT ON STREET PEOPLE, AND FOUND THAT I COULD BUILD AN ARMY.
MOTHER GAIA SPRANG FROM THE DARK WOMB OF CHAOS, AND AS A RESULT, FORMED US FROM THE VERY SOIL OF HER BEING. WE GO ABOUT EACH DAY, DREAMING AND CONSTRUCTING MYTHS THAT JUSTIFY OUR EXISTENCE, BUT THE TRUTH IS THERE IS NO TRUTH, NO REASON OR PURPOSE BUT TO REVERT BACK TO THE BEGINNING, BACK TO THE DARKNESS OF CHAOS.
THE HEARTS OF MEN MUST BE IN TUNE WITH THE DARK CHAMBER SO THAT IT MAY REVEAL THEIR BLACKEST SECRETS. THE WONDERFUL THING IS, I HAVE ALREADY ACCOMPLISHED THAT. THE SPECTRE OF WAR CREATES NIGHTMARES OF UNCERTAINTY IN THE HUMAN SOUL.
NOW A NEW AGE HAS COME, AND THE WORLD CAN BE REBORN, AS IT WAS MEANT TO BE - WITH ME AS RULER OF THE ASHES. YOU AND YOUR PETTY CONQUESTS. I AM TARTARUS, THE DARKNESS OF THE TRUE UNDERWORLD, AND MY NIGHT IS MUCH GREATER THAN YOURS.

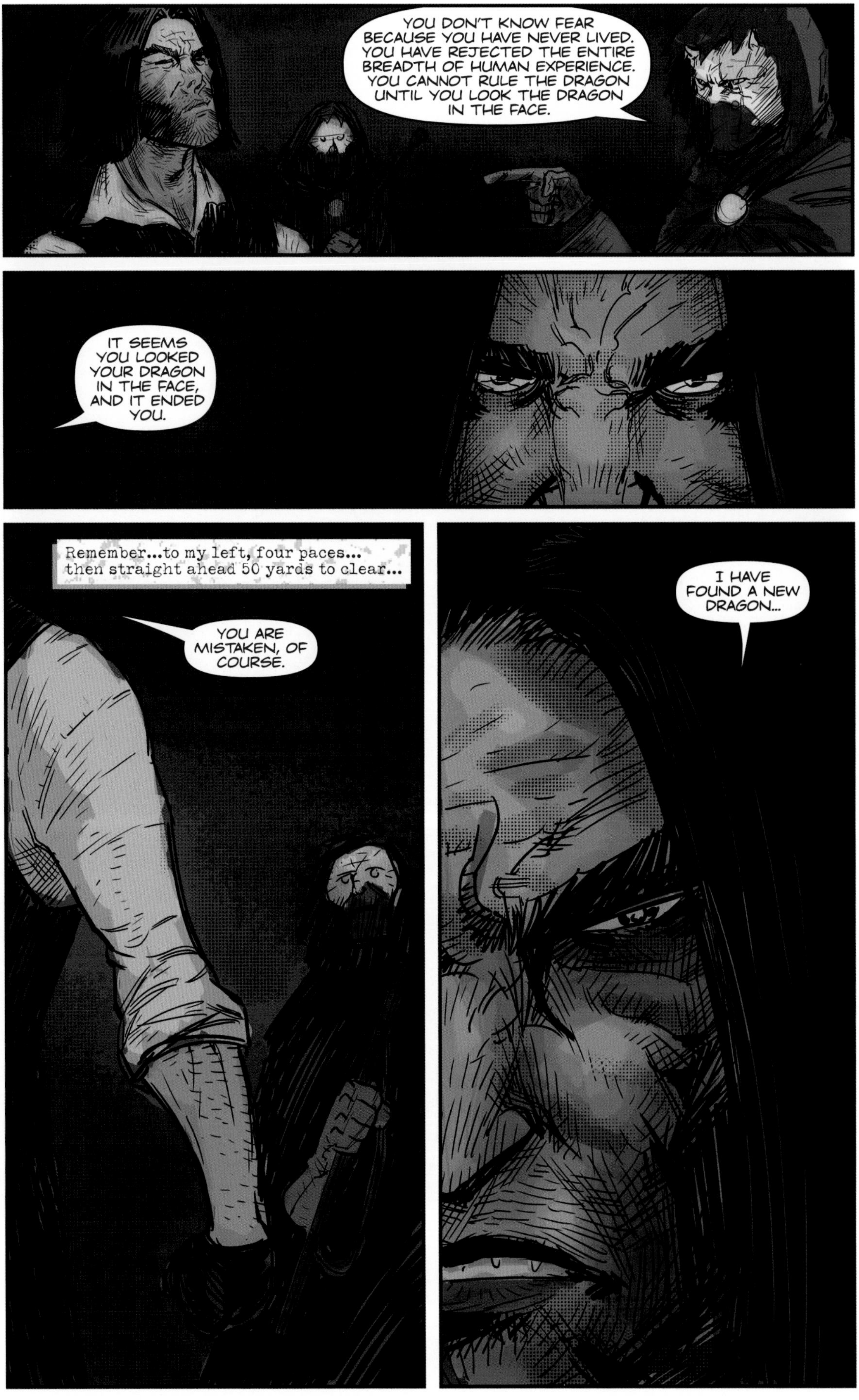
YOU DON'T KNOW FEAR BECAUSE YOU HAVE NEVER LIVED. YOU HAVE REJECTED THE ENTIRE BREADTH OF HUMAN EXPERIENCE. YOU CANNOT RULE THE DRAGON UNTIL YOU LOOK THE DRAGON IN THE FACE.
IT SEEMS YOU LOOKED YOUR DRAGON IN THE FACE, AND IT ENDED YOU.
Remember...to my left, four paces... then straight ahead 50 yards to clear...
YOU ARE MISTAKEN, OF COURSE.
I HAVE FOUND A NEW DRAGON...

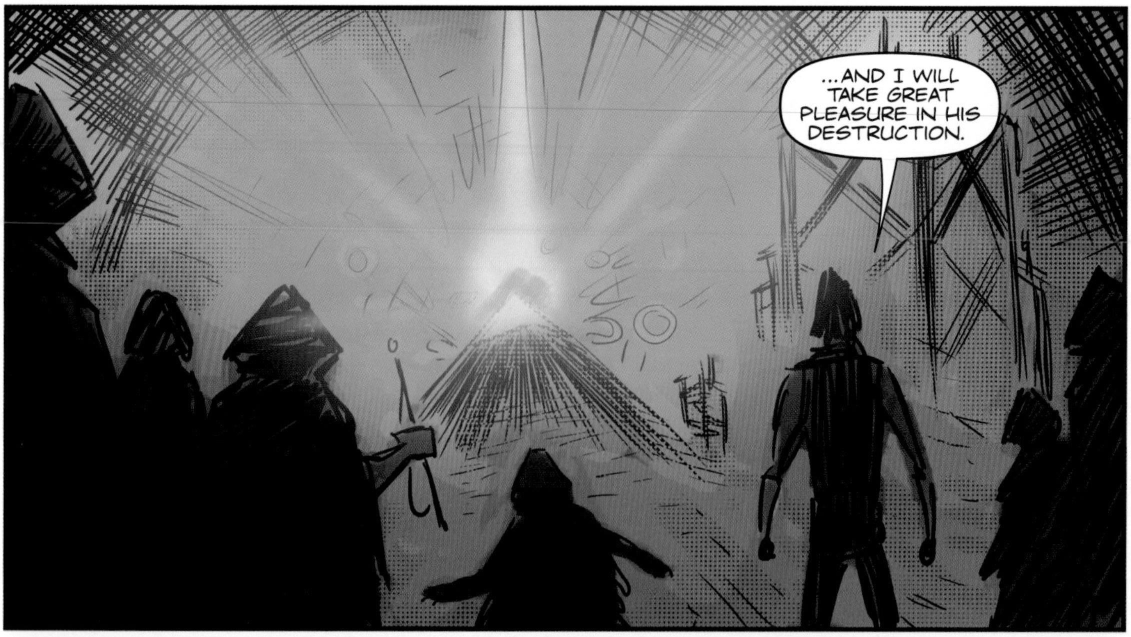
...AND I WILL TAKE GREAT PLEASURE IN HIS DESTRUCTION.

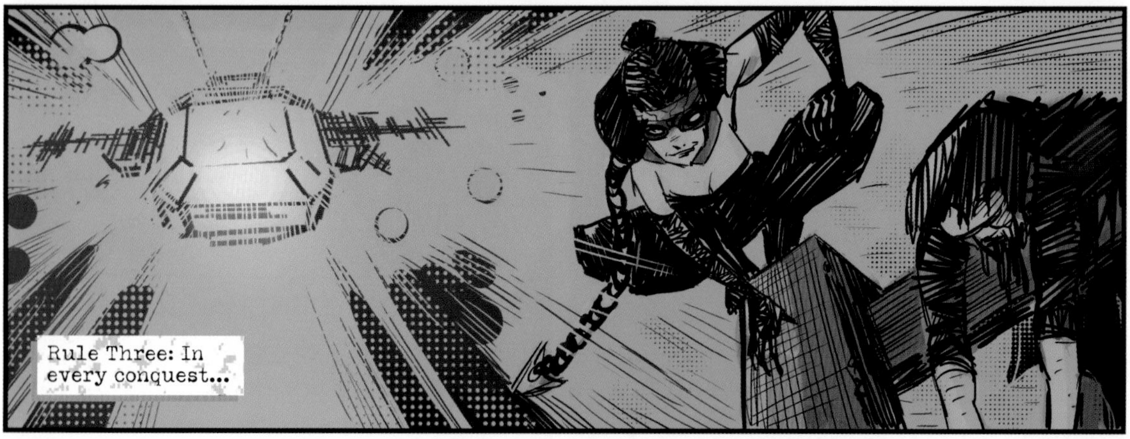
Rule Three: In every conquest...

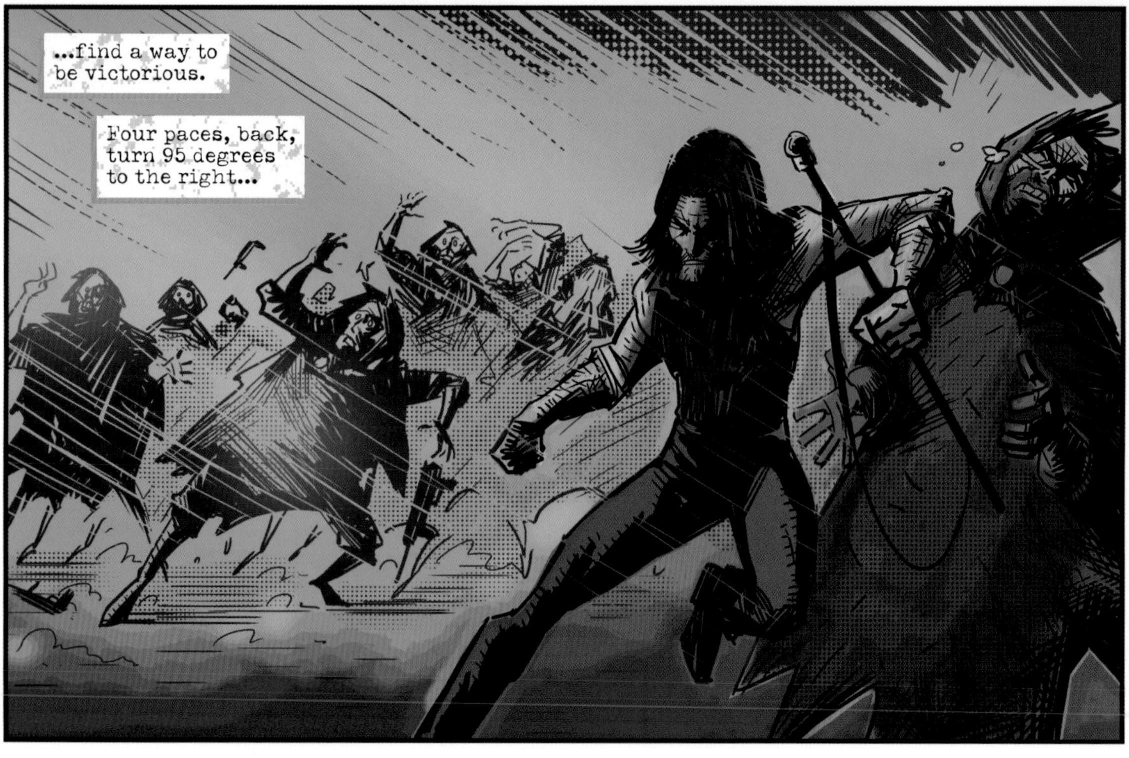
...find a way to be victorious.
Four paces, back, turn 95 degrees to the right...

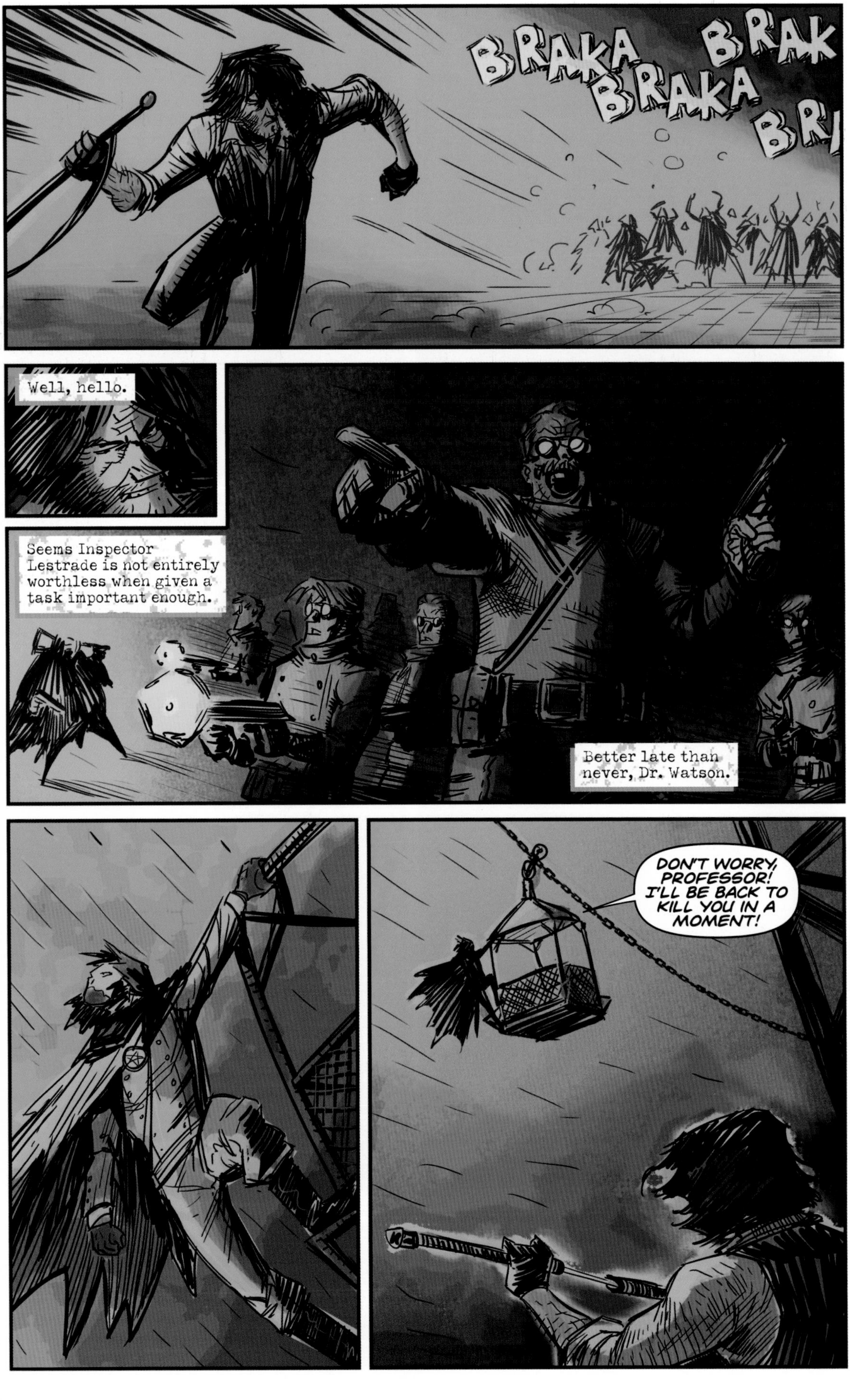
BRAKA BRAK
BRAKA
Well, hello.
Seems Inspector Lestrade is not entirely worthless when given a task important enough.
Better late than never, Dr. Watson.
DON'T WORRY, PROFESSOR! I'LL BE BACK TO KILL YOU IN A MOMENT!

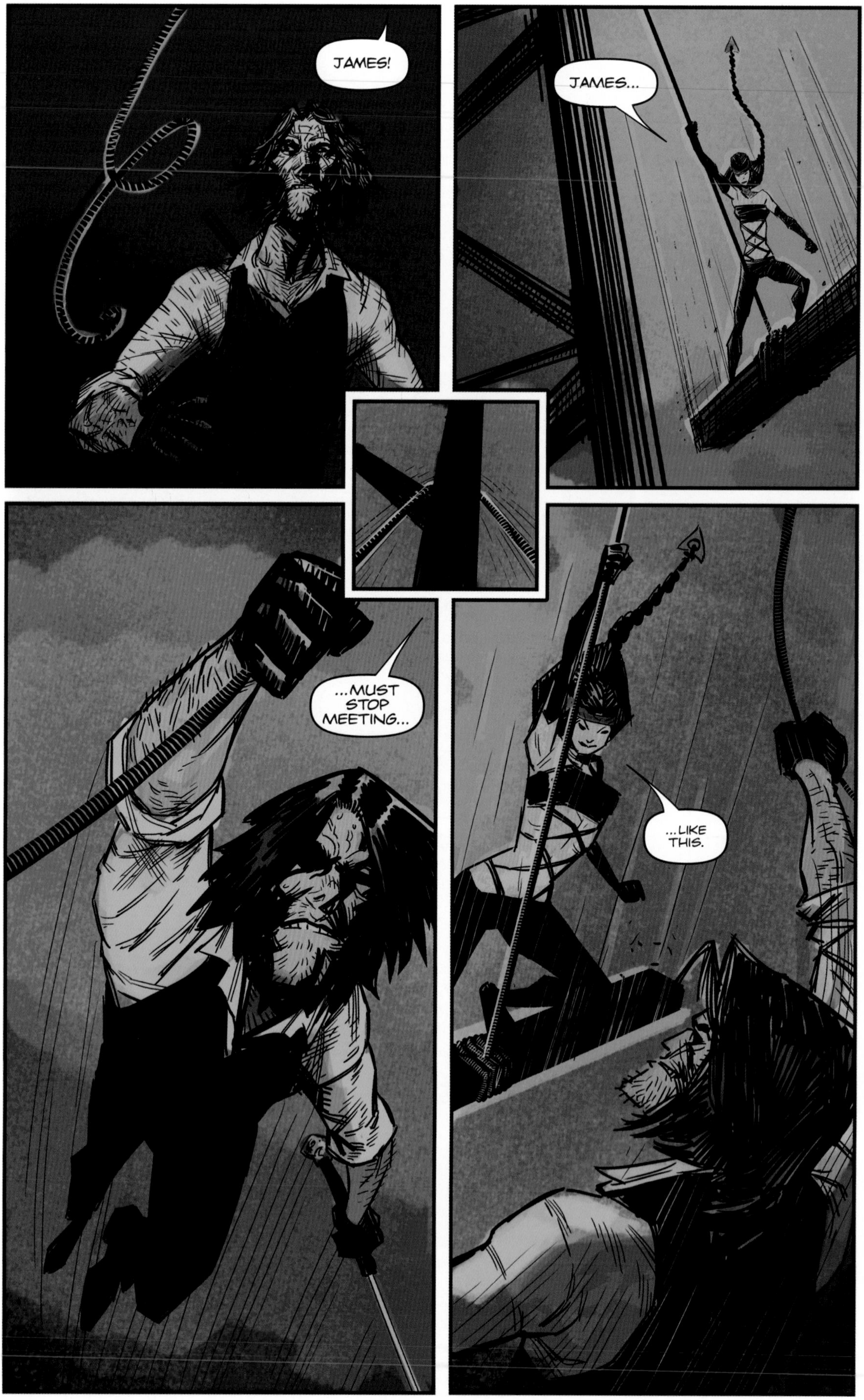
JAMES!
JAMES...
...MUST STOP MEETING...
...LIKE THIS.

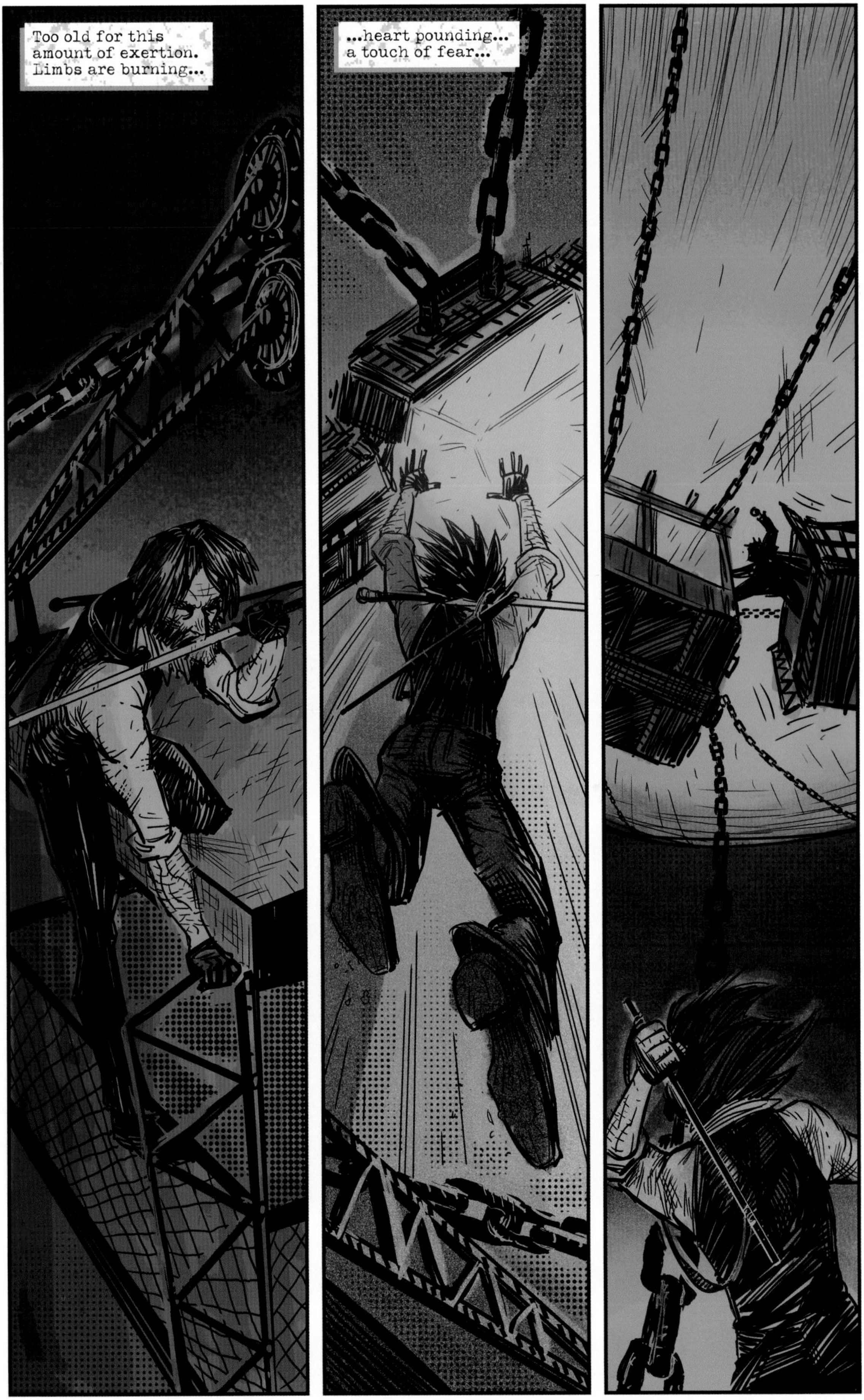
Too old for this amount of exertion. Limbs are burning...
...heart pounding... a touch of fear...

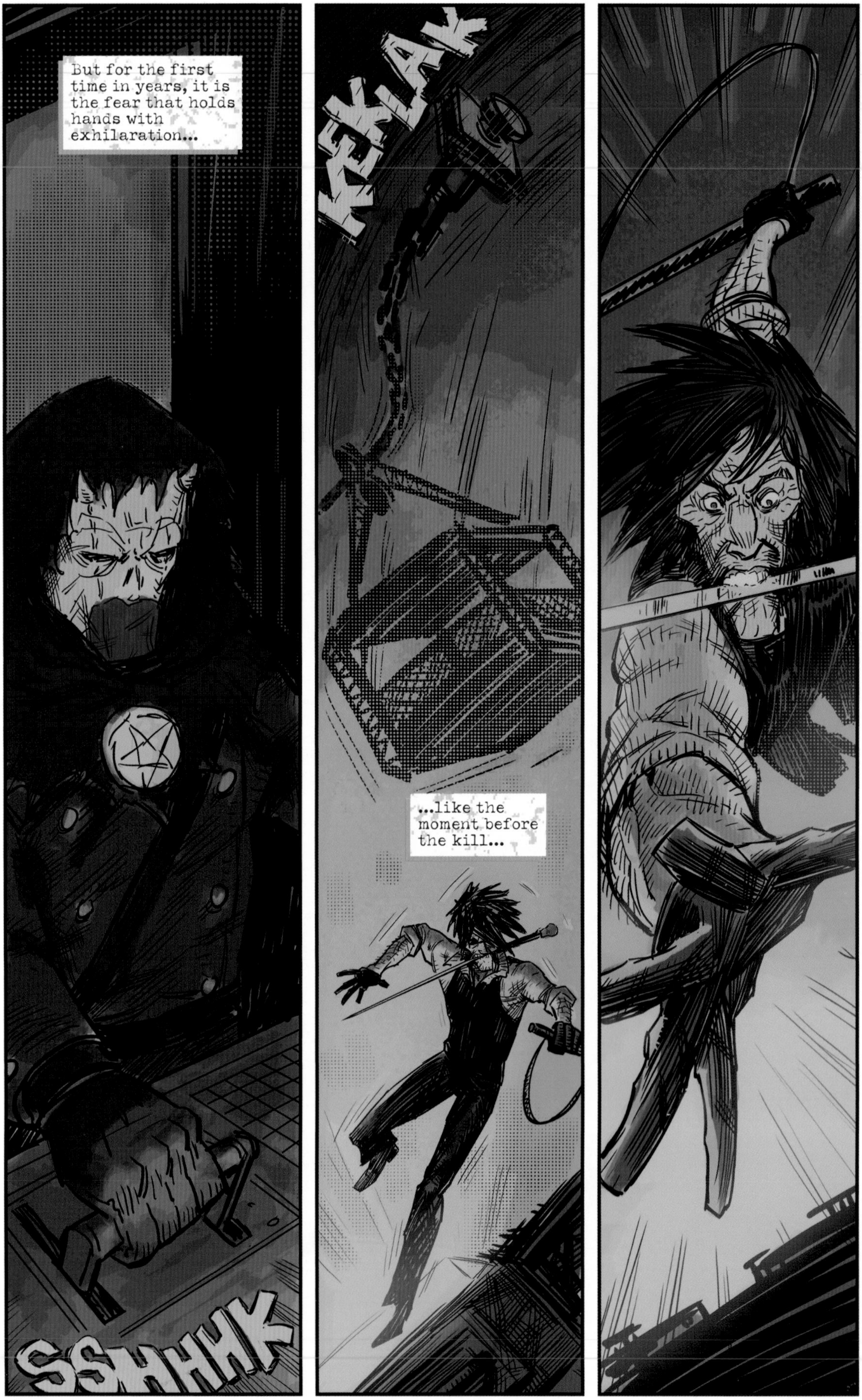
But for the first time in years, it is the fear that holds hands with exhilaration...
SSHHHK
KKLAK
...like the moment before the kill...

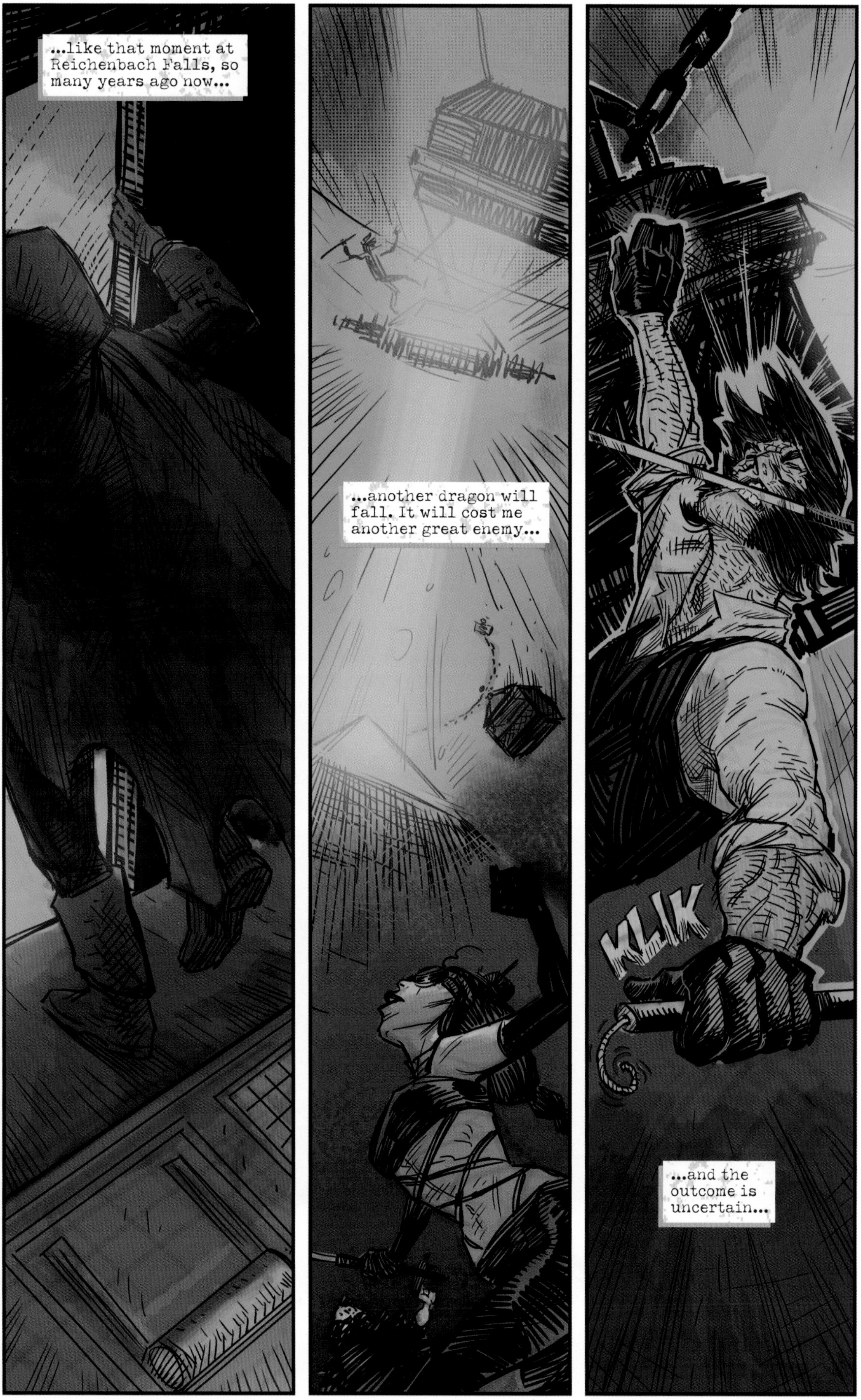
...like that moment at Reichenbach Falls, so many years ago now...
...another dragon will fall. It will cost me another great enemy...
KLIK
...and the outcome is uncertain...

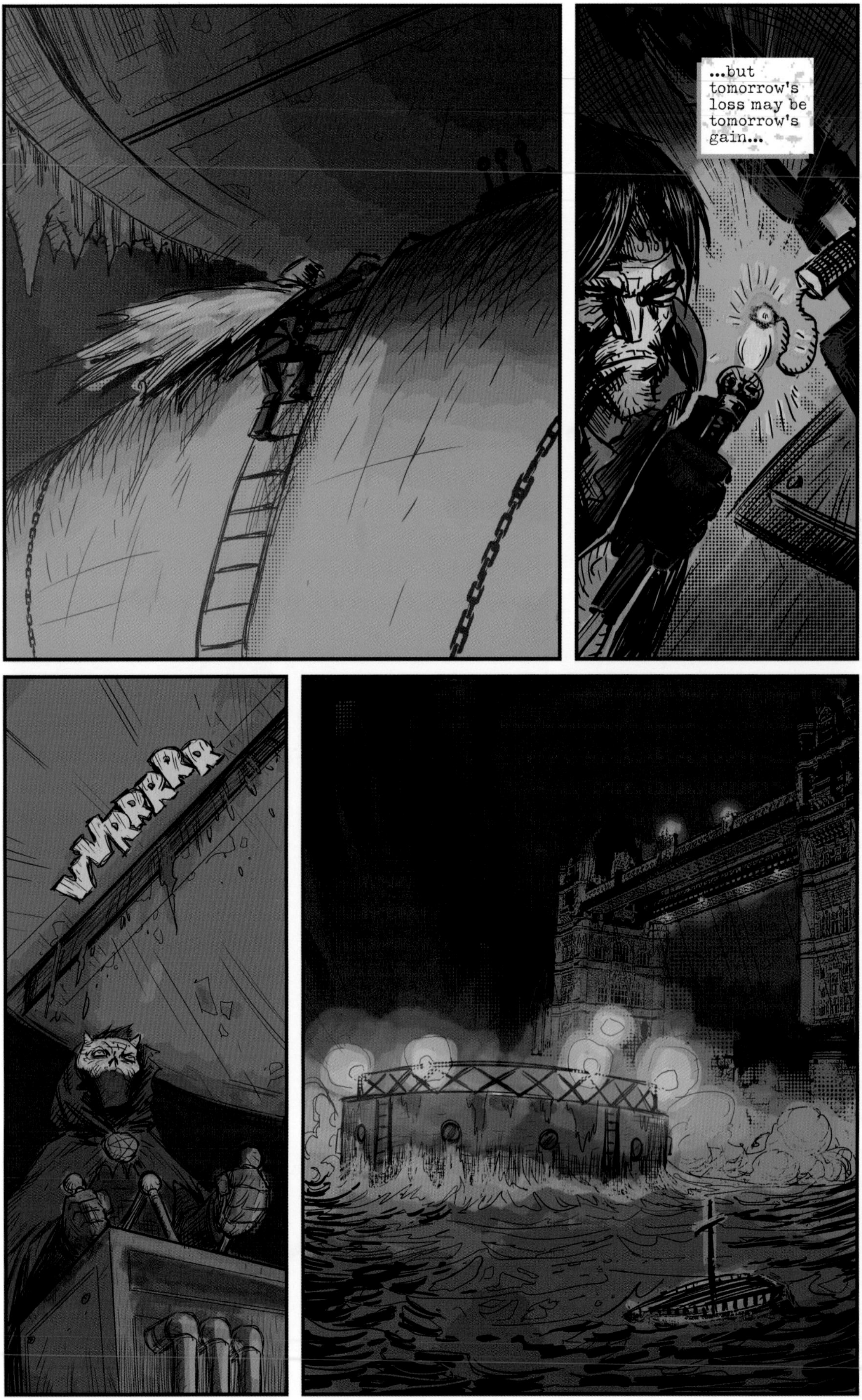
...but tomorrow's loss may be tomorrow's gain...
VWRRRR

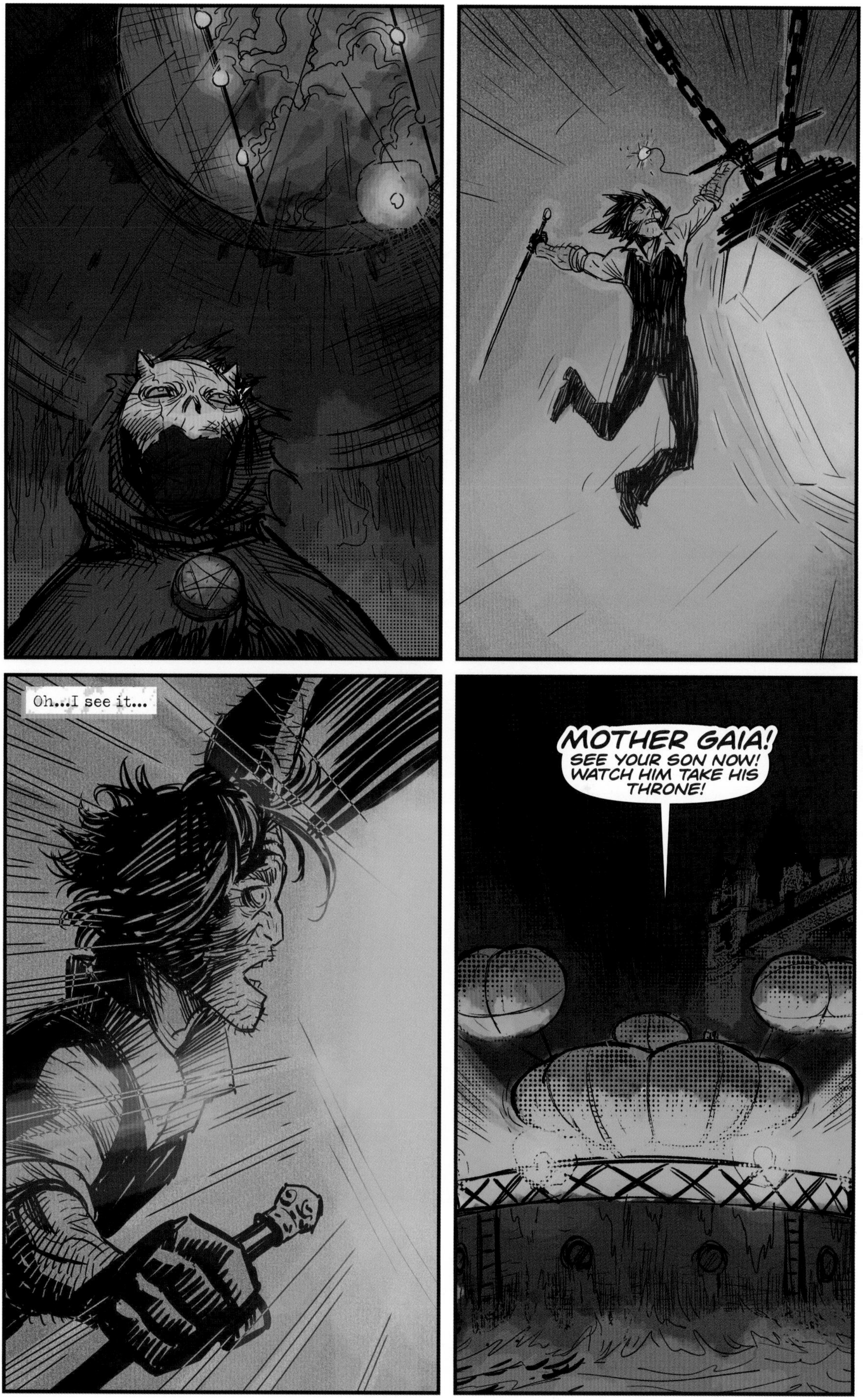
Oh...I see it...
MOTHER GAIA!
SEE YOUR SON NOW! WATCH HIM TAKE HIS THRONE!

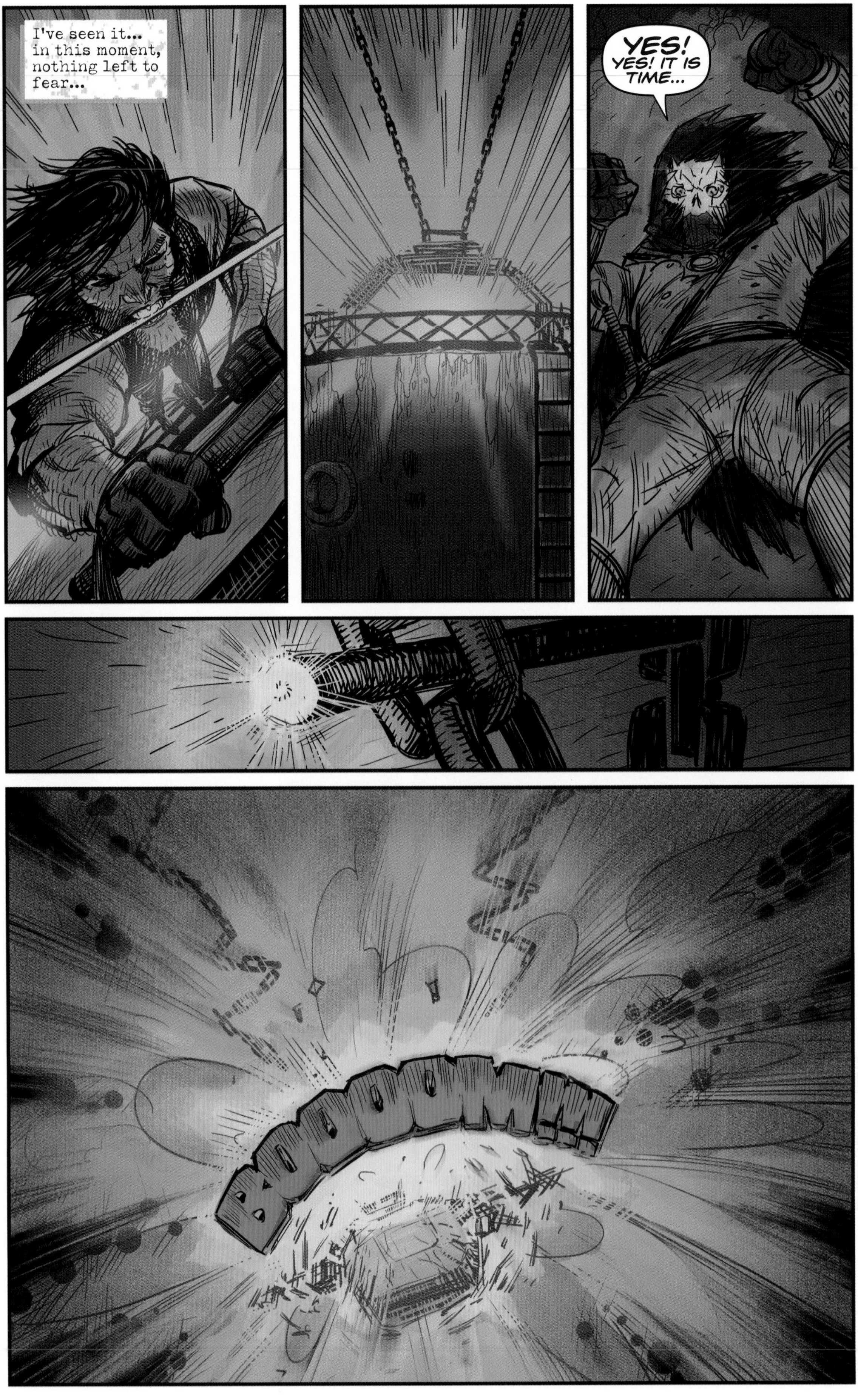
I've seen it... in this moment, nothing left to fear...
YES! YES! IT IS TIME...
BOOOOOM!!!

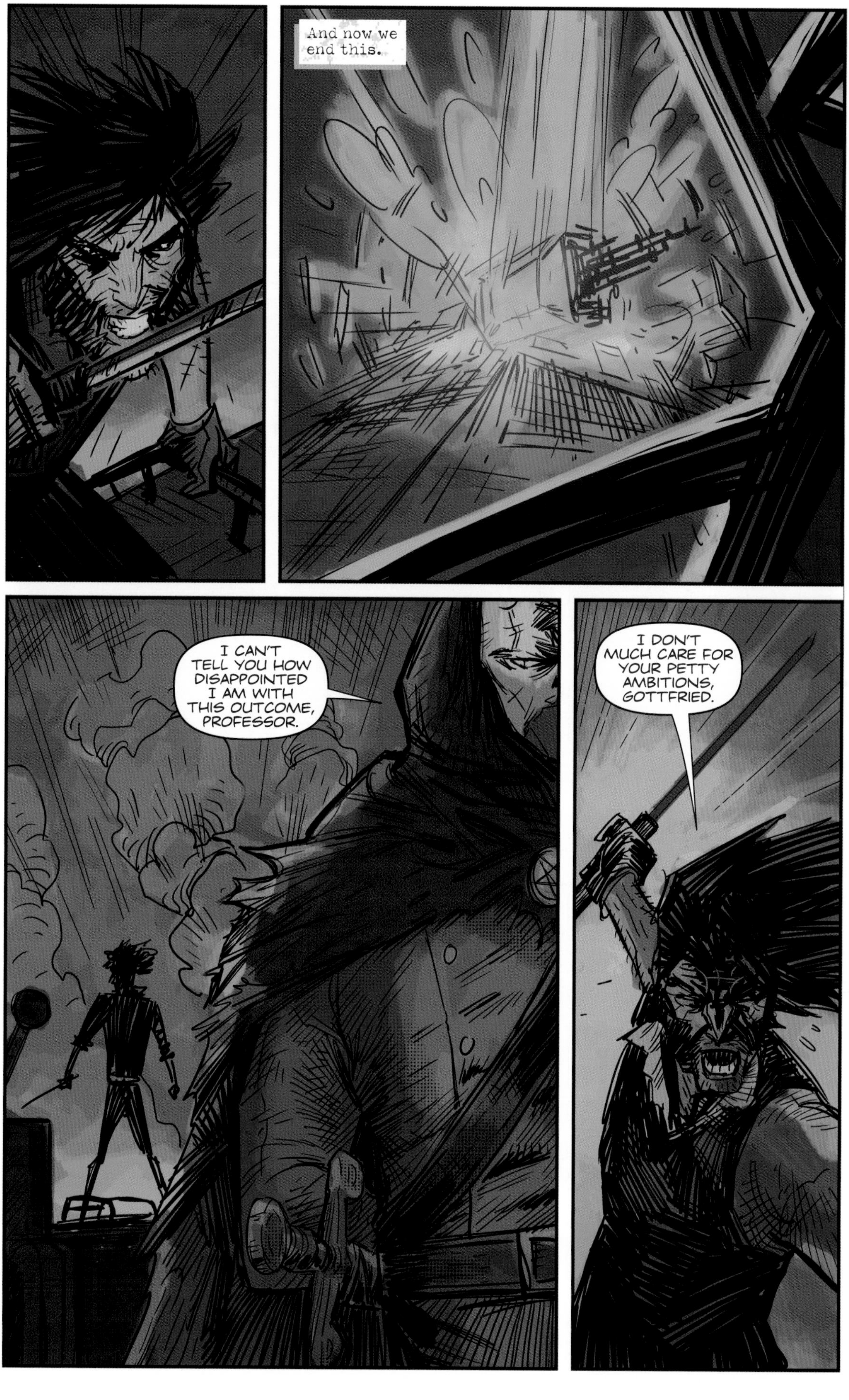
And now we end this.
I CAN'T TELL YOU HOW DISAPPOINTED I AM WITH THIS OUTCOME, PROFESSOR.
I DON'T MUCH CARE FOR YOUR PETTY AMBITIONS, GOTTFRIED.

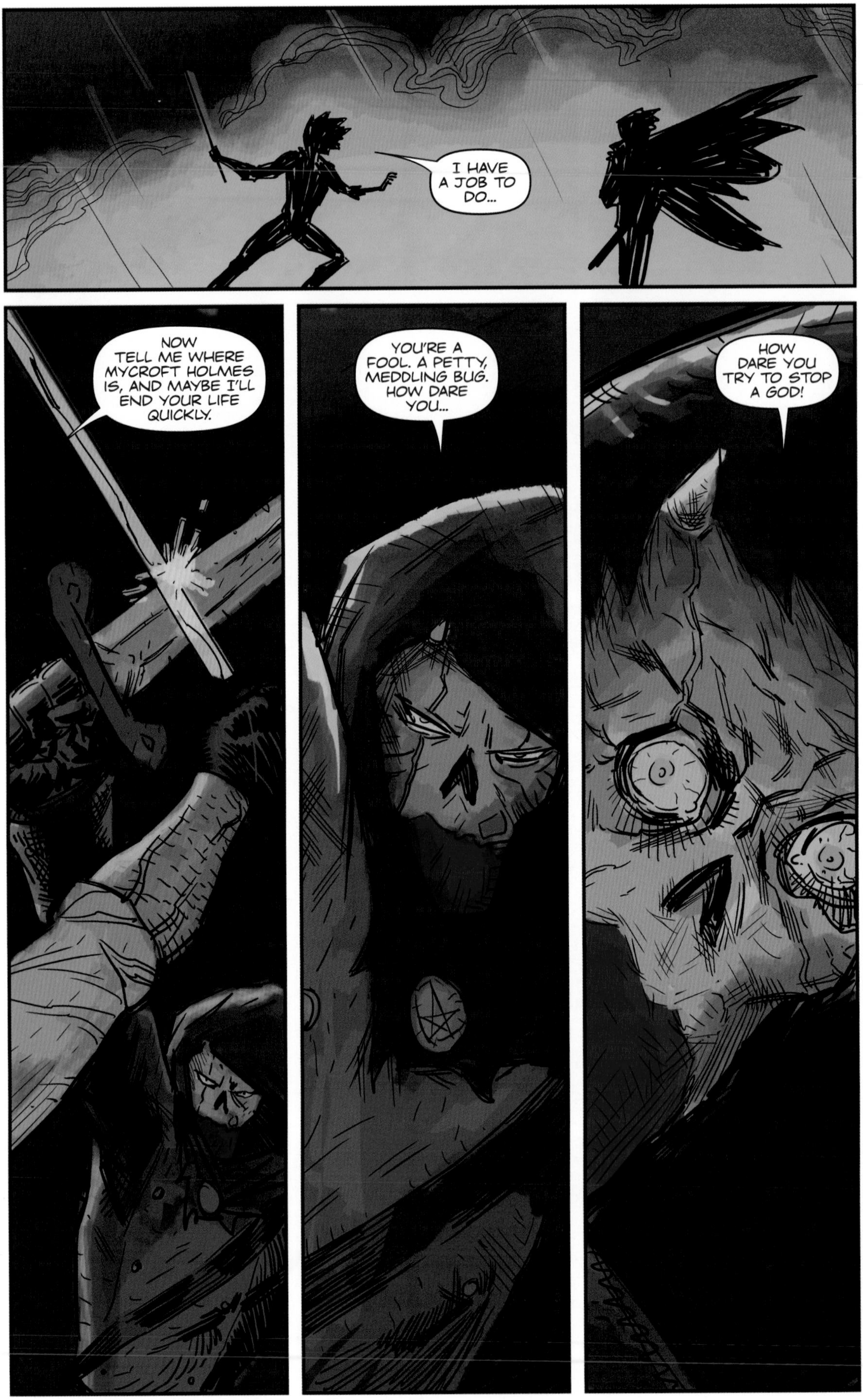
I HAVE A JOB TO DO...
NOW TELL ME WHERE MYCROFT HOLMES IS, AND MAYBE I'LL END YOUR LIFE QUICKLY.
YOU'RE A FOOL. A PETTY, MEDDLING BUG. HOW DARE YOU...
HOW DARE YOU TRY TO STOP A GOD!

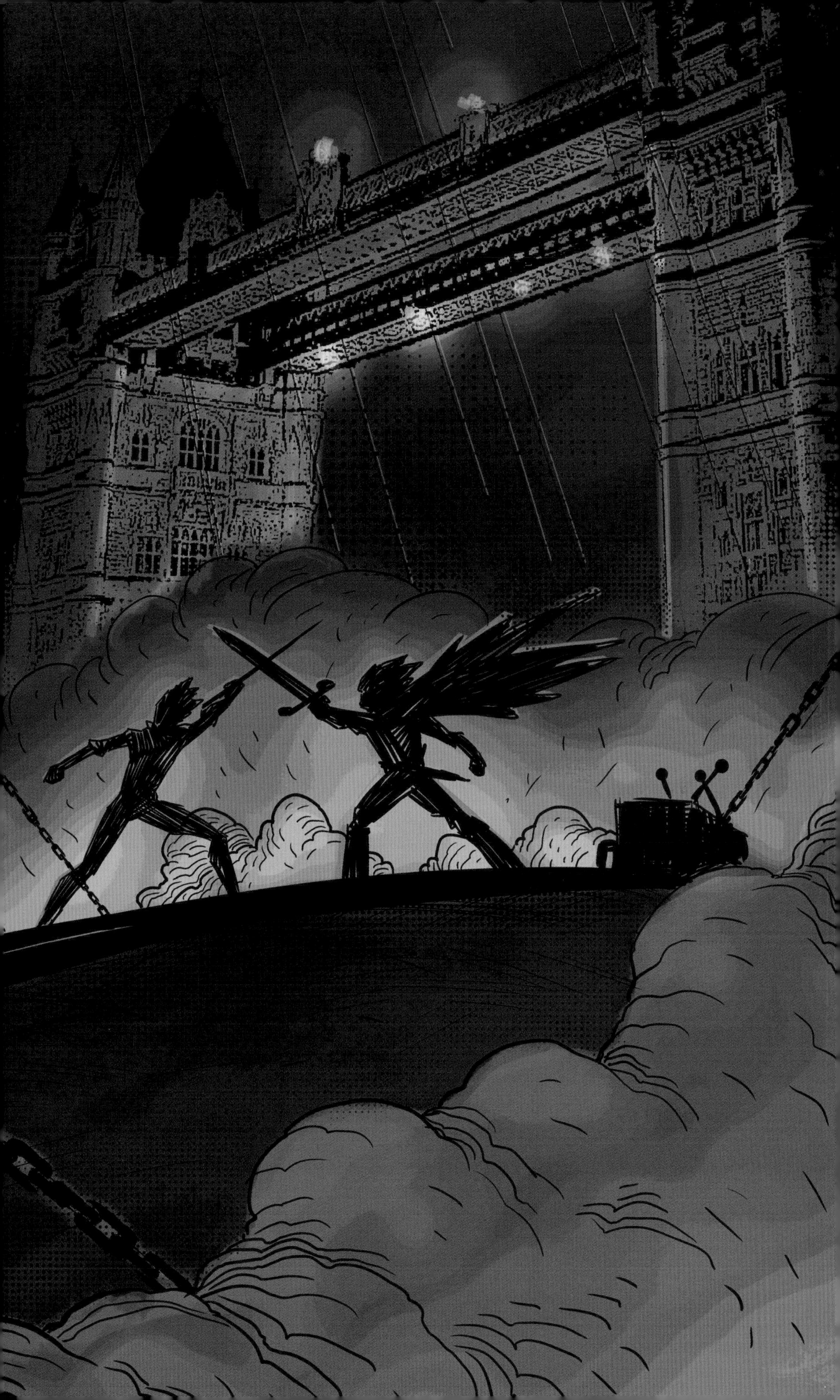

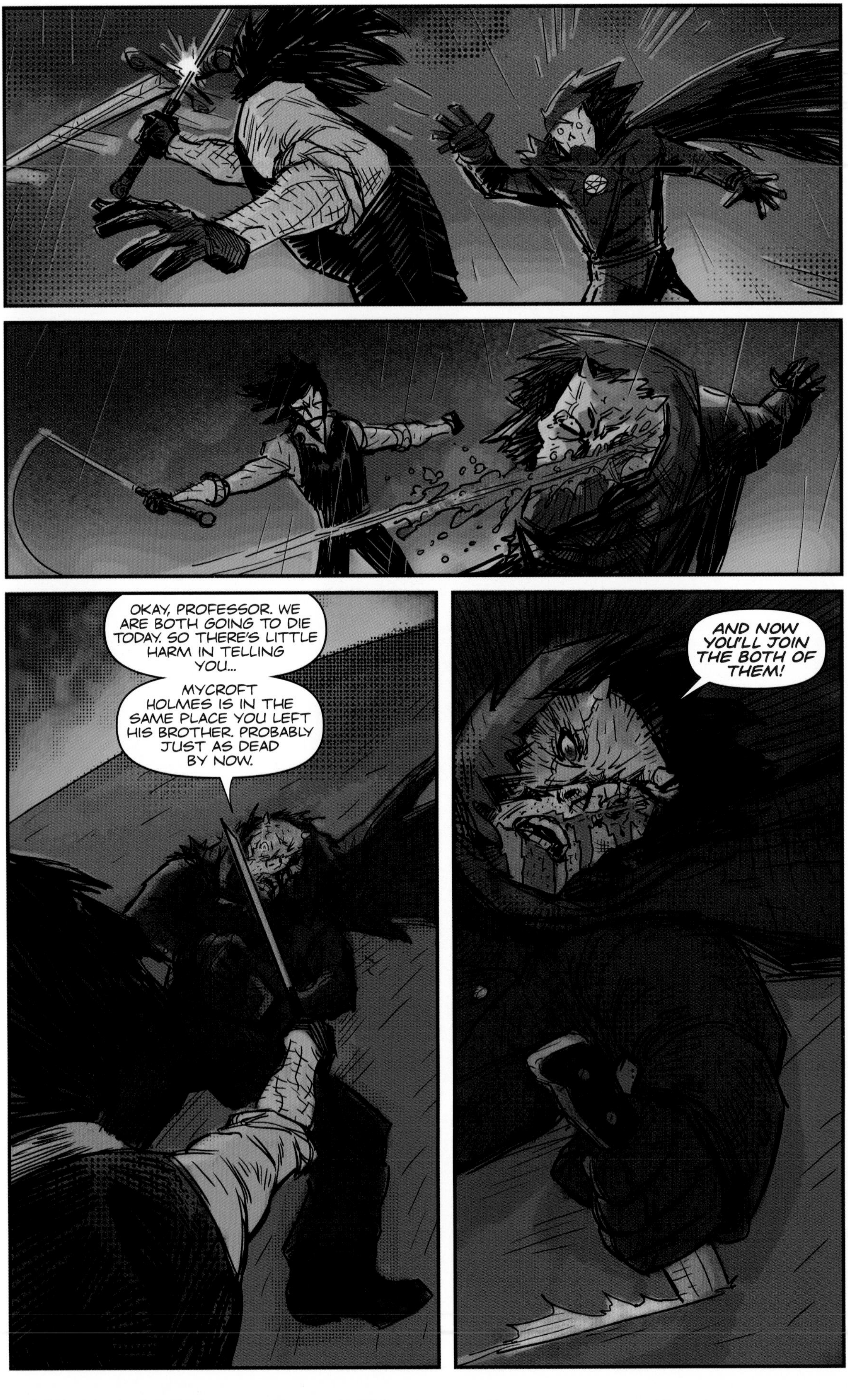
OKAY, PROFESSOR. WE ARE BOTH GOING TO DIE TODAY. SO THERE'S LITTLE HARM IN TELLING YOU...
MYCROFT HOLMES IS IN THE SAME PLACE YOU LEFT HIS BROTHER. PROBABLY JUST AS DEAD BY NOW.
AND NOW YOU'LL JOIN THE BOTH OF THEM!

This would be a most agreeable moment for death...

...but it is not destined to be...

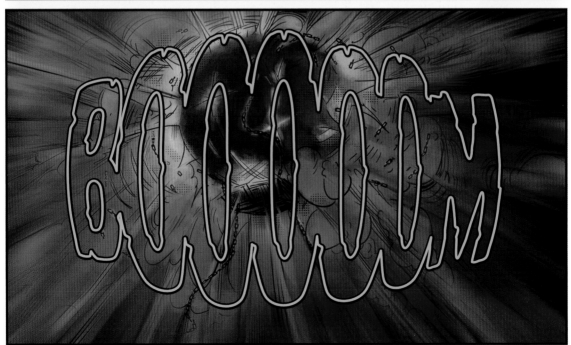

BOOOOM

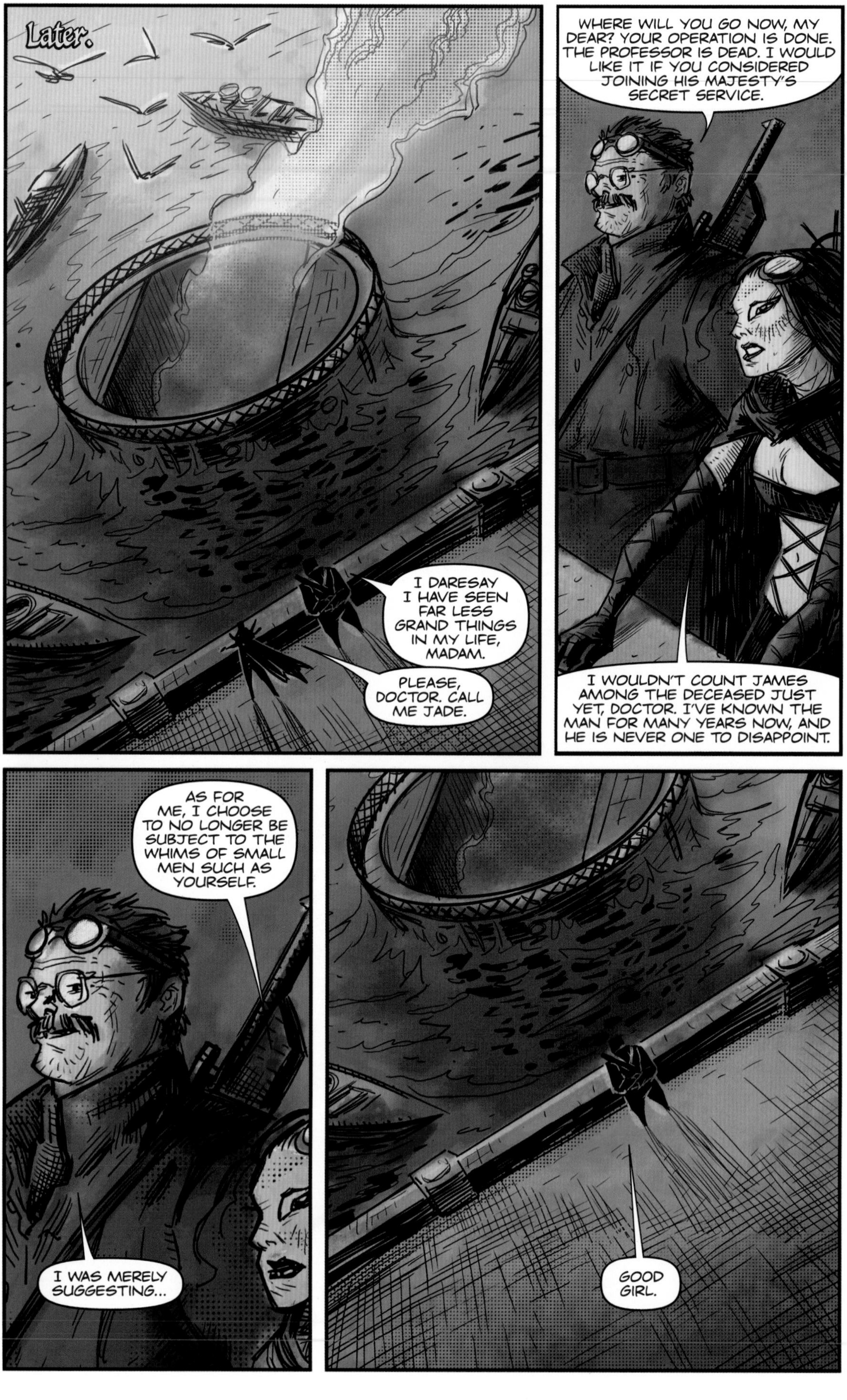
Later.
I DARESAY I HAVE SEEN FAR LESS GRAND THINGS IN MY LIFE, MADAM.
PLEASE, DOCTOR. CALL ME JADE.
WHERE WILL YOU GO NOW, MY DEAR? YOUR OPERATION IS DONE. THE PROFESSOR IS DEAD. I WOULD LIKE IT IF YOU CONSIDERED JOINING HIS MAJESTY'S SECRET SERVICE.
I WOULDN'T COUNT JAMES AMONG THE DECEASED JUST YET, DOCTOR. I'VE KNOWN THE MAN FOR MANY YEARS NOW, AND HE IS NEVER ONE TO DISAPPOINT.
AS FOR ME, I CHOOSE TO NO LONGER BE SUBJECT TO THE WHIMS OF SMALL MEN SUCH AS YOURSELF.
I WAS MERELY SUGGESTING...
GOOD GIRL.

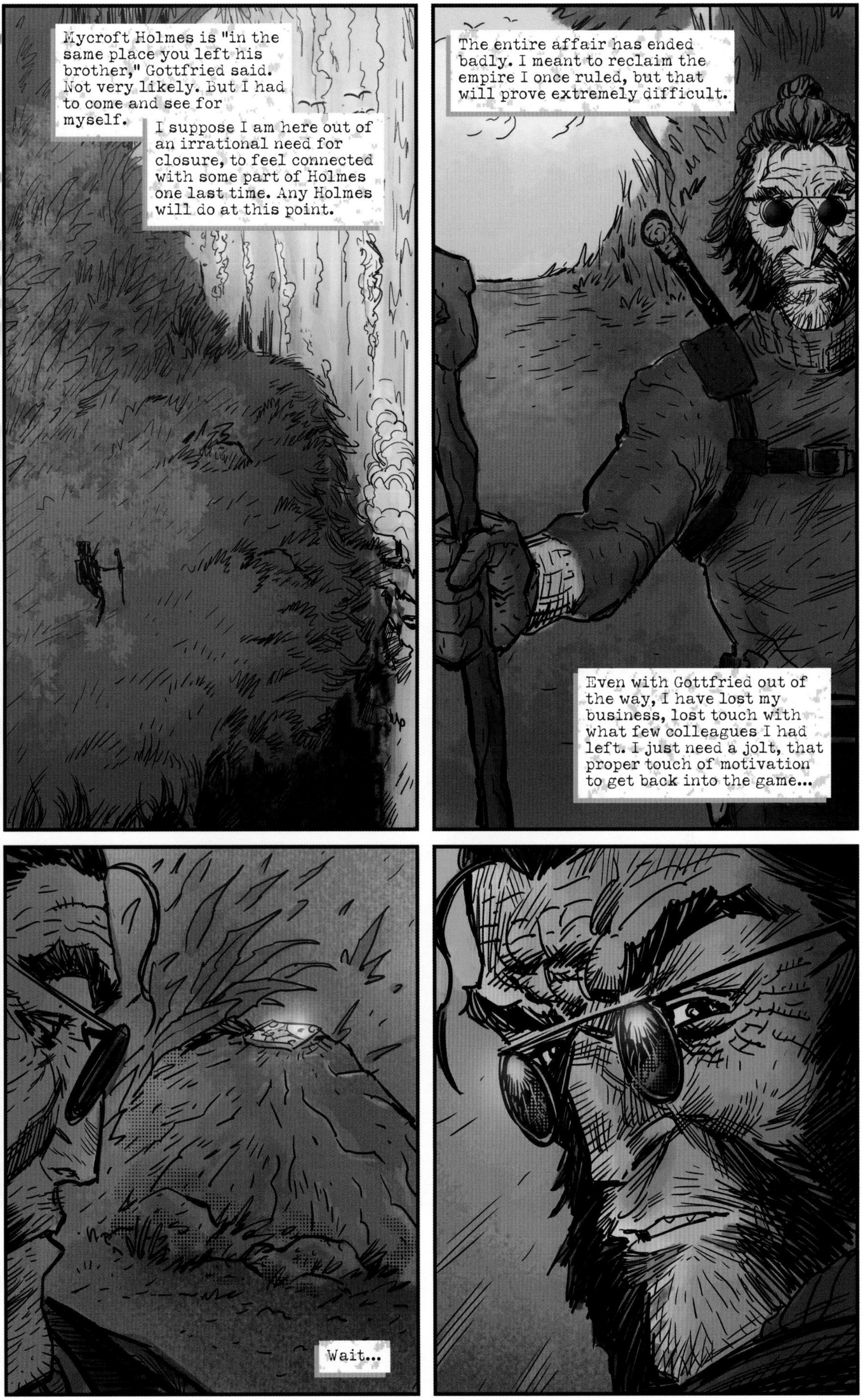
Mycroft Holmes is "in the same place you left his brother," Gottfried said. Not very likely. But I had to come and see for myself.
I suppose I am here out of an irrational need for closure, to feel connected with some part of Holmes one last time. Any Holmes will do at this point.
The entire affair has ended badly. I meant to reclaim the empire I once ruled, but that will prove extremely difficult.
Even with Gottfried out of the way, I have lost my business, lost touch with what few colleagues I had left. I just need a jolt, that proper touch of motivation to get back into the game...
Wait...

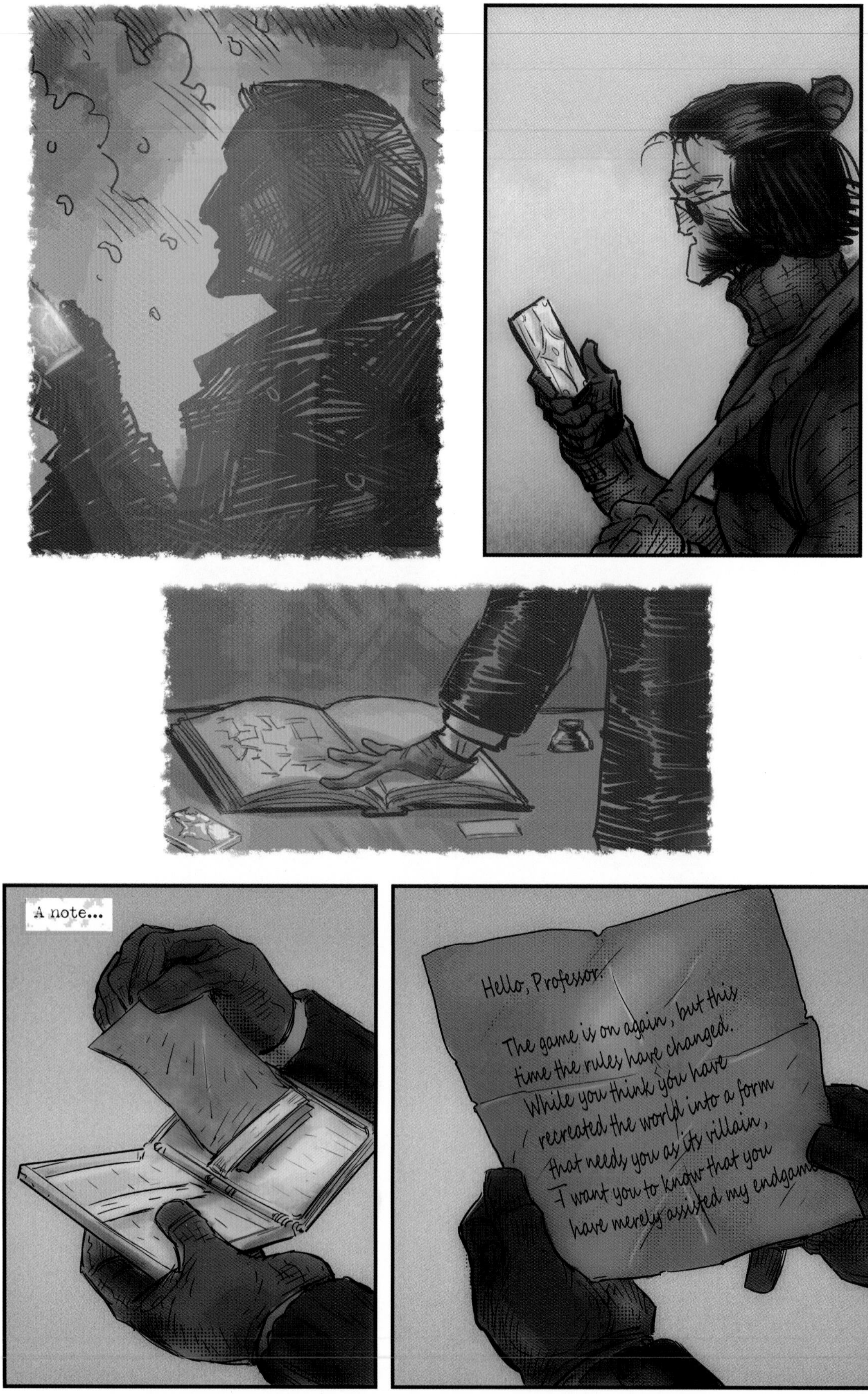
A note...
Hello, Professor.
The game is on again, but this time the rules have changed.
While you think you have recreated the world into a form that needs you as its villain,
I want you to know that you have merely assisted my endgam

"From now on, I will be the one lurking in the shadows, thwarting your every move."

"I trust that I have calculated your arrival here correctly, and have seen to it that the police will as well."

"By now you must know that it was I who masqueraded as Mycroft this entire time. Rest assured, Brother Mycroft is safe and sound on a much-needed holiday abroad."

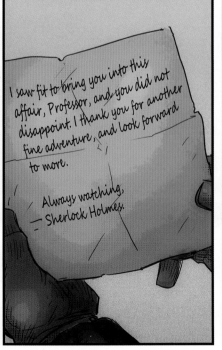

I saw fit to bring you into this affair, Professor, and you did not disappoint. I thank you for another fine adventure, and look forward to more.

— Always watching,
— Sherlock Holmes.

STAY WHERE YOU ARE!

I didn't kill the dragon. It was still lurking in the shadows all along.

I leave the affair of the Dark Chamber behind knowing one thing that I shall cherish above all else...

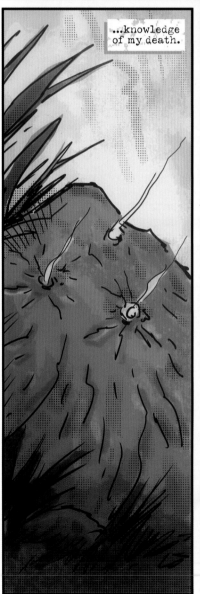

...knowledge of my death.

In the Cyclops Eye, I saw how, I saw when...

...and not even Sherlock Holmes can defeat the one man who knows the secrets of the Dark Chamber.

The End.

Moriarty SKETCHBOOK BY ANTHONY DIECIDUE

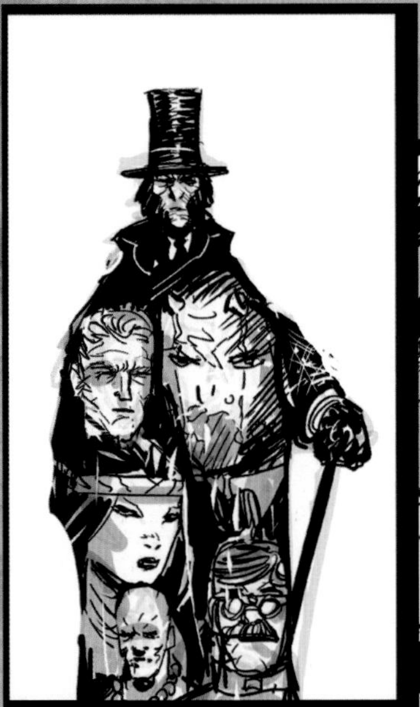

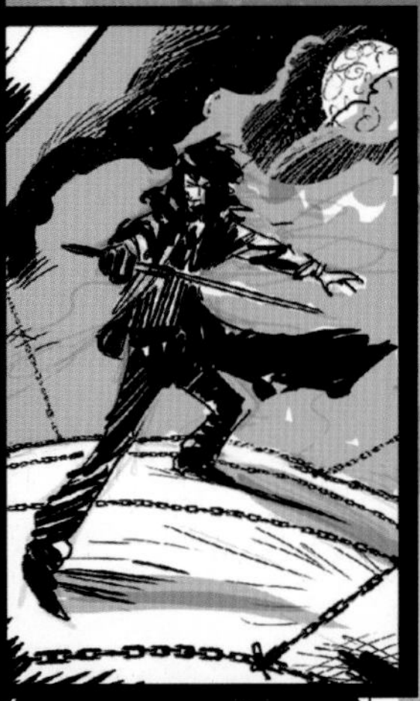

VARIOUS COVER CONCEPTS INCLUDING SOME FOR THIS TRADE. THIS IS WHAT I SHOW DANIEL FOR APPROVAL BEFORE MOVING ON TO THE FINAL INKS.

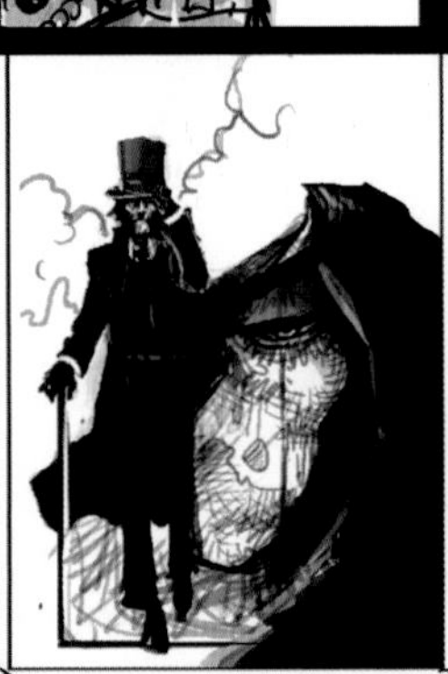

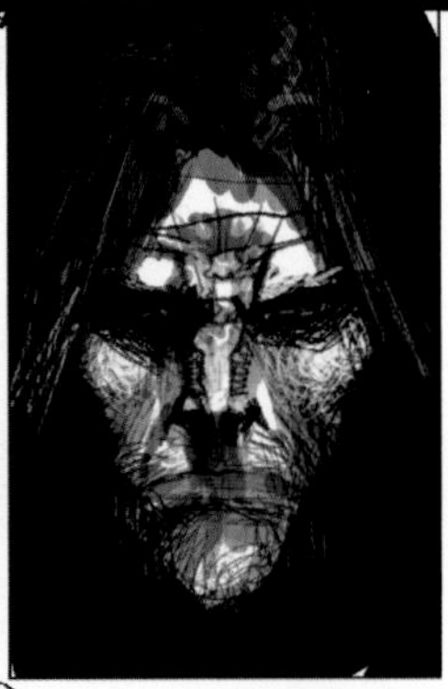

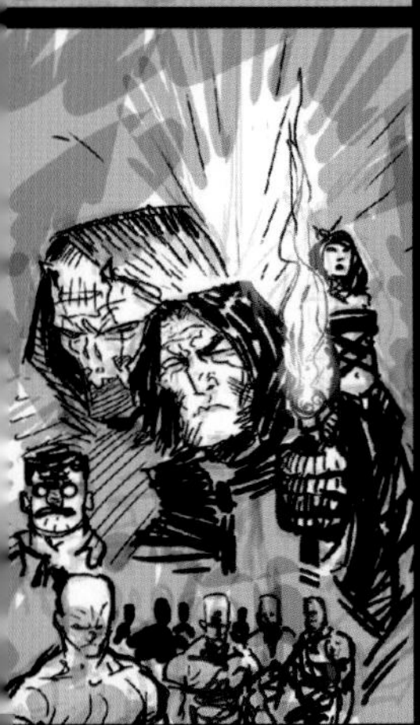

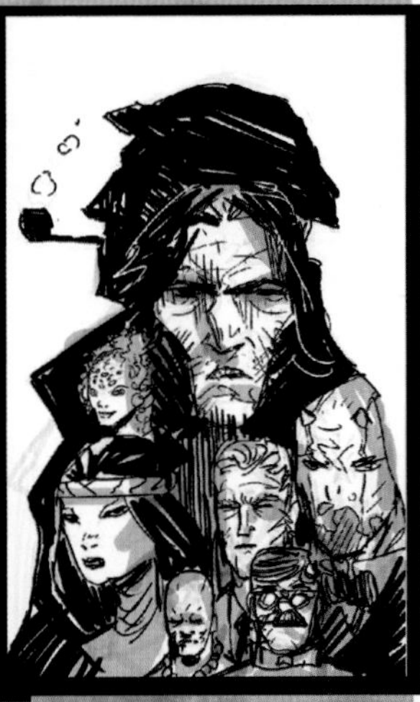

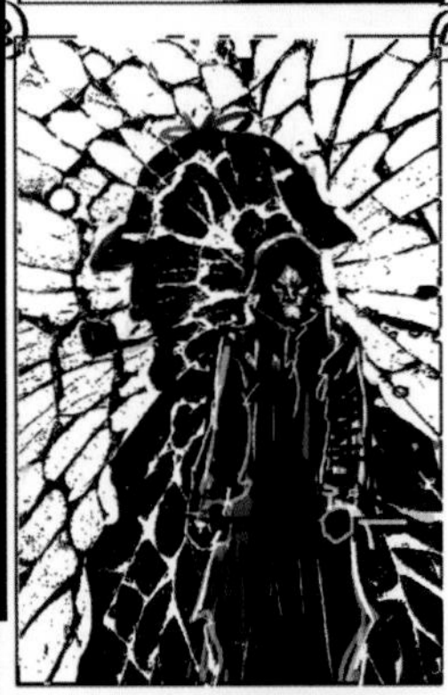

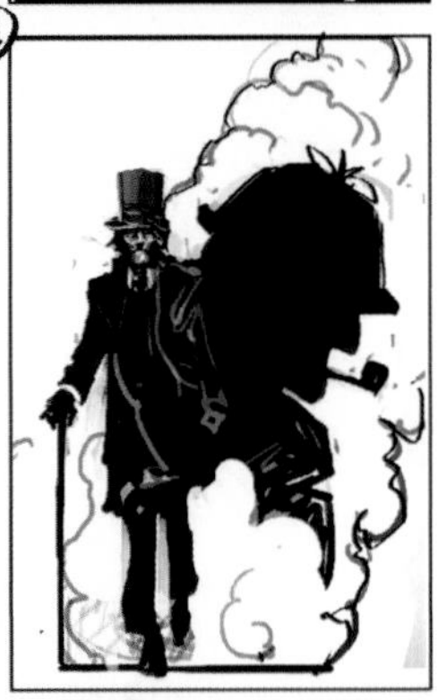

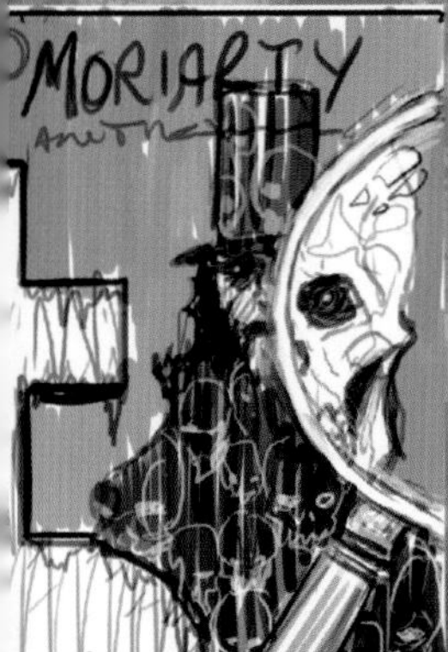
MORIARTY
OLMS

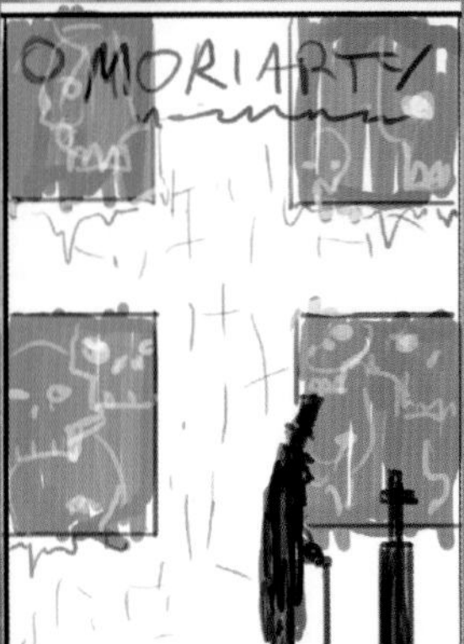
MORIARTY

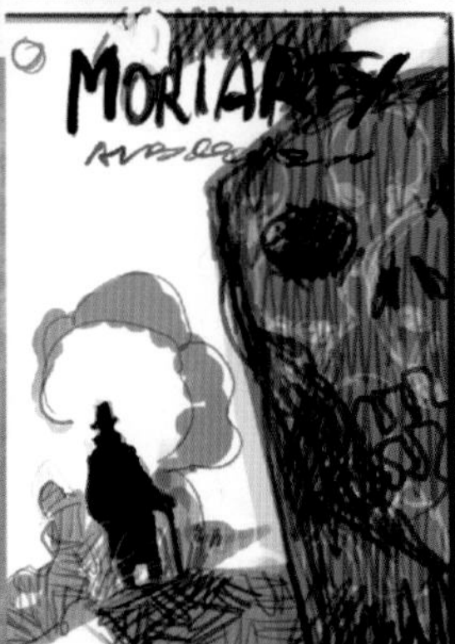
MORIARTY

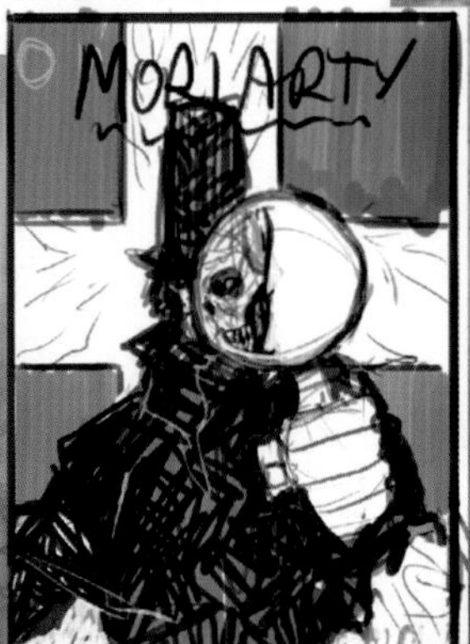
MORIARTY

INITIAL CHARACTER DESIGNS. THESE CHANGED OVER TIME AS I GOT MORE COMFORTABLE WITH THE CHARACTERS AND AS THE STORY MOVED ALONG. EVEN BY THE TIME THEY SHOWED UP IN THE SCRIPT MY IDEA OF WHAT THEY SHOULD LOOK LIKE CHANGED.

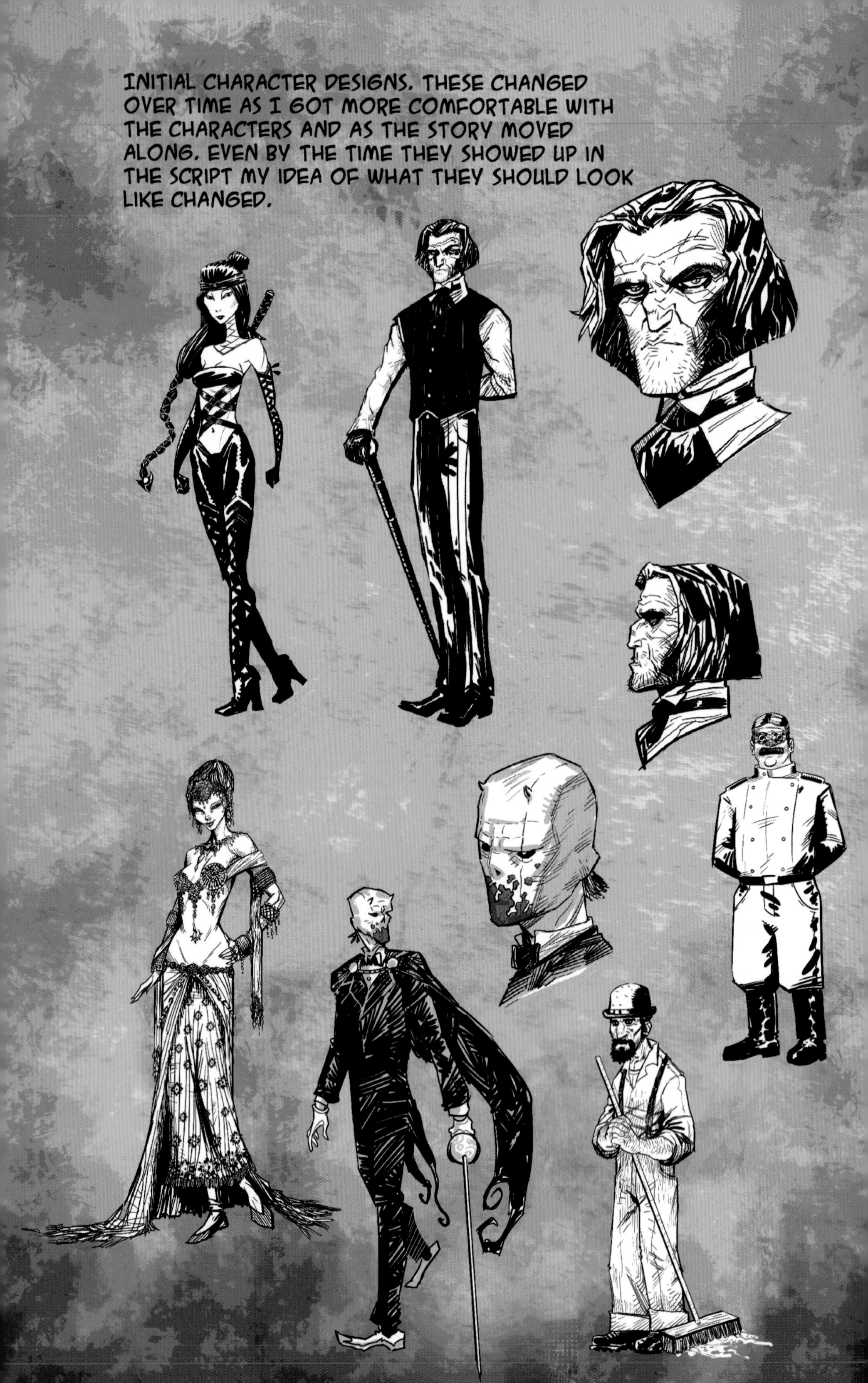